THE PROPHETIC
ANTI-GALLIC LETTERS

François Deschamps

THE PROPHETIC
ANTI-GALLIC LETTERS

Adam Thom and the Hidden Roots
of the Dominion of Canada

*Translation and Editing
by Robin Philpot*

🕮 *B a r a k a   B i b l i o*

Baraka Biblio is an imprint of Baraka Books

© Baraka Books

ISBN 978-1-77186-091-8 pbk; 978-1-77186-095-6 epub; 978-1-77186-096-3 pdf; 978-1-77186-097-0 mobi/pocket

Book Design and Cover by Folio infographie

Translation/adaptation of Chapters 1-3 and notes by Robin Philpot

Legal Deposit, 4th quarter 2016
Bibliothèque et Archives nationales du Québec
Library and Archives Canada

Published by Baraka Books of Montreal
6977, rue Lacroix
Montréal, Québec H4E 2V4
Telephone: 514 808-8504
info@barakabooks.com
www.barakabooks.com

Printed and bound in Quebec

We acknowledge the support from the Société de développement des entreprises culturelles (SODEC) and the Government of Quebec tax credit for book publishing administered by SODEC.

Financé par le gouvernement du Canada
Funded by the Government of Canada | Canada

Trade Distribution & Returns
Canada and the United States
Independent Publishers Group
1-800-888-4741 (IPG1);
orders@ipgbook.com

CONTENTS

1

THE HISTORICAL
AND POLITICAL CONTEXT[1]

The historical and political context, both locally and internationally, in which Adam Thom wrote the *Anti-Gallic Letters* is crucial to understanding the letters and their importance.

The fifty years that preceded their publication were characterized by revolution and war in Europe and in North and South America. These earth-shaking events left their marks in the hearts and minds of people everywhere.

When, for example, France and Great Britain went to war early in February 1793, British authorities in Lower Canada feared the arrival of French spies, especially because revolutionaries in Paris were petitioning for the recovery of lands that the monarchy had abandoned. Citizen Edmond-Charles Genêt, delegated by the government of France to the Philadelphia Congress, wrote to the *Canadiens* on behalf of the "Free French" with a clear invitation to rise up. "Today we are free, we have reclaimed our rights, our oppressors have been punished, all parts of our administration have regenerated, and, strengthened by the justice of our cause, by our courage and by the immense means with which we are preparing to defeat all tyrants in the world, it is finally within our power to avenge you and to render you as free as we are, as independent as your neighbours the Americans of the United States. Canadians, follow their example and ours, the route has been cleared, and magnanimous determination can make you leave the state of abjection in which you have been plunged." Putting those words to action, a small French fleet weighed anchor in Chesapeake Bay and set out to "liberate" Quebec. It was already late in the year and stories of the harsh Canadian winter prompted the commander to change course and set sail for Bordeaux.

The French threat gave rise to a hunt for spies, foreigners, and French sympathizers in Lower Canada. A new law was passed to reorganize the militia, a reform that upset many *Canadiens* and resulted in loud demonstrations of disapproval.

Many English leaders proposed that Quebec become English. The columns of the weekly *Quebec Mercury* ran attacks on the *Canadiens*. In the edition published on October 27, 1806, a certain "Anglicanus" bluntly stated that, "This province is already too much a French province for an English colony. To *unfrenchify* it, as much as possible, if I may be allowed the phrase, should be a primary object, [...] My complaint, is against the unavoidable result of an unnecessary cultivation of the french language, in a country, where common policy requires its diminution, rather than its further dissemination. [...] After forty seven years possession of Quebec it is time the Province should be english." In answer to these attacks, the *Canadien* leaders launched the first newspaper published in French only, *Le Canadien*.

James Craig was a military officer appointed Governor in 1807. He held the demands of French-speaking members in deep contempt. Craig saw conspiracies everywhere. Some in his entourage proposed to adopt measures to assimilate the French-speaking population as quickly as possible, such as uniting Upper and Lower Canada with weighted representation favouring the British minority so that they would hold a majority in the House of Assembly.

Fear of—sometimes hate for—France and the French was widespread. Isaac Brock, who Canada has made into the hero of the War

of 1812, expressed his motivation for fighting that war in his proclamation of July 12, 1812:

> [I]t is but too obvious that, once estranged from the powerful pro-
> tection of the United Kingdom, you must be re annexed to the
> dominion of France, from which the provinces of Canada were
> wrested by the arms of Great Britain, at a vast expense of blood and
> treasure (…). This restitution of Canada to the empire of France, was
> the stipulated reward for the aid afforded to the revolted colonies,
> now the United States; the debt is still due, and there can be no doubt
> but the pledge has been renewed as a consideration for commercial
> advantages, or rather for an expected relaxation in the tyranny of
> France over the commercial world. Are you prepared inhabitants of
> Canada to become willing subjects or rather slaves to the despot who
> rules the nations of continental Europe with a rod of iron? If not,
> arise in a body, exert your energies, co-operate cordially with the
> king's regular forces to repel the invader, and do not give cause to
> your children when groaning under the oppression of a foreign mas-
> ter, to reproach you with having so easily parted with the richest
> inheritance of this earth—a participation in the name, character,
> and freedom of Britons! (Tupper, 1847, 210)

In Lower Canada's House of Assembly, the majority of French-
speaking members joined the Parti Canadien founded early in the
nineteenth century. Louis-Joseph Papineau was elected Speaker of
the Assembly in 1815 and soon became leader of the Parti Canadien,
renamed the Parti Patriote in 1826.

The Parti Canadien feared that London would propose to unite
Upper and Lower Canada to the detriment of the *Canadiens*. The
leaders also were convinced that people who were opposed to the
Canadiens would misinform Westminster. Alexis de Tocqueville
later echoed this fear in a letter to a friend, who was clerk of the Privy
Council in London. Replying to a request for advice on how the
Crown should respond to the 1837 rebellion, Tocqueville wrote: "In
short, my dear friend, do not trust what the English who have settled
in Canada nor the Americans from the United States have to say

about the Canadien population. Their views are coloured by incredible prejudice and any government that would take those views only would be courting disaster."

The idea of uniting Upper and Lower Canada was hotly contested. When Papineau and John Neilson went to London to explain why the two colonies should not be united, they saw that the unionist representative, Andrew Stuart, was applying tremendous pressure push through the union bill tabled in 1822. Stuart claimed that Lower Canada was mainly inhabited by a population that still could be considered foreign more than sixty years after the Conquest. In his opinion this population had made no progress towards assimilation with their fellow citizens of British stock.

Two events occurred in 1832 to aggravate matters. A by-election in Montreal pitted Patriote Daniel Tracey, an Irish doctor who ran the newspaper *The Vindicator*, against Loyalist Stanley Bagg. On Monday May 21, the magistrate and ultra-Tory George Moffatt, pretexting a riot, called in the military. The soldiers commanded by Lieutenant-Colonel Macintosh shot and killed three innocent passers-by, all *Canadiens*. The French-language newspaper, *La Minerve*, denounced the killing saying that *Canadiens* should "Never forget the massacre of our brothers." Adam Thom lauded the commander Macintosh and the soldiers who opened fire in the *Anti-Gallic Letters*, while Governor Aylmer congratulated the officers who gave orders to fire on the crowd

Tensions escalated the following year when the Parti Patriote led by Louis-Joseph Papineau published its list of demands. Among their "Ninety-two Resolutions," the members of the House of Assembly demanded an elected legislative council, expulsion of magistrates from the Executive Council, control of the civil list, and much more. Their denunciations also targeted the stacking or plurality of responsibilities, army intervention during elections, increased government spending, and poor management of Crown lands. The general elections held in fall 1834 bore witness to the widespread discontent among the *Canadiens*. The Parti Patriote won 77 of the 88 seats in the House of Assembly.

Archibald Acheson, Count of Gosford, to whom Adam Thom addressed the *Anti-Gallic Letters*, was appointed Governor of Upper and Lower Canada and head of a Royal Commission of Inquiry into the situation in the two colonies. Troubles were not confined to Lower Canada as agitation was also spreading to Upper Canada. To curry favour among *Canadiens* who backed Papineau, the King's new representative invited a majority of French-speaking people to celebrate St. Catherine's Day on November 25, 1835. Ultra-Tory English Montrealers saw this as pandering and loudly expressed their disapproval of this policy of conciliation. This in fact reflected changes occurring in the Imperial Parliament in the wake of the 1832 Reform Bill.

In the *Montreal Herald*, Adam Thom called on English people to prepare for an uprising by the *Canadiens*. "The French faction's rashness and your lordship's weakness have rendered the struggle no longer political but purely national," wrote Thom under the *nom de plume* Camillus. "A French state shall not be permitted to exist on this English continent. Five hundred thousand determined men will speedily repeat that declaration in voices of thunder."

When 200 or more banner-carrying English citizens marched to music and converged at a meeting a few weeks later, it was clearly a call to arms. In March 1836, an armed group marched through the streets of Montreal to mark the founding of the paramilitary Doric Club. A toast was proposed: "Death rather than French domination."

Confrontation was thus inevitable. The crisis reached a climax when London adopted a series of resolutions in April 1837. On the initiative of Lord John Russell, Secretary of State for the Colonies, Parliament had adopted extreme measures to end the quarrel over subsidies and settle the problems in Lower Canada once and for all. Electing the Legislative Council was ruled out. Russell's eighth resolution ignited the fire. It authorized the Governor to take funds from the House of Assembly when necessary and without its authorization to pay for "the established and customary charges of the administration of justice, and of the civil government of the said province."

Papineau and his supporters began to mobilize. Since import duties were among the main sources of revenue for the colony, they called on people to boycott all imported goods. Meetings were held to protest Russell's resolutions and Louis-Joseph Papineau rose as the most convincing speaker. An emergency meeting of the Executive Council was called to adopt a proclamation prohibiting these seditious assemblies, but the proclamation was ignored. Members of the House of Assembly were convened for a new session in mid-August. Many entered the House of Assembly dressed in cloth of the country to demonstrate their refusal to wear imported material.

Members of the Doric Club regularly paraded fully armed through the streets of Montreal. Young Patriotes refused to ignore these provocations and founded a rival organization, the *Fils de la Liberté*.

Patriotic assemblies or rallies were held everywhere and produced resolutions directly challenging the government. The largest rally attended by thousands of people took place at Saint-Charles, in the Richelieu River Valley east of Montreal. A freedom tree was planted adorned with a Phrygien or Liberty Cap, made famous during the American and French revolutions. Armed militiamen stood at attention when Papineau dressed in cloth of the country took the stage. In a powerful speech, he proposed to pursue the constitutional means that had not yet been exhausted, which was a subtle warning against taking up arms as some were already suggesting. Wolfred Nelson, who led the Patriotes of neighbouring Saint-Denis, believed otherwise. "Well I differ with Mr. Papineau," he declared. "I maintain that the time has arrived to cast our tin spoons and plates into bullets." The 5000 people attending the rally realized that the banner of revolt had been rolled out.

Acting quickly, Governor Gosford issued arrest warrants for twenty-six Patriotes on November 16, 1837, and offered a reward for the arrest of Louis-Joseph Papineau. Since the Patriotes in Saint-Charles had started to build fortifications, orders were given to the army to march on that town before it was too late. The army arrived at Saint-Denis, the town just downstream on the Richelieu River from Saint-Charles, on November 23. Wolfred Nelson and his group of poorly armed Patriotes managed to beat back the advancing army. Papineau had left the town shortly before the confrontation. The Patriotes were defeated two days later, on November 25, after which the British troops and English-speaking irregulars wreaked havoc and destruction throughout the area. Martial Law was applied in the District of Montreal on December 5. On December 14 the Patriotes of Saint-Eustache, in the Deux-Montagnes area northwest of Montreal, were also defeated. The British troops under John Colborne brutalized the Patriotes who sought refuge in the Church and laid waste to the farmlands in the area. Martial Law was lifted in April 27, 1838 but only after 515 people had been arrested.

The following year was a completely different story. Divisions plagued the Patriotes who had escaped arrest by seeking refuge in the United States. Robert Nelson took over as leader of the Patriotes who wanted to continue fighting. During a brief incursion into Lower Canada on February 28, 1838, Nelson proclaimed the independence of the Republic of Lower Canada.

The revolt in the fall of 1838 failed and hundreds of Patriotes were jailed. After summary military trials, twelve Patriotes were hanged in Lower Canada and more than fifty were banished to New South Wales in Australia.

After the clash in 1837, London sent Lord Durham to Canada to study the situation and produce a report. Although Durham would have preferred uniting all the British colonies in North America, his two main recommendations called for the union of Upper and Lower Canada and the sending of as many immigrants as possible to the colony. These two recommendations would, in his view, ensure the gradual assimilation of the French-speaking population and effectively make them a minority when Upper and Lower Canada would be united. His outlook on French Canadians echoed that of Adam Thom who had helped draft the report. It has become famous. "They form a people without history and without literature. (...) The language, the laws and the character of the North American continent are English and every other race than the English race is in a state of inferiority. It is in order to release them from this inferiority that I wish to give the Canadians our English character."

London took Durham's recommendations seriously. The Act of Union was sanctioned in 1840 making Upper and Lower Canada into a single province known as United Canada. The colony would have a single Legislative Assembly comprising 84 members, with 42 coming from each of the former colonies. This was flagrantly unjust for Lower Canada where the *Canadiens* outnumbered the British population of Upper Canada by more than 200,000. A majority of members of the future Parliament would speak English, whereas the majority of the population of the new United Canada spoke French.

The debts of the two colonies were consolidated into a single debt. This too was grossly unjust since Upper Canada had incurred an enormous debt of some 1.2 million sterling pounds for the construction of roads and buildings. Lower Canada owed only 95,000 sterling pounds. In short, people of Lower Canada would pay for the development of the neighbouring colony.

The final injustice was Article 41 that made English the only official language of government. Adam Thom, in the *Anti-Gallic Letters* called for a "second conquest." His wish had come true.

2

WHO WAS ADAM THOM?[1]

Adam Thom was born in Scotland in 1802. He received an MA degree in 1824 from King's College, University of Aberdeen, who also granted him a law degree (LLD) in 1840. Thom immigrated to Montreal in 1832 at the age of thirty.

His career before he joined the *Montreal Herald* in late 1834 is difficult to trace. When he arrived in Montreal, he took courses in law given by the Attorney General, C.R. Ogden. He also articled under James Charles Grant, a prominent member of the British-American community in Montreal who published in November 1836 as Chairman a striking *Report of the Select general committee of the delegates of the constitutionalists of Lower Canada.*

In 1833, Thom was appointed editor of the *Settler, or British, Irish and Canadian Gazette,* which ceased publication in December 1833. That publication clearly reflected Thom's deep contempt for the *Canadiens* and his approach to the interests of the British Empire, which he developed later in the *Anti-Gallic Letters.* He was fighting to make Lower Canada a truly British province. During that time, he had been named secretary of the Beef-Steak Club, an association of some thirty leading merchants of the city.

In May 1834, when many British Montrealers were bitterly opposed to the 92 resolutions proposed by Papineau and the Parti Patriote, Thom was a member of the delegation sent to meet

Governor Aylmer in Quebec City about those resolutions. In December 1834 or January 1835, the Archdeacon of Quebec invited him to teach Hebrew and oriental languages at McGill College, but without pay.

Thom was an avid defender of the Anglican Church. He admitted that he earned the disapproval of almost all the Constitutionalists in Montreal for refusing to support William Walker, the British Party's candidate in the West Ward of Montreal against Robert Nelson of the Parti Patriote in the elections of 1834. Walker lost that election, but later became a reformer and even defended his erstwhile rival, Robert Nelson, before the courts. Adam Thom was on the Executive Committee of the Constitutional Association of Montreal in 1837 and the General Committee in 1838.

Appointed editor of the *Montreal Herald* in January 1835, he led the journalistic assault on the vast French-speaking *Canadien* majority and on the British government's "conciliatory" policy towards the majority leading up to the rebellions of 1837-1838 and the violent repression following which Canadian political institutions were redefined. This was the period during which Thom, under the *nom de plume* of "Camillus" borrowed from the Sack of Rome by the Gauls, wrote the *Anti-Gallic Letters* to Governor General Lord Gosford and published them in the *Herald*. The *Letters* appeared in book form in 1836 but have been out of print ever since.

Adam Thom was admitted to the bar in 1837. When Lord Durham was appointed to replace Colborne, who headed the military government after the revolts and Gosford's resignation, Thom offered his services and was named assistant-commissioner of the municipal commission. In that capacity, he produced a paper that was incorporated in Lord Durham's Report. He returned to England in December 1838 to work on the final draft of Durham's Report.

A lawyer, Thom was appointed to a judicial position in Red River (now Manitoba) in 1839. His job was to reorganize the judicial system there. Considering his past in Lower Canada and his contempt for everything that was French, he not surprisingly entered into bitter conflict with the local population, a majority of whom were French-speaking *Canadiens* or Métis, including Louis Riel, Sr.

While in the Red River, Thom also penned a defense of British claims to the Oregon Territory, entitled *The claims to the Oregon Territory considered* (1844). This document contains many concerns about the future of the British Empire first developed in the *Anti-Gallic Letters.*

Adam Thom returned permanently to the United Kingdom in 1854. He died in London in 1890.

3

INTRODUCTION
"A Transatlantic Voice of Thunder"

"if Camillus should write a history of Canada, for the purpose,
to an indignant, a contemptuous, a scornful posterity"
(Adam Thom, *Anti-Gallic Letters*, XXXV).

"Deep memories yield no epitaph."
Melville, *Moby Dick*

A Repudiated Oracle

Adam Thom was editor-in-chief of the *Montreal Herald*, the newspaper with the widest circulation in the entire British North America, from January 1835 to July 1838. He wrote under a number of *noms de plume*. His *Anti-Gallic Letters* series, which ran from September 1835 through January 1836, are his best-known work. It has earned him a bad name in Quebec historiography. His close links to the regime of terror of the Doric Club secret police and to the military caste commanding British North America from December 1837 until 1841 and the pro-assimilation views that he shared with Lord Durham made Adam Thom a prime target. The first to fire the shots was Patriote Party leader Louis-Joseph Papineau (2006, 402 and 408).

In English Canadian historiography, however, Thom and the influence he had during those years, so crucial in the development of the political institutions in what became the Dominion of Canada, have been buried or forgotten—that is until recently. No mention is made of Adam Thom in the recent erudite works of Philip Buckner (2005), Bruce Curtis (2012) or Brian Young (2015). Paul Romney (1999), who waxed indignant about how Canadians have forgotten their past, totally ignores Adam Thom.[1] Moreover, Elinor Senior (1981) only deigns to mention him in order to disassociate the serious plan of creating a volunteer British Rifle Corps in December 1835 from "such braggart terms" used by the pamphleteer Thom.

Michel Ducharme (2010) broke with this widespread forgetfulness when he published *The Idea of Liberty in Canada during the Age of Atlantic Revolutions, 1776–1838*. His defence of the idea of constitutional freedoms in the perspective of triumphant liberalism earned him the Sir John A. Macdonald Prize for scholarly excellence. His challenge was daunting. It meant proving that the modern Canadian notion of freedom and the related constitutional freedoms was a victory won during the 1830s when Quebec civil society was growing ever more revolutionary. Readers of the *Anti-Gallic Letters* will be able to appreciate this radicalization that spread like wildfire throughout grassroots organizations, which were divided into rival factions. The gratuitous military assassination of three innocent French-speaking *Canadiens*[2] on rue Saint-Jacques during the May 21 by-election was a critical turning point. Michel Ducharme nonetheless describes the *Anti-Gallic Letters* by Adam Thom, alias "Camillus" as "one of the best defences of the Canadian Constitution published in the colony" (2010, 167). That Ducharme should put Adam Thom front and centre is not a mere coincidence. As Editor-in-chief of the *Montreal Herald* and spearhead of the select group of disgruntled merchants, magistrates, militiamen, and gentlemen banded together in the Constitutional Association of Montreal (CAM), Adam Thom was at the heart of the action.

Why has Canadian history forgotten Adam Thom and retained others? Is it unconscious avoidance, active forgetting, or writing history to bury the past? One might think that in order to remember some historical characters, others had to be erased from the record. Yet Adam Thom claimed to be the authorized representative of all citizens of British extraction in the colony, and even in the entire British North America that was developing. Thom can be seen as a misunderstood or unwanted messenger, or perhaps someone that historians have tacitly disavowed. The fact that his newspaper was widely and scornfully taxed as "Tory"—Colonel Grey described the *Herald* as "a very violent ultra-English Paper"[3]—surely helped push Thom out of historical record. Adam Thom was aware of this scorn, and was equally scornful in 1835 about the description of "an honest man's contempt and scorn of the existing administration" as being "ultra-torish and illiberal (XXVIII).[4] The term "Tory" undoubtedly still bore traces of sectarianism or the Orange Order in the collective memory. In reaction to Thom's editorials, Edmund O'Callaghan, the Irish leader in Lower Canada and ally of Louis-Joseph Papineau, did not hesitate to publicize widely the alleged collusion between the civil and military lodges of the Orange Order, which was then rapidly spreading among the patriotic societies, particularly the St. Andrew's and St. George's societies. For example, Peter McGill and George Moffatt, two leading English-speaking Montrealers on the Executive Committee of the Constitutional Association of Montreal, were also honorary presidents of these two patriotic societies.[5]

Another more bothersome issue can explain why Adam Thom and his *Anti-Gallic Letters* have been buried and forgotten. As Ducharme points out (2010, 169), the ardent editorialist was equipped with rhetorical skills and a linguistic prowess that allowed him to lash out viciously when replying to attacks by republicans and demagogues or when unabashedly defending armed violence during the confrontation of two national communities living within a single territory. This has surely irked historians and helped push Adam Thom out of our collective memories. His identification with Camillus, under whose name all the letters are signed, and the Gallic

Sack of Rome is not coincidental. Though Camillus—like Thom in his own eyes—was "suspected and insulted and injured" by his enemies, his gifts of clairvoyance enabled him to predict that the Capitol would be taken back "not with gold but with iron" (VI).[6] Yet the authorized creed on the birth of Canadian political institutions obscures or totally buries the founding violence under a mound of compensatory myths. The *Anti-Gallic Letters* are thus an invitation to dig into that mound and see clearly what lies beneath.

The avoidance of Adam Thom is also linked to the discomfort arising from the influence, be it real or alleged, that this unwanted prophet had in his own adopted community. In the absence of close scrutiny, his claim to be the authorized spokesman of the "English inhabitants of this province" has caught some people off guard. That claim needs to be taken with a grain of salt. Ducharme's generalizations on this point hint that the Constitutionalists were all of the same opinion. Readers of the *Anti-Gallic Letters* will observe however that they were far from unanimous and that signs of discord abounded. Adam Thom's diatribes clearly exacerbated the tensions within the Constitutional Association of Montreal. As early as October 1835, the polemic with the *Morning Courier* that Thom cites is proof of the discord. Distancing itself from Thom, the *Morning Courier* denies, "[...] the assumption so singularly set forth and industriously maintained in the columns of the *Montreal Herald*, that the *ultra* opinions therein enunciated are in harmony with the sentiments of the Association, or those of a large majority of the Executive Committee" (*HA*, 20 October, 1835).

When the establishment of the British Rifle Corps failed then, Thom stigmatized "the dishonest neutrality of selfish constitutionalists" (LIX). Dr. William Robertson, past Chairman of the Executive Committee of the Constitutional Association, echoed Thom and warned that: "The threatening aspect of the times demands action; neutrality, the usual resource of ordinary minds, will not be attended by an immunity from danger" (*HA*, 23 January, 1836). This is not a mere coincidence. The recurring jabs at those who claimed to remain neutral with respect to rival factions are critical as they show that the radical Tories in Montreal likened their fight to a kind of "civil war." Thom was targeting both Commissioners Gosford and Gipps and the liberals in the Constitutional Association who were ready to give the benefit of the doubt to the British imperial policy of conciliation. To the former, he inveighed: "They are the beings whom Solon's sagacious law against the cowardly or the dishonest babblers about neutrality would have hanged in the forum of Athens or driven into the gulph of Salamis at the point of the 'red pursuing spear'".[7]

The *Morning Courier*'s attacks on "the slanderous *Herald* and time-biding *Gazette*" (*HA*, 26 August, 1836) continued in 1836 after the "schism" in the Constitutional Association of Montreal in the spring.[8] The plan to unite the legislatures of Upper and Lower Canada (now Ontario and Quebec) was by no means supported by all. The November 1836 General Meeting was held in an empty hall. Adam Ferrie, spokesman for the secessionist liberal current, did not mince his words when he asserted that the liberal principles and feelings he defended were not to be likened to those the "High Flown Tories" were championing. People from the two neighbouring colonies spoke up as well in opposition to "the wisdom or policy of the course which has been pursued here – a course, which has disunited the British *population, and left the Constitutional Association the mere remnant of a party, the minority of a minority at variance within itself, and powerless for the end for which it was called into existence*" (*HA*, 28 January, 1836).

The radical Tory wing's takeover of the executive was absolute. On the eve of the dual insurrection of November 1837, discord had reached such heights that the themes of "neutrality" and violence came back to haunt the members. "Hampden"[9] lashed out at the constitutionalists who considered it wise to keep their distance from the ruffians and rioters in the Patriote camp and leave it up to the authorities to act:

Well, merchants, lawyers, doctors, tradesmen, of British and Irish origin, what say ye? Will you not turn out and face these rough-handed people? Take my word for it, you will not meet Monsieur Papineau, you must expect sterner stuff; or, gentlemen! do you expect your battle to be fought for you by our rough-handed artisans and poorer fellow citizens? if such be your coward thoughts, your selfish intentions, blush, if blush ye can, for your disgrace. Eyes are upon you, and tongues are asking, why are these people not out with us? The muttered curse will burst upon your ears in thunder, should our supineness *now* be cause of defeat. Say, are you really afraid of blows and blood? (K*MH*, 14 October, 1837).[10]

The fundamental divisions in the Constitutional Association suggest that Tory patricians were far from enjoying the unanimous support of the British community in Montreal. Adam Thom himself confirms that he had been tacitly rejected as a sort of unwanted and disavowed visionary. When he was about to leave his position of Editor-in-chief of the "slanderous *Herald*" in July 1838, he lamented:

> [W]e had almost resolved to let the good folks of Montreal make out their own case in their own way, for, with certainly one exception and perhaps two or three others, they have met our public labours of the last three years and upwards with nothing but discouragement and neglect (*HA*, 7 July, 1838).

The radical Tories' visceral opposition to the policy of conciliation adopted by the Whig-Radical "Frenchified cabinet" in control in Westminster is clearly revealed to attentive readers of the *Anti-Gallic Letters*. Just as the Patriotes used the catchall but imprecise term "*Bureaucrates*," Adam Thom's polemical lumping together of the so-called "French faction" must be broken down. An impartial reading of the *Anti-Gallic Letters* also reveals that Thom, the gagged oracle, establishes an explicit link between political agenda and recourse to arms. From the first *Anti-Gallic Letters* (III et V), he unequivocally supports insurrectional violence backed by the army with the aim of wresting once and for all British interests in North

America from control of any possible future French majority. As a straight shooter, Adam Thom is hard to beat. Three years before the 1837 mutiny and the "second conquest" foretold, Thom uncovered the ultra-sophisticated networking that the Tory magistrates and loyalists, in cahoots with the military command and regiments, would use to settle the crisis and advance their own political agenda.[10] The *Anti-Gallic Letters* are thus a perfect illustration of how the "garrison mentality" still held sway in the 1830s. As F. M. Greenwood brilliantly demonstrated, the garrison mentality remained strong and pervasive until the end of the Napoleonic wars (1815) and the establishment of *Pax Britannica*.

Greenwood's thesis is revealing. He set out to show how the Tories' paranoia about security ended up permanently jettisoning the fragile alliance of liberal reformers in the 1780s. The liberals' program can be summed up in four essential points: independence of the judiciary from the executive branch, restrictions to suspension of habeas corpus, extension of trials by jury, and control of the budget by the House of Assembly. The Tories, however, lived in fear that revolutionary France or the United States would invade, but they also shivered at the possibility of a fundamentally disloyal *Canadien* militia being mobilized. The sombre schemes hatched outside the country would also include and count on a hostile fifth column within.

The expression "reign of terror" came to refer simultaneously to two sources of fear. First was the fear that *Canadien* militia would carry out their deep desire to inflict "Sicilian Vespers"—to use Governor Craig's term for a sort of apprehended ethnic cleansing—on the English inhabitants of Lower Canada (Greenwood, 1993, 236). Second was the dictatorial behaviour of Craig himself, who could count during his reign from 1807 to 1811 on the unfettered complicity of his legal councillors to gag any opposition and arrest people arbitrarily. Greenwood even submits that, "With some few exceptions but hardly any among English judges Baconianism characterizes the Lower Canada Bench down to at least 1839" (1993, 258). The "baconian" method in the administration of justice, unlike that of Francis Bacon's contemporary Edward Coke, is characterized by its eminently partisan and vindictive approach. Other governors who were known to behave like proconsuls followed in the steps of Craig, including Dalhousie and Colborne in particular. Significantly, during the entire period from 1810 to 1839, the *eminence grise* of these three military governors was none other than Judge Jonathan Sewell.

In this regard, Ducharme's conclusions are ironic, disconcertingly so. Whereas he sets out to celebrate the supposed victory of the idea of modern freedoms in Canada and challenge the negative image of Canadian institutions in comparison with American republicanism, he ends up extolling the virtues of the military despotism that characterized the period he describes. Once again, a careful reading of the *Anti-Gallic Letters* shows first that Ducharme glosses over the real conflict between republicanism and monarchism that brewed within Montreal Tory ranks. Furthermore, Ducharme completely ignores the consequences on the governing of the Empire that changes in the British parliamentary system were producing in the wake of the 1832 Reform Bill. Thom, on the other hand, accurately prophesied these changes in the *Anti-Gallic Letters*.

The *Anti-Gallic Letters* are prophetic in several ways. They uncover the secret "design" of the Melbourne cabinet to grant the *Canadiens* a majority in both the Legislative Council and the House of Assembly. That revelation heralds in some ways the "plot" that the former Governor of Upper Canada Francis Bond Head railed against in the House of Lords in 1839.[12] They develop concisely the idea of the commercial empire of the St. Lawrence, so dearly defended by Donald Creighton (1937). The *Anti-Gallic Letters* are also a forerunner to the fundamental elements of the Durham Report regarding the assimilation of the *Canadiens* through the massive emigration from the "British Isles" to make Quebec British. It should be remembered that Adam Thom was later a member of Lord Durham's Commission of inquiry and wrote some of the report. Perhaps even more important in terms of prophesy are Thom's fear of the possible dismembering of the Empire, his loathing of mass democracy and his concomitant appeal for racial homogeneity as crystallised in the notion of "Englishmen." On these questions, before many others, he defines the traits that would define triumphant Anglo-Saxon imperialism as expressed by Charles Dilke (1868), Disraeli (1872), J. R. Seeley (1883), and others.

A Metaphorical Mind that Predicted "Crisis"

The best approach to the *Anti-Gallic Letters* is to take the author at face value and focus on his style. Little can be gained by looking for consistency and coherence. His writings abound with contradictions, which in fact are more enlightening than any overarching plan that some might try to extract from them. Although he defends the British liberties guaranteed under the Constitutional Act of 1791, he fulminates against the principle under which the former Province of Quebec was divided into Upper and Lower Canada and which was sanctioned by the very same "obsolete parchment" (XXXIII; "musty," XXXIV). While he holds dearly to the Crown's privileges as one would to an "unbuttoned cloak" (XXXV), he has the perspicacity to depict with striking insight what a responsible government would be under the "despotism" of a Patriote majority.

He rises to the defence of "equal rights," but does so in order to exclude the *Canadiens* by keeping them "prostrate" at the feet of "the English inhabitants of this province." While boasting about how the people he says he represents display "well-tried and well-known fidelity" to the Crown, Thom blithely compares the Montreal Tories' situation to that of the American revolutionaries of 1776. His posturing as an unprejudiced but critical intellectual is simultaneously the *hubris* of someone with an ultra-partisan view of the world.

Thom's billowy style sets the tone in the first letters as he jumps from one subject to another appearing to have no particular object-ive. As an editorialist, he must be flexible and versatile, moving like a boxer with political events and punches that can inevitably rewrite even the best of agendas. Thom is a master improviser. Though he couches his writing in obsequious and high-flown language, he unfailingly concludes his digressions with short, pithy proposals that broach no misinterpretation. His rhetorical skills allow him to glide from a dry analysis of some obscure principle to vibrant emo-tional pleas, especially when discussing easily offended honour (XXXI-XXXII) by a wide variety of "insults" (the word comes back again and again). The most instructive quirk in the sensitivity of a British expatriate like Adam Thom is his acute sense of the intoler-able. The *enfans du sol*, in comparison, are in his eyes an indolent, easily manipulated, and easily satisfied people. The main chords Thom strikes are shame and loud, fiery indignation. Any sense of duty or allegiance should by no means be taken for granted, nor should it be interpreted as some sort of affection for another person (III). As with the fiery editorials in the *Montreal Herald* up to and after the 1837 uprisings, the *Anti-Gallic Letters* resuscitate all the pathos of treason in the British cultural tradition. The coded refer-ence to Hamlet's famous soliloquy in Letter XXXV is a shining example.

Behind Thom's apparent nonchalant attitude can be found none-theless an extremely meticulous analysis of Governor Gosford's Speech from the Throne, which, like a wolf with its prey, he cites obsessively as he tears it apart. So doing, he claims legitimacy since he is faced with adversaries who are masters of the "jesuitical lan-guage" (XLI), starting with the recipient of *The Letters,* Viceroy Gosford himself, who headed both the Executive and a Royal Commission of Inquiry. Master of the understatement, Thom knows very well that words both conceal and reveal thoughts and feelings. Having control of oneself and of one's temperament is crucial, because words hide weapons: "with the pen as with the knife, it is temper that cuts keenly, deeply, fatally" (XXXV). He hopes to wield the well-sharpened words so as "to break through the misty veil of your lordship's language into your lordship's breast" (XLIV)—or better yet, "into the very marrow of the dastard's soul [Papineau]" (XLIII). Words can even, in some cases, turn into bayonets. His premonitory and exalted foresight of the savage repression of 1837 and 1838 prompted him to write about the *habitans* who would dare to take up arms: "They would be hemmed in by a gradually closing circle of English breasts and English bayonets" (XI).

Despite, or perhaps because of, Thom's erratic course, he manages to turn full circle and contemplate the very sources of his own call for action. We learn for example that the first eight letters target the secret compromise reached between the imperial authorities and the leaders of the "French faction." His review of the peaceful measures that could be taken to solve the crisis is little more than an appetizer: emptying the coffers, smuggling goods from south of the border, re-appraisal of customs duties in favour of Ontario, and more. The following eight letters justify his use of the term *Anti-Gallic* to qualify his editorials.[13] Next he examines various symptoms of the crisis and the violent means to solve it.[14] As he proceeds, his own icy disillusion inspires some of his finest strokes applied to the "Frenchified trucklers" who pull the strings of conspiracy in Westminster.

A succinct sample of his style can be very telling. Thom refers to the "malady" that affects society. The Colonial Office's policy of conciliation, he claims, will "ultimately aggravate the malady, which it professes to cure" (II). "[T]he homeopathic principle of modern liberals" (XXIII) is how he spells it out. Moreover, Thom even stoops to use it himself, in an attempt to exaggerate. Elsewhere, he refers to the particular type of viral infection (XXVIII) or, borrowing from the *New York Albion* to hammer his point home, "the system of palliations" (XXXIII) that leads directly to the autopsy room. Just as with Rousseau, the remedy for Thom is in the evil itself (the necessary violence and aggressive passions) for which the "physical resistance" of the "English inhabitants of this province" is the advance warning sign:

> [T]hat 'evil' has roused the indignation and stiffened the sinews of 'the English inhabitants of this province', I venture to console your lordship with the assurance, that such 'evil' will be productive of 'good' as well to this colony as to the whole empire. (XLVIII).

His approach gives us a glimpse of what he really thinks: the salvation of the Montreal Tory oligarchy must be radical and they must defend violent means. The symptoms of an imminent resolution of the "crisis" are evident. Over and above the empty coffers of the state, which depend mainly on money from the merchant classes in Montreal and Toronto, he perceives two possible options before the metastases ruin everything. Either the Imperial Parliament intervenes directly in the internal affairs of the colony (the peaceful solution) or, if by chance the Patriote camp carries out their threats of rebellion, they must turn to the much more powerful military solution in the wake of the military killing of three innocent *Canadien* after "The Riot that Never Was," as James Jackson so accurately described it.[15]

Adam Thom's characteristic trait is always to anticipate what might happen based on his own reading of "facts or analogies that may cast the shadows of coming events" (XXVIII). From the beginning, the *Herald*'s pugnacious editorialist goes straight to the point declaring that he "confidently anticipates the day, when the undying perseverance of true Englishmen will make French factions and Frenchified cabinets quail in terror and dismay" (III). If no "appeal to the sword" is made, the consequences of the "secret compromise" appear to him to be very clear, namely "the temporary establishment of French supremacy in this colony, the not very remote horrors of civil war, the dismemberment of the British empire, the decay of British influence, and the ruin of the British navy" (VIII). Elsewhere, while once again referring allegorically to the military option—he alludes to "the tools of a forsaken profession"—he can "draw aside the veil of futurity, and see through not a very long vista the inevitable workings of an awful retribution" (XXXIV). Interpreting "facts or analogies" inevitably leads Thom to foresee and foretell the necessary violence. What is more, his *nom de plume* Camillus combined with his Latin sources give impetus to his prophecies. Under the promise of a new era of prosperity and happiness, he sees flowing "tides of blood *Cerno ipsum spumantem sanguine Thybrim*." (War, fierce war, I see: and the Tiber foaming with much blood) (Virgil, *Aeneid*, VI, 87).

The *Anti-Gallic Letters* are undoubtedly fatalistic. They wilfully link the logic of concessions made by the "Frenchified" imperial authorities to the "French faction" with the irreversible and imperceptible movement that grows, expands, and intensifies until the final dénouement. "Every step in the march of conciliation leads to another step still more fatal—smooth water is gradually quickened into a rapid; and the rapid again dashes itself into pieces in the foaming form of a cataract. To recede, my lord, is impossible" (XVI).[16]

Classical rhetoric and culture are the means by which the *Anti-Gallic Letters* express interests and passions. Thom's emphasis on links between sensitivity, imagination, and memory—be it "the most treacherous" (XXIV)— is an intimate part of his defense of the English language (XXV). Speaking many languages makes no difference. People neither think nor feel the same things in different national languages, especially when they are in foreign lands. Thom's rhetoric breathes new life into old worlds. He is moved by memories of his native Scotland, but also by his homesickness. To compensate for the difficulty in adapting, he turns to dreaming with quotes from a poem by Walter Scott about "my own, my native land" (LIII).[17] Like Wordsworth in *Tintern Abbey* (1798), the "nostalgia" he feels and expresses in English provides the perfect lever "to raise national and patriotic feelings of every man of British blood in British America" (XLIII et XLVII).[18]

When Thom is at his best, he appears convinced that in the era of mass media— Anderson's famous "vernacular print-capitalism"— the power of ink on paper is decisive. Like Benjamin Franklin, he submits that careful use of the media could have prevented the bloodbath of the American Revolution (III). Yet nothing says that the same could not happen if "'the English inhabitants of this province' were to vindicate their right by an appeal to arms" (XXXIX). His proof once again can be found among the British soldiers in the garrison. Never in such a case, claims Thom, would they dare shoot upon their fellow "countrymen," for they are not "cannibals" after all and "they have eyes to read, hearts to feel and heads to understand" (*Ibid*).[19] Though he may have hoped that his pen and ink would deter those in power from implementing the policy of conciliation, he very soon loses hope and vigorously appeals for the release of dark forces: *"Flectere si nequeo superos, Acheronta movebo"* ("Hell will I raise, if Heaven my suit denies").[20] While awaiting the predicted arrival of Gosford's successor and the "second conquest" by arms of 1837 (XXXVI), he reaches the conclusion that his perseverance in trying to convince Governor Gosford has in fact been "more foolish than St. Anthony's homily to the fishes" (LIV).

Crisis of imitation

Although Thom emphasizes the ethnic and cultural divide in Lower Canada, in fact, both the Patriotes and the Tories refer to the American Revolution in their speeches on organization and strategy. So similar are they in their discourse that one might gather that they were suffering from a crisis of imitation. Both hearken back to the revolutionaries of 1776; both threaten boycotts and possible recourse to a convention or congress; both establish national societies (the Société Saint-Jean-Baptise in July 1834 for the moderate Patriotes and reformers; St. George's, St. Andrew's and "German Society" for the Tories); both revere Common Law and the right to resist and the duty to obey only the laws that they had voted for; both demand comparable sworn affiliation to unrecognized paramilitary organizations (Fils de la Liberté and Frères Chasseurs among the radical Patriotes and the British Rifle Corps, the British Legion and the Doric Club for the radical Tories).

Adam Thom makes two references in the *Anti-Gallic Letters* to recent events in American history in order to prepare the ground for his attacks. First is the Quebec Act of 1774 marking the beginning of the despised policy of "conciliation" towards the *Canadiens*. Second is the parallel he draws with the American revolt against taxation without true representation. Republican sentiments therefore were not held by the Patriotes alone; the Montreal Tories were also inspired by them. The allusion is clear. The discontented gentlemen of the Tory Oligarchy, judging by the *Montreal Herald* editorialist's observations, quite enjoyed identifying with the revolutionaries of 1776. Understatement does not hide the message. The conciliatory approach to the *Canadiens*, which underpinned the creation of the Province of Quebec in 1774, led straight to the Boston Tea Party, Bunker Hill, and the revolutionary war of 1776. The colonial authorities were blind and deaf to the Thirteen Colonies in 1775 and they are doing it again in 1835. Moreover, further concessions to the plebeians in the democratic faction, according to Thom, will inevitably provoke the English settlers in Lower Canada to rise up.

When Thom likens the Montrealers' situation to that of the American revolutionaries he is marching in lockstep with the founding manifesto of the Constitutional Association of Montreal.[21] He reveals a kind of emotional ambivalence prevalent among some Tory merchants, who also enjoy showing off their patrician manners. It appears they are divided between a deep attachment to the Crown of England, which they enthusiastically applaud, and the republican aspirations of the Americans with whom they share their British heritage. For them, it would seem better to avoid forcing a choice between their condition as taxpayers and their visceral anti-democratic rejection of the "unholy

coalition" between the imperial authorities and the "French faction."
Thom, on the other hand, can live with the ambivalence in identity,
convinced as he is that in the end if the crisis is exacerbated and the
possible national independence of the colony dramatized enough (III),
the Imperial Cabinet will have no other choice but to rely on the members of the Montreal Tory Oligarchy and English bayonets to maintain
the link with the Empire (III; VI; XI ; L).[22]

What is more, Thom sees the republican flights of oratory in
the Patriote camp as little more than noise. If money is the key to
victory in the crisis at hand, the Montreal Tories have nothing to
fear. What is scandalous for Adam Thom is the fact that those who
are active in trade and business and who fill the public coffers by
their habits as consumers have no say on how the money is spent.
Worse yet, these same British subjects subsidize the very people who
are trying to shut them up (V; VI; VII). Another aggravating factor
for Thom is the "democratic prejudices" in favour of the *Canadiens*
that fly in the face of the most basic notions and sentiments of the
high degree of perfection of English culture. Ethnic considerations
are mixed with the rational calculation of economic interest.

> [T]o assume, that a French Canadian contributes as much as an
> Englishman to the public revenue, is to confound indolence with
> enterprise, barbarism with civilisation, contented ignorance with
> ambitious intelligence (V).

Three years before the Parti Patriote raised the strategy of con-
traband, Adam Thom alluded to the possibility that such a system
could be used drain the public coffers: "an empty treasury is one
mode, and perhaps the only mode, of compelling the government
and the faction to surrender at discretion" (III). By smuggling in all
the goods required from New York, it would be easy also to favour
the massive migration of American settlers and capital into the
"Eastern Townships." Thom was convinced that time was working
in favour of the Anglo-Scottish merchants. He couldn't wait for the

day when "the universal indignation of your lordship's robbed and insulted countrymen in both provinces shall have made the receiver general of Lower Canada the guardian of a beggarly account of empty boxes" (VIII). When Thom uses such a republican and insurrectional tone he actually becomes seditious. Before the end of 1835, the creation of a rifle corps and threats of boycott should, in his mind, lay the foundations for a Convention or a Congress for which the network of associations would be the basis:

> The organization, that it may combine both moral determination and physical force, must be as well military as political. There must be an army as well as a congress; there must be pikes and rifles as well as pens and tongues; there must be valour as well as wisdom. The sooner that this double organization is exhibited, the less likely is it to be needed (*HA*, 23 December 1835).

The Theory of a Democratic Plot

The *Anti-Gallic Letters* is a layered document. In addition to the notion of two national communities (British versus *Canadien*) vying for power, Adam Thom develops the idea of a democratic conspiracy. Setting his sights on the many instances that the "unholy coalition" acted against the British community, he lumps together the least radical reformers and the moderate Patriotes who were disenchanted or had broken with Papineau's party. That coalition includes not only Viceroy Gosford, but also the "Frenchified" Melbourne Cabinet in London and the radical-Whig supporters in the Imperial Parliament. Their collusion is aimed to provide nothing less than a double majority for the *Canadiens* in the Legislative Council and the House of Assembly. Though Thom fears the French "revolutionists" and "demagogues," what irritates him the most is the infiltration of moderate Patriotes in the executive where they will be invested with the imperial authority of appointing people of their own ilk to well paid positions in the judiciary. He fulminates against the claims that these upstarts might be able to pose as neutral arbiters between the two radical factions, the Tories and the Patriotes (XXVII).

Thom's catchall term "French Revolutionists," like the Patriote's term "*Bureaucrates*," needs to be broken down. The leaders of the majority party in Lower Canada's House of Assembly in Quebec City cannot be considered to be the same as the group of dissidents who were willing to take a chance with the conciliatory approach or even those "moderates" who remained in solidarity with the Patriote Party but who had accepted some imperial largesse. The latter and the reform wing of the Patriote Party simply cannot be dealt with as a single entity. These are the "moderates" who make up, in Thom's words, "your lordship's 'French allies'" (XL, XLIX, LIV, LVI). They are part of "the unholy coalition" (XXXV; LIII), which Thom also calls "your 'Excellency's faction'" (XXXIX; XL). They are "miserable trucklers" in his view. Significantly, the transfer "of all executive authority" (XXXIX) under the authority of "great body of the people" was devised to be to their advantage. Thom was aiming particularly at the "shameless" owner of *L'Écho du Pays*, P. D. Debartzch, who is on the receiving end of Thom's most colourful—and scornful—rhetoric: he is a "viper" (XVII), a "Hessian mercenary" (L), and has the "dog-face impudence of the monster" (L), and more.

The Tories also have several other people in mind. They include Sabrevois de Bleury, who commanded the Canadian Rifle Corps, Pierre de Boucherville, road surveyor, Elzéar Bédard and Vallières de Saint-Réal, who had been appointed to the King's Bench, Hughes Edmond Barron, one of the Gosford Guards, but also Jacques and Denis-Benjamin Viger, respectively Mayor of Montreal and Legislative Councillor.[23]

Thom however touches on a key point in Letter XXVI. When the Melbourne Cabinet placed "the administration of 'the laws by which society is held together' at the mercy of the French faction"—

including the party holding a majority in the House of Assembly and the loyalist "shameless traitors" from the Patriote camp who were playing the conciliatory card—, the Cabinet was betting on the wrong horse. As early as the third *Anti-Gallic Letter*, Thom reassures Gosford that sooner or later the ultra-Tory radicals in Montreal, thanks to the means at their disposal (arms and money), would make it known "in a Transatlantic voice of thunder" (XXIV) that they themselves were the exclusive custodians of the colonial link.

A close reading of the *Anti-Gallic Letters* also shows that behind his haughty pronouncements about the Crown's privileges and the balance of different powers, Thom had already perceived in the throne speech the dynamic and perhaps perverse effects on the British Parliamentary system that stemmed directly from the Reform Bill of 1832. The evolution underway at that time proved him right. Thirteen years before Canada obtained "responsible government," the importance of which Canadian historiography has cravenly overstated—John Ralston Saul has likened LaFontaine and Baldwin to no other than Mahatma Gandhi and Nelson Mandela[24]—, Adam Thom tears it apart as he predicts what will arise from the "despotism" of the majority in the reformed English system. The authority of the Crown will be but a formality. Only the Imperial Parliament will hold sovereignty. The trio of "King, Lords, and Commons" will be substituted by another three-pillared structure: electoral body, Commons, Cabinet. The majority vote would make and break governments from then on. The problem for Thom is that, unlike Upper Canada with its "homogenous" population where defeat at the hands of the majority is part of normal parliamentary activity, in Lower Canada the Patriote Party led by Louis-Joseph Papineau, working as a compact block, had consolidated its position more at every election (XVII). This tendency explains why the Constitutionalists demanded massive immigration from the British Isles. It also explains why they reactivated the project of a legislative union of Upper and Lower Canada. This was the only way they could defeat

the Patriote majority.[25] The irreversible decline of the Crown's privileges is matched by the rise of the Prime Minister as the central
figure. As head of a responsible, elected cabinet standing together,
the Prime Minister would control the legislative and executive
branches and is in charge of appointments to the judiciary and the
civil service, not to mention all the patronage appointments.[26] The
conventional notion of the balance of powers in a mixed monarchy
as defended by the American revolutionary John Adams (XXX) had
gone out the window.

This development did not escape Adam Thom's sharp eyes. In
his first remarks, he notes that, "henceforward the provincial patronage of the crown is virtually to be vested in the French demagogues,
as the organs of 'the great body of the people'" (XXIII). The principle,
once established, will inevitably provoke a multitude of ruinous
consequences:

> [w]hen, therefore, the French demagogues shall demand all executive
> and judicial appointments, your lordship will, of course, receive
> 'precise instructions' to make Mr. Papineau your successor, as the
> last in a scale descending from Dalhousie downwards, to make
> Mr. Viger Speaker of the legislative council, to make Mr. Lafontaine
> chief justice of the province, to make Mr. Debartzch deputy post-
> master general (XXXIV).[27]

Drawing a parallel in Letter XXXVII with republican institutions, Thom continues to argue both for better coordination between
the three branches of the government and for greater powers for the
elected assembly. A few days later, however, frightened by the logical
outcome of his own analysis, he changes his mind and concludes:
"Instead of *wholesome separation and independence*, my lord, your
new system will establish *complete connexion and dependence, a
perfect identity of purpose, an undivided unity of action*" (XL Thom's
italics). Even though Thom, in his fast-moving, unbridled prose,
foresees exactly how the modern parliamentary system would work
in coming decades, something in him prevents him from believing

that in the eyes of the authorities in the Mother Country the *Canadiens*, being the "great body of the people," will be the natural and legitimate beneficiaries of these developments. Thence springs in Thom's fertile imagination the idea of a conspiracy. Either Gosford is "the passive and perhaps unconscious tool of your noble and right honorable employers" (XLIV), or he is underhandedly operating "in the unenviable light of a conspirator against the independence of the minority of the assembly, and of the majority of the legislative council" (XXI). What Thom and the purged Constitutional Association of Montreal feared the most came to be in October 1837 when Governor Gosford made new appointments to the Legislative Council:

> [...] both councils are now decidedly French, so that the "English inhabitants of this province" have now no hope of safety but in such a broken reed as "precise instructions" emanating from Downing Street. The local government is exclusively Anti-British; and its various branches, however much they may disagree on civil lists and revolutions, are all ready to unite against every thing savouring of the proud isles of the ocean. The absurd idea of nationality is not less vivid in the minds of French loyalists than in those of French revolutionists, — an idea, that will pervade, corrupt and poison all the proceedings of the local government (*HA*, 4 November 1837).

Four years later, in August 1839, Adam Thom's fears would echo loud in the British House of Lords when the former Governor of Upper Canada, Francis Bond Head, addressed the House. In Bond Head's view, as in Thom's, the loyal subjects of the Crown:

> [H]ave seen the Ministers of the Crown, in spite of warning or remonstrance, resolutely insist on elevating over the heads of the loyal population the ringleaders of the conspiracy – they have seen the arch-agitator of each of the Canadas offered to be rewarded – the insulters of her Majesty's representative officially shielded from punishment ; in short they have seen the Ministers of the British Crown actually fan into a flame the embers of rebellion, which the

representative of the Sovereign, but for the encouragement shown to agitators, would easily have extinguished (*HA*, 15 August 1839).

Defenders of the 1791 Constitution? Making the Case for Upper Canada (Ontario)

Adam Thom saw the conquest of Canada by Wolfe's and Amherst's armies in 1759 and 1760 as a founding act. Yet the imperial authorities repeatedly made concessions to the *Canadiens* (1774 and 1791) that betrayed the spirit of the Royal Proclamation of 1763. The lack of homogeneity in the population and the institutions exacerbated the hybrid nature of the colony. Since he foresaw no possibility of positive interaction between the two national communities (XXIV), Thom built his case on the logic of communicating vessels. Any concession made to one group would automatically penalize the other. As a result, the *Canadiens:*

> [...] were petted too, my lord, at the expense not merely of abstract principles but of the natural rights and the covenanted claims of His Majesty's English subjects. [...] For the gratification of 'His Majesty's Canadian subjects', these English subjects were doomed to live under the foreign laws [...]. Every year, in short, has seen the vanquished become more and more able to dictate terms to the victors. So long as the conciliatory system is continued, its natural effect must continue to gain strength. THE CONCILIATORY SYSTEM, THEREFORE, MUST BE ABANDONED (IX; XXIV)

Errors always come in bunches. The fundamental *faux pas* of the imperial legislators in 1791 might well have been dividing the Province of Quebec into two entities (Lower and Upper Canada). Adding insult to injury, they also failed to annex Montreal to Upper Canada (Ontario) when they drew the line between the two colonies to the west of the Ottawa River.[28] The bitter negotiations over the division of customs duty revenues under the Canada Revenue Act of 1831 might prompt Upper Canada to turn to New York and the

Hudson River to obtain access to the ocean. Although Thom does not address the theme of legislative union of Upper and Lower Canada directly, he quite clearly counts on eventually seeing the day "when French influence ceases to be supreme in the provincial legislature" (XII). This issue was laying dormant after the two failed attempts of 1810 and 1822, but was reactivated in June 1835 in a blistering article published by *Blackwood's Magazine*. Among other targets, the House of Assembly, whose "days are numbered," received some of the most scathing attacks:

> The catalogue of its crime and its follies is long enough to justify, not alone the cashiering of the Assembly, but the castigation of its leading members. [...] We trust, however, its days are numbered, and that soon it will be heard of only as among the things that have been. We have heard much of conciliation, but we hold the word to have been abused and the mode to be impracticable.[29]

Since they understood perfectly the demographics of the new parliamentary legitimacy, Thom and the leaders of the Constitutional Association looked forward with serenity to a future where, thanks to the anticipated immigration from the British Isles, the question of which nationality would dominate would be definitively settled. Some fifty years later, riding on the same prophetic wave as the *Anti-Gallic Letters*, Cambridge historian and champion of the British Empire, J. R. Seeley, compared "the Frenchmen and Catholics in the midst of a population mainly English and Protestant" to a foreign body, adding that, "[...] here too the alien element dwindles, and is likely ultimately to be lost in the English immigration, and also that its animosity has been much pacified by the introduction of federal institution."[30]

Encircled: The Two Faces of the Garrison Mentality

The *Anti-Gallic Letters* clearly had an important, though virtually unknown and unrecognized, influence on the transformation of

British North America into the Dominion of Canada. They provide clear link between the rowdy debates about imperial administration that followed the Seven Years' War, the Treaty of Paris, and the Royal Proclamation of 1763 and the imperialist cant about "Greater Britain," very much in vogue between 1870 and 1900.[31] In the narrower context of the end of what some call the "Atlantic revolutions," the *Anti-Gallic Letters* bear witness to much more that a minor discord between the imperial representatives of the Melbourne Cabinet in Westminster and the handful of disgruntled merchants, bankers, and gentlemen in the Tory Oligarchy of Montreal. The *Anti-Gallic Letters* are proof positive of total mutual disagreement within the same culture as to the symbolic representation of power. Whereas the Melbourne Cabinet and other reformers, in the wake of the Reform Bill of 1832, believed in the gradual and harmonious transfer of British parliamentary values and institutions to a majority community of a different culture—"the great body of the people" as Governor Gosford described them in his throne speech in French—, the Montreal Tory Oligarchy and its mouthpiece Adam Thom, torn between fear and bravado, apprehended the worst while still espousing the same imperial mission and British commercial interests worldwide. Seeing Montreal as the pivotal point of the entire British North America that was developing, they brandished the spectre of the dismemberment of the Empire by the creation of a French Republic on the shores of the St. Lawrence River or by the pure and simple annexation of Upper and Lower Canada to the powerful republic to the south. Preventive armed action to force those pulling strings at Downing Street to back down was therefore, in their view, fully justified.

Adam Thom's perception of the reach and power of the British Empire is central to his arguments. It is based on factual data but also on a fertile imagination. The army, trade, and the banks are to spearhead the development of the Empire. The British had irrevocably overcome the insurmountable barrier of the Atlantic Ocean; its "manifest" destiny was to reach across North America to the Pacific and from there it could expand in all directions. Its planetary sphere of influence would be the protective envelope of all the subgroups that it would encompass. Letter LII of December 24, 1835 describes it brilliantly.

Montreal, which represents a fundamental axis of development, is the lynchpin of this vast and complex geostrategic network. It is located at the head of the only navigable waterway into the interior of the continent. Since Upper Canada (Ontario) has no direct access to the Atlantic, its economic development necessarily depends on transit through Montreal. With the lucrative trade from the Midwest being turned towards Montreal, the city would become the metropolis of the entire British North America and would compete directly with New York. Calling for the special rights for British expatriates, Thom draws an interesting parallel between the British settlers in Montreal and their fellow subjects settled in Bombay who were outraged to see the imperial authorities grant extended privileges to "foreigners," meaning the indigenous population of India, at the expense of subjects of British stock.[32]

The planetary expansion of the British commercial empire provides Thom with the means to develop an up-to-date version of the garrison mentality. In his *Remarks*, he anticipates an opinion expressed by Alexis de Tocqueville at the same time in the first volume of *Democracy in America*: "From Gaspé to Hull, the Canadians are surrounded by men of British origin" (1835, 5).[33] The Crown lands in the "Eastern Townships" were therefore a vital issue for the Montreal district.[34] Thom wanted the flow of immigration from the British Isles to counterbalance the equally spectacular population growth of the *Canadiens*. The British American Land Company nonetheless faced two economic and cultural obstacles: the seigneurial land regime, which delayed normal capitalist development of the territory and particularly on the Island of Montreal, and the peasant mentality of the "*enfans du sol*," who resisted settling elsewhere, as the British settlers themselves were doing—and so were the American pioneers along the "frontier" in the Midwest (L et LVIII).

The minority position of the Montreal Tory Oligarchy in the House of Assembly, however, turned the sense of being encircled upside down. Combined with the favourable position the authorities in the Mother Country had towards the "anti-British faction," which dominated as a result of the official policy of conciliation, the struggle to obtain the upper hand transformed the British settlers' urge to expand into its opposite. Though they were the conquerors in 1759 and 1760, they now felt they were under siege by a foreign population deeply hostile to their interests and development. This feeling of being under siege thus justified the close cooperation of the military command and regiments with the Tory magistrates (Thom saw it as a natural tight networking of the Orange and Masonic lodges). Here we get a glimpse of the hard inner core of the garrison mentality. Taking the position of victim inescapably led them to call for the civilians of British origin to take up arms and enrol in paramilitary organizations. The year 1835 saw, for example, the British Rifle Corps, which enjoyed the full approval of the executive committee of the Constitutional Association of Montreal, make a public appearance in preparation for a special congress of all the loyalist forces in Lower and Upper Canada. When this paramilitary organization marched in the St. Andrew's Day parade and thereby made the festivities a military event, Thom's prophesying reached new heights. He was not off mark:

> The appearance of yesterday's band of brothers convinces me, my lord, that the provisions of that bill [withdrawal of soldiers guarding the polls during elections], if they ever come into operation, will, in less than three years, give your lordship's oppressed and insulted countrymen the exclusive possession of the island of Montreal and of any the communications with Upper Canada both on the Ottawa and on the St. Lawrence (XLIII).

The anticipated failure of the attempt to intimidate the executive would nonetheless prompt Thom to project his dreams of violence into some foggy future. Despite the sleepy old tale we are told, the

Canadian political institutions in fact find their roots in the prophetic words of Adam Thom. In his letter of November 18, 1835, he refers to the statue of Wolfe and Montcalm in Quebec City burning their flags, thereby heralding the "second conquest" of Quebec that Gosford's successor, John Colborne, will be called upon to command (XXXVI). A few days later he hammered his point home, unequivocally. Pooh-poohing the idea of a victorious insurrection led by the democratic "demagogues," Thom cuts to the quick. Only a call to arms (on the condition that the regiments provide support) will allow the "English citizens of this province" to claim their rights. Thus:

> An English insurrection, however, a conciliatory cabinet may wisely dread—an insurrection not against a British King but against a French Viceroy. Such an insurrection is to be dreaded, not only as comparatively probable, but as absolutely certain of ultimate success (XXXIX).

The Montreal Tory faction's attempt to awe the Governor with the establishment of a volunteer rifle corps ended, as we know, when Governor Gosford censured them in January 1836. However, the question of the people of British stock taking up arms would remain at the core of their conflict with the colonial executive right up until the Proclamation of Martial Law in the district of Montreal on December 5, 1837.

In another work, I demonstrated that the torpedoing of the governor's plan for civil involvement immediately prompted the volunteers to mutiny with the support of the military command.[35] Mutual distrust was so intense that J. S. McCord and the disgruntled gentlemen in the Tory Oligarchy were threatened with another proclamation. In his capacity as the go-between who linked the military command and Attorney General Ogden, McCord was in a strategic position. His testimony is therefore crucial. In a highly emotional speech, McCord stated that:

> [...] with what deep anxiety did we watch the proceedings of a wilfully blind Executive, ever crying out peace, peace, when there was

no peace, — whilst treason openly marched through our streets, and men, self-styled patriots, were permitted, in open day, to drill and organize themselves for the avowed purpose of overthrowing everything we held sacred, whilst the services of our loyal fellow-citizens, eagerly tendered in the hour of need, were not only coldly refused, but their energies attempted to be crushed by *proclamation*, as if there were treason in the offer to defend our country (Cheers.)[36]

Adam Thom's prophetic insurrection resonates curiously in the anecdote "A Loyal Scotchman." Somebody had asked him

[...] whether the English inhabitants of Montreal, *now that they had got arms in their hands*, should not demand the removal of Lord Gosford. I replied, that such a step would be unjustifiable mutiny but that he or say any other person was at perfect liberty to make the removal of Lord Gosford the condition of taking up or laying down arms as a volunteer (*HA*, December 6, 1837).

Much more than the simple "removal" of Gosford was at play here. When George Moffatt and William Badgley went to England in the spring of 1838, the two ultra Tories made their case to Lord Durham:

[...] we believe that the existence of a separate French Government would not be tolerated on the continent of North America, we must in candour state to Your Lordship our firm persuasion, that the Provincial inhabitants of British origin in Lower Canada are resolved to submit no longer than they shall be compelled to the predominant power of French Canadian ascendancy by which the resources of the Province have been blighted and its advance in the scale of Colonial improvement retarded [...] No longer delay therefore in effecting the Union of the Canadas should be contemplated.[37]

Conclusion

As noted before, in 1883, some fifty years after the publication of the *Anti-Gallic Letters,* Sir John Robert Seeley, historian and champion of the British Empire, wrote essentially the same thing as Adam Thom about the indigenous French-speaking population of Canada. In Seeley's view, creation of the Dominion of Canada under the British North America Act of 1867, despite minor concessions, had not changed—and would not change—the fundamental course of history foretold by Adam Thom. Seeley wrote: "here too the alien element [the *Canadiens*] dwindles, and is likely ultimately to be lost in the English immigration, and also that its animosity has been much pacified by the introduction of federal institution."

Although the sun did set on the British Empire—while rising on the American—both Thom and Seeley have proven to be visionaries as regards the descendants of the *Canadiens*. Demographically, politically, and economically, Quebec has almost steadily lost power within Canada ever since the 1830s. Careful readers of the *Anti-Gallic Letters* will thus understand why the title of this edition includes the word **Prophetic.**

The *Letters* also help understand Canada better. F. Murray Greenwood, as noted above, explained that a "garrison mentality" dominated the hearts and minds of British authorities in Canada almost from the time of the Conquest until 1815, while Senior talked about the alliance between the garrison and the British (Tory) party lasting until 1849. The "garrison mentality" that these two historians describe arose from fear of a potentially disloyal and majority population of *Canadiens*, the possible return of revolutionary France to North America, and the American Revolution. Moreover, knowing that Canada later adopted the paramilitary Northwest Mounted Policeman as a national symbol, one might conclude that the garrison mentality has lasted much longer.

Northrop Frye, probably English-speaking Canada's greatest literary critic, identified in 1971 what he described as a "garrison mentality" in the Canadian imagination. He wrote, "A garrison is a closely knit and beleaguered society, and its moral and social values are unquestionable." Margaret Atwood also perceived a similar mentality in English-Canadian literature in her 1972 book, *Survival: A Thematic Guide to Canadian Literature*. Some have linked this mentality primarily to anti-Americanism stemming from the Loyalist population who fled north during and after the American Revolution. Others, including Frye, see it as being an offshoot of the wildness of the natural environment in Canada and the terror it inspires. Readers of *The Anti-Gallic Letters* will see the "garrison mentality" is also, if not primarily, an offshoot of Canada's relationship with the "alien element" within, as Thom and Seeley put it.

Publication of this new annotated edition of the *Anti-Gallic Letters* will hopefully provide new insight on the roots of Canada's political institutions and on the difficulty Canada has in dealing this "alien element," concentrated in Quebec.

Walter Benjamin, in *Sur le concept d'histoire*, wrote that, "the true image of the past flits by."[38] Citing Dante, he adds that it is a "unique and irreplaceable image of the past that fades with each present that has failed to recognize itself as its aim." This new annotated edition of Adam Thom's *Anti-Gallic Letters* and the still-to-be-heard "voice of transatlantic thunder" will possibly be silently ignored—if not censored—in Canada's prevailing historical conscience. Yet once historians and attentive readers have perused this work and reflected on the context, they will inescapably feel challenged now that the evidence has been made available.

4

ANTI-GALLIC LETTERS

ANTI-GALLIC LETTERS ;

ADDRESSED

TO

HIS EXCELLENCY,

THE EARL OF GOSFORD,

GOVERNOR-IN-CHIEF OF THE CANADAS,

BY

CAMILLUS.
MONTREAL :

PRINTED AT THE HERALD OFFICE.

1836.
Price 2S. 6D

Anti-Gallic Letters Addressed to His Excellency, the Earl of Gosford, Governor-in-Chief of the Canadas by CAMILLUS.

PREFACE.

The following letters, originally published in the *Montreal Herald*, are now re-printed for sale in the Canadas, and for gratuitous distribution in the Lower Provinces and the United Kingdom. For any inaccuracies and inconsistencies, that may be discovered, the circumstances, under which the letters were almost necessarily written, may form some apology. With two trifling exceptions, they were composed amid the noise and confusion of an office open to all comers; and hardly one of them, unless as a proof, was ever read by the writer either in manuscript or in print.

ADAM THOM, A. M.

Herald Office

1st February, 1836.}*

---

* This annotated edition comprises eighty percent of Adam Thom's original Letters. The original punctuation and spelling has been maintained.

No. I.[1]

My Lord,

As Governor of Lower Canada, your lordship may be sometimes compelled to act without sufficient deliberation; as a Royal Commissioner, you are solemnly bound to collect on every point the fullest possible evidence.

The very appointment of Royal Commissioners[2] necessarily restricts your lordship's functions as Governor within the narrowest possible limits, and justifies the English population in expecting, that no executive measure, which can be postponed, shall be carried into effect either with or without the concurrence of your lordship's fellow-Commissioners. But for the prevalence of certain rumours, I should not have expected, that the slightest interference of the junior Commissioners with your lordship's executive duties would have been either attempted or tolerated. These two functionaries are only competent to inquire, and, even if competent to act, can do so only within their own sphere and after the most minute and most patient investigation. For the acts of the executive, your lordship must, therefore, be alone held responsible; and I cannot but infer from facts, without paying any attention to mere rumours, that your lordship has already incurred the very heavy responsibility of effecting a secret compromise[3] with a part—a large part, I admit, but still only a part—not of the Assembly, as a legally constituted body, but of the members of the Assembly.[4]

The report of the *Canadien*[5] as to the intended elevation of Mr. Viger[6] or Mr. Lafontaine[7] to the judicial bench, followed up, as it was, by an unambiguous confirmation in your lordship's English organ,[8] clearly justifies the strongest suspicions of a secret compromise. What that compromise substantially is, the most ordinary intellect cannot fail to discover.

The French enemies of the English name, while they clamour, and perhaps sincerely, about an elective council, are meanwhile peculiarly eager for a large share of the public revenue in the shape of illegal contingencies and official emoluments. The English cabinet, on the other hand, from the very moment of Sir Robert Peel's mention of a Royal Commission, has been chiefly, if not solely, desirous of being extricated from pecuniary embarrassments by the grant of a civil list.[9]

The compromise, therefore, must be the barter of a civil list for illegal contingencies and official emoluments; and the intended promotion of Mr. Viger or Mr. Lafontaine, proves, to a certain extent, *the nature of the compromise*, as clearly as the sources of the report prove *its existence*.

Had your lordship resided long enough in the province to form mature opinions in regard to the provincial politics, I might have been prevented by ignorance from combating your excellency's motives for such a compromise; but, as matters do stand, I am fortunately able to refer your lordship's conduct to the fatal principle, if principle it can be called, of conciliation.[10] I do not mean to say, that your lordship's conduct is not warranted by the letter of your instructions; but, as your lordship well knows, that those instructions were dictated by fears, which your lordship must have already found to be groundless and ridiculous, you cannot fail to see, that a little delay in waiting for other instructions is within the limits of sound and justifiable discretion. Be this as it may, I shall only discharge the duty of a good citizen, in submitting to your excellency's consideration a few strong objections against the contemplated arrangement of what may be called the official grievances of the Government and the French faction.[11]

By granting the contingencies on any grounds, however weak or however strong, your lordship manifestly throws away almost the only peaceable means[12] of inducing the assembly to grant English claims, however just, and to redress English grievances, however severe. The want of money distressed the faction not less than it distressed the provincial executive; while his Majesty's government had, what the assembly had not, a direct remedy at its own disposal in resuming the crown duties by an imperial statute.[13]

In negotiating with the leaders of the assembly, your lordship seems to have forgotten that there is a legislative council; and your lordship can hardly expect, that the members of that body will sanction a compromise, which is essentially objectionable on principle, and is effected by means derogatory to their own dignity and subversive of their own independence. The legislative council, therefore, will, as a matter of course, carry the rejection of any supply bill founded on a secret compromise, as the only mode of affording adequate protection to its virtual constituents. Thus will your lordship have surrendered the revenue and lowered the dignity of the bench without any equivalent whatever.

Your lordship, moreover, will be exchanging a lesser evil for a greater. The French faction may refuse to appropriate any portion of the provincial revenue to the maintenance of the provincial government; but the English population can, if it be unanimous, prostrate the provincial government and the French faction, by cutting off the very sources of the public revenue.[14] Your lordship may have been led to believe, that the avowed determination of the constitutionalists, to resist the extension of French domination, was merely an empty threat;[15] but they have not forgotten, that the glorious fields of Cressy, Poictiers, Agincourt and Minden were won by "miserable" minorities of Englishmen over vast majorities of Frenchmen[16]. At present, however, milder weapons, than the sword and the musket, will be sufficient to distress the enemies of the English population, not by the artificial poverty of an overflowing treasury, but by the real pressure of empty coffers.

In my next letter, I shall convince your excellency of the practicability of such a measure without the slightest violation of the law.

I have the honour to be,
My Lord,

Your Lordship's most obedient humble servant,

CAMILLUS.

***

No. II.

Montreal, 29th Sept., 1835.

My Lord,

In my letter of yesterday, I drew your excellency's attention to the fact, that the secret compromise, into which you appear to have entered with the French faction of the provincial legislature, would, like every other conciliatory expedient, ultimately aggravate the malady, which it professes to cure.[17] I stated to your lordship, what I doubt not will prove to be the fact, that the English members of the legislative council, who are the virtual representatives of the English population, will never so far forget the just claims of their compatriots or so far sacrifice the constitutional privileges of their own body, as to become "patrons of seditious conventions[18] and accomplices in public robbery" by sanctioning the barter of illegal contingencies for a civil list. Should your lordship be tempted to neutralise those virtual representatives of the English population by an infusion of French revolutionists,[19] your lordship will be pleased to observe, that every Englishman, as well as every French supporter of English connexion, would be literally an outlaw[20]—always excepting the patriotic protection of a bending, cracking, breaking reed of an executive.[21] It is, my lord, the principle of liberals, so far as liberals have any permanent principle, that freeborn men are bound to obey only those laws, which they have a voice in framing;[22] and, though I may not carry this principle to its full extent, yet I will carry it so far, as to admit, that, when a hundred thousand inhabitants of this colony, who possess far more than an average share both of property and of intelligence, are deprived of any and every share of legislative power without their own consent, they may fairly avail themselves of the foregoing convenient principle of liberals. They may do so still more fairly, if they are outlawed by the delegates of the very state, to which they are zealously and faithfully attached. If the old colonies were oppressed, they were at least spared the insulting degradation of being oppressed through the instrumentality of Frenchmen; and yet it may be well for your lordship to reflect, that the dread of such degradation, excited by the conciliatory act of 1774,[23] was the very drop, that made the cup of American discontent overflow. May I presume to draw your lordship's most serious attention to the fact, that the FIRST step towards the establishment of French supremacy in this province, led to the political independence of the OLD colonies. What the LAST step may effect in the NEW colonies, I shall leave to your lordship to conjecture and to time to determine.[24]

As the secret compromise, which at present forms the main subject of these letters, affects the disposal of the provincial revenue, I shall proceed to shew, that, according to the established doctrines of the most liberal radicals, it is cruelly unjust towards the English population of this province. You will agree with me, my lord, that those who furnish the greater part of the public revenue, ought to have some control over the public expenditure. Granted, as a matter of course. With this concession, then, can your lordship reconcile the establishment of a system, by which those, who pay hardly any part of the revenue, shall spend the whole of it according to their will and pleasure, and by which those, who fill the public treasury, shall tamely see it pillaged by traitors, equally beggarly and greedy. Let me solemnly implore your lordship to believe, that such a system will not be suffered[25] to exist.

I shall reserve for my next letter the detail of the peaceful means of overthrowing such a system, and close this communication by proving, that the French inhabitants of Lower Canada pay but a very scanty portion of the provincial revenue.

On what does a French habitant pay duty? Is it on woollen stuffs of his own manufacture? Is it on wooden shoes, the produce of his own bush? Is it on tobacco, the growth of his own fields? Is it on sugar, the juice of his own maple-groves? Is it on wine, which he never tastes? Is it on books, which he cannot read? Is it on spirits, distilled from his own grain, and coloured and flavoured in to very palatable and very wholesome rum? To all the questions but the last, I must answer in the negative; and to the last question I reply, that the French habitant does pay on his rum a duty of about one penny, Halifax currency, per gallon as a gallon of real rum, which pays 6d. sterling and 6d. currency per gallon, flavours almost any given quantity of native spirits. If we reckon 80,000 families of French habitans and allow each family half a gallon per week, we shall derive from them a gross annual revenue of £8,666 13s. 4d., Halifax currency, being a trifle more or less than the annual contingencies of the assembly. That the compound of native spirits and West India rum has already entirely supplanted the use of the latter ingredient in its pure state, I do not mean to assert; but I do assert that, before many years shall have elapsed, the aforesaid compound will be the rum of every French habitant. An alarming decrease in the quantity of imported rum is gradually taking place. As to the cause of the decrease, wise men differ. Some blame the stratagem of importing rum of double strength to evade the payment of full duty; others very foolishly babble about "the state of the West Indies", as if there were no rum to be had in Jamaica for love or money.

In regard to the French inhabitants of cities, your lordship and the junior commissioners must have already observed, that they do not yield a revenue by any means proportioned to their numbers or their wealth.

You will, therefore, come to the conclusion, that the greater share of the revenue is paid by the English inhabitants of the province; and I may take an early opportunity of shewing your lordship that such share ought not to go exclusively into the treasury of Lower Canada.

I have the honour to be, my Lord,

Your Lordship's most obedient humble servant,

CAMILLUS.

***

No. III

Montreal, 30th Sept. 1835.

My Lord,

The provincial revenue is, almost exclusively, paid by the English inhabitants of the province, whether as consumers or as importers. In behalf of my compatriots in their character of consumers, I have already appealed to your lordship's sense of justice; and I now beg to direct your lordship's sense of expediency to their power of affecting the amount of revenue in their character of importers.

With the exception of the half-crazy delegate of the East Ward of Montreal,[26] there is not a single English merchant in Lower Canada, who does not view the French faction, even in its present state of weakness, as a deadening incubus on the spirit of commercial enterprise, and who has not reason, even on the selfish ground of personal interest, to endure gladly any temporary sacrifice, that may humble the French demagogues and all the official patrons of the French demagogues in the dust. The nature of the secret compromise, my lord, proves clearly, that an empty treasury is one mode, and perhaps the only mode, of compelling the government and the faction to surrender at discretion; for it would be uncharitable, my lord, to suppose, that either the government or the faction would require stronger motives to act equitably, than what it may deem sufficient to justify secret pillage.[27]

That your lordship may estimate the readiness, with which enlightened merchants can submit to temporary sacrifices for the sake of ultimate advantages, I beg to apprise your lordship, that the merchants of New York have cordially approved the scheme of enlarging the Erie canal, either at the temporary sacrifice of the greater part of their western trade or at the expense of carrying on the present trains by more circuitous and more costly routes. These enlightened New Yorkers must suffer loss and inconvenience for several years; but one year's perseverance on the part of the English merchants of Canada would compel the government and the faction to surrender at discretion. What have they to do? To import from New York, everything which can be so imported. The partial loss of the trade of Upper Canada, which Montreal must thus sustain, would be more than counterbalanced, even in a commercial view, by the rapid influx of American settlers and American capital. True it is, that duties, and higher duties too, are payable on the boundary line than at Quebec or Montreal; but it is not quite so easy, on an artificial line of great length as it is at a single point, to ascertain, that duties *payable* are *actually paid*. Reflect then, my lord, that outlaws, who are not protected by the law, are not themselves morally bound to *protect* and hardly even *to obey* the law. Reflect, my lord, on this, and be assured, that the English inhabitants of Lower Canada, if placed under the legislative and executive control of a French faction, will remain, and that only for a time, subjects of Great Britain rather from motives of policy and affection, than from a sense of duty and allegiance.[28] Permit me, however, to explain to your lordship, that these oppressed subjects of his Majesty are devotedly attached to British connexion and British institutions, and that they anticipate any decisive change in their political relations, as a matter not of choice but of necessity, as an evil more tolerable than the combined insult and injury of a French yoke. Such a yoke, your lordship, I am sure, must confess to be truly intolerable. Let me contrast with such a disposition the avowedly rebellious feelings of the French faction. The *Vindicator* of yesterday quotes with approbation an editorial article of an American newspaper, published in the district of Columbia, which contains the following remark:—"Almost to a man would the French Canadians rejoice to throw off the English yoke." Study this confession, my lord, and compare it with the *Vindicator's* "Samples of constitutional Loyalty." Ask yourself, then, whether of the two races in Lower Canada is the more likely to maintain the connexion of the mother country and the colony.[29] By increasing the power of the French faction, you inevitably dismember the empire;[30] by shielding your compatriots from oppression, you preserve British America for many years to come as a happy and prosperous appendage of the British Isles. Englishmen, my lord, are neither stocks nor stones. Can Frenchmen love England, as men of British blood, however far removed by space or time, love her?

The Frenchmen, my lord, confess, that they aim not at a redress of grievances, but at the establishment of national independence.[31] Did ever an English colonist say so much? Did not Benjamin Franklin, in his quaint way, acknowledge, that England could have retained America for a century longer by the judicious use of a little pen, ink and paper?[32] The Americans, even after the commencement of the civil war, still yearned with affection for "Old England", and were willing and anxious to return to their allegiance under an adequate guarantee against future oppression. On the 19th April and 17th June, 1775, respectively, were fought the battles of Lexington and Bunker's Hill; and yet on the 2nd July, 1776, the colonists of New Jersey put forth the following declaration, which still forms part of the constitution of that state:—

"Provided always, that it is the true intent and meaning of this Congress, that, if a reconciliation between Great Britain and these colonies should take place, and the latter be again taken under the protection and government of Great Britain, this charter shall be null and void, otherwise to remain firm and inviolable."

The Englishmen of New Jersey, my lord, did not object to the "government" of Great Britain, but to the "absolute domination" of the British Parliament. Do the Frenchmen of Lower Canada speak in an equally moderate tone? No, my lord, they "would rejoice to throw off the English yoke", not because they are oppressed by England, but because they hate English institutions and the English name. They cannot, in justification of their conduct, point to the battle-fields stained with the blood of their fathers, brothers and sons, shed by English bullets and English bayonets— unless, indeed, the ungrateful traitors attempt to make a grievance of the Plains of Abraham, which a 'miserable minority' of English foreigners drenched with the blood of a vast majority of true and faithful Frenchmen. Encourage their intimacy, my lord, and hear them style the heroic Wolfe a bloodthirsty ruffian.[33] Such language would be quite in keeping with the character of a party, whose leader— the very being with whom your lordship appeals to have held private communication—so often stigmatised Lord Aylmer as a murderous tyrant, and once styled Colonel Mackintosh a "fanatic brute."[34]

The long digression, into which I have been inevitably led, has prevented me from showing in this letter, that, when Upper Canada gets her fair share of the import duties, Lower Canada will not have sufficient revenue to defray the expenses of the legislature and the executive. In my next letter I shall make this very clear, and thus point out to your lordship a third peaceful mode of prostrating both the executive government and the French faction. It is better, far better, for the loyal inhabitants of this province, that there should be a scanty revenue, than that an ample one should be employed by greedy and dishonest revolutionists as an instrument of oppression and a feeder of rebellion. I for one beg to assure your lordship, that, if my suspicions of a secret compromise be confirmed by facts, I shall incessantly devote my moral and physical energies to unite Upper Canada its one man in the untiring demand of a fair share of the import duties, whether by a division of receipts or a distribution of ports of entry. This, my lord, is the declaration of a man, who has never sacrificed his political consistency and never faltered in his political career, and who confidently anticipates the day, when the undying perseverance of true Englishmen will make French factions and Frenchified cabinets quail in terror and dismay.

Your lordship's course, so far as it can be gathered from the language of your lordship's organs, English and French, will doubtless accelerate that day. Here again I must allude to the American revolution.[35] When the surrender of Montreal had released the English colonists from the terror of their French neighbours, Mr. Jonathan Sewell, father of the present chief justice of the province,[36] as also of the present speaker of the legislative council, and grand-father of many a junior servant of his Majesty, remarked to John Adams, that the English government, unless resisted by a demonstration of force, would attempt to subdue the colonies to its arbitrary will. Mr. Sewell's sentiment was soon spread by the aid of unwise legislation on the part of Great Britain; and the English government at last kindled discontent into rebellion by the Frenchifying act of 1774. Whether England intended by that act to use the French Canadians as instruments for oppressing America, I do not know; but I have made it evident, that the Americans put such a construction on that statute and ACTED ACCORDINGLY.

I have the honour to be, my Lord,
Your lordship's most obedient humble servant,

CAMILLUS.

***

(...)

No. V

Montreal, 2nd October, 1835

My Lord

There are various principles, on which the import duties may be divided between the two Canadas. Some persons would have these duties to be divided in proportion to the respective expenditures on account of the legislature, the executive and the judiciary; others in proportion to population; others in proportion to consumption of taxed articles. On each of these methods I shall offer a few remarks.

So long as the crown duties, which were expressly destined for the support of the civil government and the administration of justice, were expended under the direction of the commissioners of the treasury, these duties at least ought to have been divided between the two provinces according to the spirit, if not the letter, of the first method. I say the spirit, my lord, and not the letter, because the literal application of the principle would have held out a premium to extravagance, and would have made the more economical province contribute to the expenditure of her more extravagant neighbor. For instance, my lord, while the speaker of the one assembly receives only £300 a year, the speaker of the other,[37] by a compromise equally secret and disgraceful, robs the public of a salary five times as large. So far, therefore, as these salaries are concerned, the literal application of the first method of division would reward the profligacy of the one legislature with a dollar, and punish the economy of the other with a paltry shilling. But, since the conciliatory statute of his present Majesty surrendered the crown duties to the provincial legislatures, the dominant faction in Lower Canada has so far diverted these duties from their original destination, by refusing to make any appropriation for the support of the civil government and the administration of justice, that it cannot, consistently at least, demand a division of the crown duties or of any other duties, according to the first method in proportion to the respective expenditures. It must, therefore, quietly submit to some more equitable method of division, even though that method may render necessary the imposition of direct taxes, for carrying on the government of the province of Lower Canada. Would the English outlaws, my lord, be bound, on moral or even on liberal principles, to pay taxes, to the imposing of which they could not have consented, and by the spending of which they would inevitably be oppressed? Could the French faction compel the English outlaws to pay such taxes? Certainly not, unless your lordship or some other advocate of conciliation should disgrace English soldiers by ranging them on the side of dastardly and deadly enemies, for the destruction of friends, countrymen and brothers. English soldiers, my lord, would, of course, obey orders; but, in troops less carefully trained, nature might prove too powerful for discipline. Strong feeling, my lord, must be my apology for this or any other digression.[38]

The method of dividing the import duties between the two provinces in proportion to population is almost too absurd for discussion. Were both provinces inhabited by one and the same race, the proposed method would be plausible, though not faultless; but to assume, that a French Canadian contributes as much as an Englishman to the public revenue, is to confound indolence with enterprise, barbarism with civilisation, contented ignorance with ambitious intelligence.[39] It is true, that the manufactured goods, which are chiefly consumed by the English inhabitants, pay a duty of only 2½ per cent., and that the rum, which the French Canadians, like the red *enfans du sol*, liberally quaff, pays about a shilling a gallon, being equivalent perhaps to 25 or 30 per cent.; but this argument in favour of the Canadians, as I have already stated to your lordship, has been almost annihilated by a general substitution of a compound of native spirits and West India rum, so that 400,000 French habitans will soon pay a smaller share of the import duties than 10,000 English citizens of Toronto. At the date of the next adjustment, therefore, the principle of dividing in proportion to population will be utterly inadmissible.

The division, therefore, must be effected in proportion to the consumption of taxed articles. How is that consumption to be ascertained? The principle of population may be here introduced, so far as to make the respective numbers of consumer tests of the respective consumptions. The French agitators estimate the French population of Lower Canada at 525,000 and the English at 75,000; but if I diminish the former so as to double the latter, I find only 150,000 such consumers as Upper Canada contains, If I reckon the French population as equivalent to 50,000 such consumers, I find here altogether 200,000 consumers, or little more than half the population of Upper Canada. At the date of the next adjustment, therefore, Upper Canada will have a clear right to fully two thirds of the import duties, for an adjustment, that is to continue in force for four years, ought, in justice to the more rapidly increasing province of Upper Canada, to be fixed in reference rather to the probable circumstances of the middle of the quadriennial period than to the actual circumstances of its commencement. The adjustment ought either to be fixed on this principle or to be fixed every year. It is sufficiently galling for Upper Canada to be dependent on Lower Canada; but it is still more galling for the former to pay tribute as well as homage to the latter.[40] For many years, however, such has been the humiliating fact. The share of Upper Canada has risen from 20 per cent, to 25, from 25 to 33£, and must, in two years, rise from 33 1/3 to at least 50 per cent. During the first period, she should have received 22½ per cent.; during the second, 29 1/6 per cent; and during the present period, 41 2/3 per cent. Her least loss, therefore, is equivalent to more than the difference between currency and sterling; while at present she loses precisely one fifth of her due, or, in other words, receives four shillings in place of a dollar. If one, my lord, takes a different view of the present loss of Upper Canada, one will find that Lower Canada seizes, at the expense of her sister, eight and one-third per cent, on the whole of the divided duties, equal, by a singular enough coincidence, to a feudal fine.

To-morrow, my lord, I shall resume the consideration of this subject; and, in the meantime, I beg to assure you, that the English inhabitants of Lower Canada have a direct interest in transferring the import duties, which your lordship seems to have surrendered to an anti-commercial faction, to their enterprising and intelligent compatriots of the upper province.

Let me once again implore your lordship to reflect and pause, ere it be too late. The danger, though invisible, may yet be nearer than your lordship imagines. Revolutions, my lord, that are intended to be permanent, are not effected in a day. Let me again allude to the American revolution. Sixteen years, my lord, elapsed between Mr. Jonathan Sewell's recommendation of physical resistance to oppression and the declaration of American independence; but each year contributed its mite towards accelerating the catastrophe of a drama, in which foolish ministers were the principal actors. Even between the first instance of physical resistance and that catastrophe, there intervened the long period of three years, in each of which the plot gradually thickened. In 1773, the tea was thrown into the harbour of Boston; in 1774 the first congress met at Philadelphia; in 1775, were fought the battles of Lexington and Bunker's Hill; in the winter of 1775-6, Canada was invaded and evacuated; and on 4th July, 1776, was signed the declaration of American independence.

I have the honour to be,
My Lord,
Your Lordship's most obedient humble servant,

CAMILLUS.

***

No. VI.

Montreal, 3rd October, 1835.

My Lord,

I yesterday proved, that Upper Canada, as she was admitted to have a right to one-third of the import duties at the date of the last adjustment and would certainly be admitted to have a right to one-half at the date of the next, was entitled to receive annually during the whole of the quadriennial period the arithmetical mean between the two quantities, or, in other words, 41 2/3 instead of 33 ½ £ per cent. I, moreover, inferred, that, under the existing arrangement, she receives precisely four shillings in place of a dollar. Your lordship must perceive, that either Lower Canada is a bankrupt or that Upper Canada is a tributary. Does your lordship think, that Upper Canada will submit tamely to a system, which, besides being at present so galling and so iniquitous, becomes more oppressive every year[?] During the first of the three enumerated periods, Upper Canada was robbed of a *ninth* of her just claim; during the second, of a *seventh*; during the third, of a *fifth*. Her definite loss during the first two periods I am neither able nor anxious to specify; but during the last two years, she has been despoiled by Lower Canada of at least 100,000 dollars. In 1833 and 1834 respectively, she received, in round numbers, £60,000 and £40,000, whereas she ought to have received instead of these respective sums £75.000 and £50,000, or £25,000 more in all. This difference, my lord, would have paid more than half the interest on the sum borrowed for the construction of the St. Lawrence Canal.[41] The allusion to that magnificent work, my lord, gives me an opportunity of briefly proving, that the revenue of Upper Canada is more beneficial than that of Lower Canada to the English inhabitants of the latter province. These inhabitants are chiefly engaged in commerce, and more likely to derive benefit from the improvement of our noble river than from the extravagantly remunerated services of your personal friends,

Mr. Viger[42] and Mr. Papineau. Mark the contrast, my lord. The province, that receives less than her share of the revenue, does every thing for the promotion of public prosperity, while the province, that receives more than her due, does nothing—absolutely nothing. Your lordship must be aware, that you are doing as much, as in you lies, to establish and perpetuate the despotism of an anti-commercial and Anti-British faction. Let me call your lordship's special attention to a striking event in Roman history. A Gallic robber of the name of Brennus[43] had driven the last hopes of Roman power within the walls of the capitol. The besieged Romans, though they were a 'miserable minority', yet long withstood the fierce assaults of their savage foes; but worn out at last by famine and fatigue, they appointed a deputy to effect a compromise with the exulting and insolent barbarians. That deputy, my lord, did promise the barbarians gold. I admit, my lord, that he did so; but in justice to him, my lord of Gosford, I must add, that he stipulated for the salvation of the capitol. Can either of your organs say as much in justification of your lordship's compromise? Have you stipulated for the salvation of the capitol? No, my lord! The golden bribe, with which you have conciliated the barbarians, essentially involves the sacrifice of the capitol, the extinction of the last hopes of British connexion. But, my lord, I must proceed with the historical passage. The gold, my lord, was in the scale; many a Gallic ruffian was directing one eye in contempt on the abject deputy and another in eagerness on the glittering bribe; the audacious and dishonest leader was already giving a foretaste of violated promises, broken treaties and trampled rights. Such was the scene, my lord, when a man, whom the intended victims of Gallic avarice and treachery had suspected and insulted and injured, put an end to the compromise, and ransomed the capitol, not with gold but with iron.

That your lordship may have leisure to ponder on this digression, I shall close this letter and subscribe myself,

Your Lordship's most obedient humble servant,

CAMILLUS.

***

No. VII.

Montreal, 6th October, 1835.

My Lord,

I have already proved to your lordship, that Upper Canada, through the practical misapplication of the professed principle of adjustment, has been annually deprived of part of her admitted share of the import duties. But, my lord, that principle of adjustment, however liberally applied, would be unjust towards Upper Canada. That province is clearly entitled to a share, proportioned not to what her consumption of taxed goods actually is, but to what it would be in the event of her having a sea-board of her own. Suppose for a moment, my lord, that the two Canadas were as independent of each other in regard to maritime trade as are the states of Massachusetts and New York, and then ask yourself, how many Englishmen would be residents of Lower Canada. About a tithe of their present number. Had Mr. Pitt[44] been able to mould the face of the country to his will, so as to make the Atlantic wave dash against both provinces, he would almost literally have effected the desired separation of the French and the English, and would have rendered English Canada and French Canada respectively the rivals of Massachusetts and the land of the Esquimaux. Mr. Pitt, it is true, was not able literally to do so; but be might have done almost the same thing by giving Montreal to Upper Canada as a port of entry.[45] Mr. Pitt, however, banished Upper Canada seventy or eighty miles farther towards the west, thus preventing the desired separation of the two races, so as to make Lower Canada the arena of national struggles[46] and virtually to rob Upper Canada of part of her population.

Is it not, my lord, sufficient for Upper Canada to lose all the benefits of the private expenditure of that portion of her population—a private expenditure too, drawn from her own industry and capital —without losing also the benefits of its contributions to the public revenue?

Is not the grievance, my lord, rendered more bitter and more indigestible by the reflection, that these contributions to the public revenue are, with your lordship's aid, to swell the pride and sharpen the fangs of a faction, hostile to commerce, hostile to immigration, hostile to the best interests of Upper Canada? The organs of the faction may tell your lordship, that Lower Canada has a clear right to all the public revenue paid by her inhabitants, on the ground that she must find the means of governing and improving all her territory. So far, my lord, as the improvement of the country is concerned, the argument is entirely fallacious. When you visit Montreal, my lord, you will see an unfinished harbour, almost impassable wharves, and a canal, that does not yield a single farthing for defraying the expenses of attendance and repairs. But, my lord, my pen runs too fast. Your lordship, on your way to Montreal, may be mud-bound amid the easily deepened shallows of Lake St. Peter. Should your lordship, however, reach Montreal, and pass on towards the more westerly portion of your delegated dominions, your lordship will be able to judge for yourself, whether the public revenue has been hitherto expended for the promotion of public prosperity. If your lordship proceed by the Ottawa, you will find that almost every improvement has been effected either by private individuals or by the imperial government. Should you prefer the route by the St. Lawrence, you may ascertain the boundary by the unaided glance of your own eye. The French rapids of Lower Canada, so far as the provincial legislature is concerned, have been left in a state of nature; whilst the English rapids of Upper Canada lash the bank of the most magnificent canal on this continent, constructed by the province at vast expense, but rendered comparatively useless by the anti-commercial prejudices of a selfish and greedy faction in Lower Canada.

You, therefore, see, my lord, that Lower Canada cannot resist, at least on the alleged ground of improving the country, the just demand of Upper Canada for as much of the import duties, as she contributes, whether directly within her own limits or indirectly in Lower Canada. You also see, my lord, that, in this reasonable and just view, the English province is entitled to at least three-fourths of the import duties; and I must again repeat to your lordship, that such a principle of division would be doubly agreeable to the English inhabitants of this country, inasmuch as it would cripple the revolutionary factions and the conciliatory governments of the French province, and would lead to the more rapid and more effectual improvement of the English one.

If your lordship persevere in your intention of surrendering the contingencies, I solemnly assure your lordship, that I shall devote my power, such as it is, of stirring men's minds to the patriotic purpose of transferring the import duties from the French province of Lower Canada to the English province of Upper Canada. In so good a cause, my lord, I would even stoop to the baseness of courting popularity.[47] I would even become a demagogue, "a thing that crawls in the mire of party politics in these countries, and usually slavers like a fulsome toad the prey it gloats on, but which becomes, when it is hungry, unusually daring in its ferocity and reckless in its audacity—a thing, not like the crocodile, for it does possess the power of turning in all directions, and can twist and struggle with such facility as even to perform the Hibernian[48] exploit of turning its back upon itself—a thing, not like the serpent of Jamaica, for it does possess fangs, which are not destitute of venom—a non-descript reptile, partaking of the nature of the bull frog and the galley[-]wasp".[49]

Before I pause for a day, permit me to draw your lordship's attention to the letter of "Coz", in this day's *Courier*, which professes to expose the fallacy of my views. It is but right, that your lordship should see both sides of the question. The man's letter I have abstained from reading, lest I should be diverted from a noble quarry to the hunting of a weasel.

I have the honour to be,
My Lord,
Your Lordship's most obedient humble servant,

CAMILLUS.

***

(…)

No. XI.

Montreal, 10th October, 1835.

My Lord,

Having, in my last letter, proved that the views of the English inhabitants of this province are not more advantageous to themselves than to "His Majesty's Canadian subjects", I now proceed to prove that the success of these views can alone secure the connexion between the mother country and the colony, and maintain the integrity of the empire. Every sentence of my letters must have tended to convince your lordship of so important a fact; but I shall now enter a little more minutely and more formally into the merits of the question.

I yesterday heard, my lord, that an obscure man of the name of Malhiot,[50] whom some freak or other some time ago elevated to the legislative council, boasts of having told your lordship at a private interview, that, unless the demands of the French faction be conceded, Lower Canada will not belong to England more than thirty years. Having never before heard of the man, I take the report merely as I find it. The threat is supremely ridiculous, because *the lapse of thirty years will render the French Canadians a numerical minority.*[51] Every year, while it may legally strengthen the demagogues through the anti-national co-operation of a conciliatory government, will physically weaken them through the immigration of men of English blood from the old country and the United States. But, my lord, when, in the deadly struggle, race closes with race, party with party and man with man, legal strength will not atone for physical weakness; and your lordship must, therefore, perceive, that the demagogues, if they do intend to raise the tricolored standard of rebellion,[52] are worse than insane to defer the threatened exploit for thirty years or thirty months. But, my lord, they do not intend to do any such thing. Their threats of physical resistance are empty and false; but, for the credit of British statesmen, I am sorry to add, that they have not been altogether fruitless. Past success, my lord, inspires future audacity. The first tangible threat of a French rebellion, my lord, was embodied in some of the ninety-two resolutions[53]. The babbling Bobadils, who framed the false and foolish series, did not seem to have decided, whether they would set up for themselves with France as a model, or throw themselves into the arms of the United States. Both schemes were equally ridiculous and were intended merely to produce an effect on weak nerves. Whether they did produce any such effect, your lordship must know much better than Camillus. The scheme of uniting two races, more distinct perhaps than any other two races in the world—of which the inferior repays with jealous hatred the irrepressible contempt of the superior—elicited an almost universal burst of incredulous ridicule. Demonstration followed demonstration in the English journals to the effect, that the scheme, if carried into operation, would inevitably and almost instantly blast the fondly cherished hopes of Canadian nationality.[54] The revolutionary journals were prudently silent in regard to these unanswerable demonstrations; and yet they had the politic audacity occasionally to repeat the impracticable threat for the special benefit of conciliatory statesmen. Whether is the falsehood itself, my lord, more disgraceful to the demagogues, or the success of the falsehood to— others?

The reference to France, which was contained in the famous resolutions, displayed on the part of the revolutionists very little either of knowledge or of gratitude. The creatures forgot, that, as British subjects, they were the free grandsons of French serfs; and they were too dull or too prejudiced to understand, that any connexion with despotic France would convert the English whip, which existed only in their own crazy imaginations, into the hot and heavy reality of a French scorpion. But, if, my lord, the revolutionists had really intended to hold out the right hand of fellowship to France, they would, most probably, have paused in their career, lest they might seem, in any respect, to imitate the liberal Gallomania of hated England.

The Canadians, my lord, will never rise in arms against the British government. Your lordship's French organ, with characteristic want of tact, confessed, that the rural habitans neither felt any real grievances nor knew any of the imaginary ones. Can you, my lord, believe for a moment, that these *habitans* can be goaded by mere words into rebellion? You cannot believe so.[55] If then your lordship has the slightest reason to believe, that your instructions were at all affected by the notorious misapprehension of his Majesty's ministers, on the subject of the threatened insurrection, are you not, my lord, bound, as a man of honour and a British subject, to demand from the cabinet fresh instructions better adapted to the actual state of affairs[?].

If, however, the French Canadians should be goaded into rebellion by the specious falsehoods of shameless traitors,[56] such a rebellion would be speedily suppressed. If they should, in the first instance, shed the blood of every English inhabitant of the seigniories, they would pave the way not for ultimate success but for most awful retribution. They would be hemmed in by a gradually closing circle of English breasts and English bayonets,[57] and would, in a few short months, become the hunted of all hunters, the enslaved of all enslavers, the slain of all slayers. Their wretched leaders would wish, that they had never been born.

An English insurrection, however, a conciliatory cabinet may wisely dread—an insurrection not against a British King but against a French Viceroy. Such an insurrection is to be dreaded, not only as comparatively probable, but as absolutely certain of ultimate success. The probable consequences of such an insurrection I shall detail in my next letter; and meanwhile I implore your lordship to remember your royal master's command to Sir Charles Grey—"Canada must not be lost."

I have the honour to be,
My Lord,
Your Lordship's most obedient bumble servant,

CAMILLUS.

***

No. XII.

Montreal, 12th October, 1835.

My Lord,

In my last letter I attempted to convince your lordship, that an English insurrection against any French viceroy of Lower Canada would, most certainly, be ultimately successful; and I now proceed to point out the results of the success of such an insurrection. The loss of Lower Canada would necessarily involve the loss of all British America. The loss of British America would deprive England of her most productive fisheries, place her entirely at the mercy of foreigners for the main element of her maritime power, and leave her not a single port on this continent for sheltering her navy to the northward of Bermuda. If the colonies, my lord, be the wings of the empire, what would England, if deprived of her stronger wing, become among the nations of Europe? If, my lord, I may borrow an equally vulgar and appropriate expression from the Stock Exchange, she would become a lame duck. I earnestly implore your lordship to reflect, that such must be the result of a perseverance in the anti-national scheme of conciliating a handful of bawling and rebellious demagogues at the expense of the imperial dignity, in violation of sound principles and at the temporary sacrifice of the intelligent and loyal minority of English origin.

Having thus, my lord, exhibited the influence of farther conciliation of the French faction on the political peace of Lower Canada, I must now inquire, what influence such conciliation is likely to exercise on her agricultural and commercial prosperity. Here again, my lord, the past is the best index of the future.

Will the French faction, my lord, devote the public revenue to the improvement of the commercial facilities of the province? Will the demagogues deepen Lake St. Peter? Will they improve and extend the wharves of Montreal? Will they complete the magnificent line of communication so nobly undertaken by their tributary victim of Upper Canada? Will they make one effort to render Montreal, what nature destined her to be, the rival of New York? No, my lord; they will not do any thing, that at all tends to inundate the sacred soil of a French province with British or Irish or American foreigners. Should any funds remain, after the two contracting parties to the secret compromise are both satisfied, the French Assembly[58] will make the surplus an instrument of oppression, an engine for gagging the less patriotic portion of the outlawed minority. They will appropriate it, my lord, to local objects, which ought to be accomplished by local assessments, and thus buy the support or at least the neutrality of individuals, who are too short-sighted to see the fatal consequences of French supremacy or too selfish to sacrifice the less good of the present for the greater good of the future. Not many weeks, my lord, have elapsed, since professed constitutionalists condescended to wear the revolutionary mask in the hope of securing a giant of public money for a projected railroad. To gain their ends, they put a radical pauper of the name of Bardy in the chair and ordered their resolutions to be inserted only in the radical journals, *St. Francis Courier* of Sherbrooke,

Vindicator, Minerve and *Morning Courier* of Montreal. The sooner, my lord, that professed constitutionalists are not tempted to perpetrate such absurdities, so much the better; and the temptation will be taken away either when Upper Canada gets her fair share of the import duties, or when French influence ceases to be supreme in the provincial legislature. Thus, my lord, does every shilling of excess of revenue over and above the reasonable expenses of the legislature and the executive become a fatal obstacle to the ultimate prosperity of the province. Part of such excess, as I have just shewn, is dispensed in the shape of local bribes; while the other part of it is likely, with your lordship's consent, to swell the contingencies as pensions for Roebuck[59] and his tail, the London correspondents of the French *Vindicator.* Permit me, my lord, to remark in passing, that the secret com. promise, which your lordship seems to have sanctioned, presents an English nobleman in the character of patron to the French Vindicator, in the character of paymaster of the miserable hirelings, who have virtually recommended the assassination of British soldiers—who have stigmatised Lord Aylmer as a murderous tyrant—who have styled Mr. Spring Rice, who, according to the latest advices, was still Chancellor of the Exchequer, a notorious liar. Does your lordship remember Dean Swift's sarcastic remark on King William's motto. *Non rapui sed recepi*— "The receiver is as bad as the thief"?[60] The application, my lord, is too obvious; and I can only hope, for the honour of my country, that your lordship is innocent of the compromise, and that I am mistaken in my suspicions. I must here pause for a day; and meanwhile

I have the honour to be,
My Lord,
Tour Lordship's most obedient humble servant,

CAMILLUS.

***

(...)

No. XVII.

Montreal, 19th October, 1835.

My Lord,

The concessions, which will be successively demanded by the French faction from a conciliatory government, are the gift of the waste lands of the crown, the surrender of all executive and judicial offices and the republican blessing of an elective council. The demagogues, my lord, have already demanded all these concessions. Whether will the contemplated surrender of the illegal and iniquitous contingencies whet or cloy the revolutionary appetite of an avaricious and ambitious faction? Whet it, certainly, is the answer of your lordship. Yes, my lord, as certainly as the taste of human blood converts a tame lion into a thirsty manslayer. Unless your lordship be disposed to grant all the demands of the French faction, you will only excite indifference into discontent, warm discontent into clamour and ripen clamour into insult, by granting any one unreasonable and illegal demand. The secret compromise, therefore, drives me to one of two conclusions—either that your lordship's conciliatory disposition, in defiance of your general knowledge of human nature, gives the French faction credit for a marvellously large share of moderation, or that your lordship is ready to give the waste lands to those, who will close them against settlers of English blood, to hand over the executive authority to those, who have so systematically perverted their legislative privileges into the oppressive instruments of selfish aggrandisement, and to double and more than double these legislative privileges by filling the legislative council with the counterparts of those, who are already supreme in the assembly.[61] To one of these two conclusions, my lord, every man of discrimination must come.

If the former conclusion be correct, I shall content myself with predicting, that your lordship's favourable opinion of the demagogues will not last long—unless your lordship, like lord Melbourne, be so full of christian charity as to cherish in your bosom the very vipers[62], that may have stung you. But if, according to the latter conclusion, your lordship be prepared to grant all demands, I must do the duty of a good citizen of the British empire in pointing out to your lordship the inevitable consequences of granting each or any of the three enumerated concessions.

How would the French faction, my lord, dispose of the waste lands of the crown? The avowed resolution of the demagogues to exclude English settlers from the country and to establish a French-Canadian nationality, may enable the most superficial reasoner to return a true answer to the important question. The wastelands would be reserved in all the beautiful desolation of nature, until the seigniories should have been parcelled out into the potatoe gardens of starving myriads of a French population. This, my lord, would be bad enough; but the English outlaws of the neighbouring townships might make matters worse by bursting into the sacred reserve, axe in hand and rifle on shoulder.[63]

Without at all adverting to the legal obstacles, that stand in the way of the demanded transfer of the wild lands from the crown to the provincial legislature, I would draw your lordship's attention to the fact, that the system, which the demagogues would introduce into a British colony, does not exist even in the United States. In the American republic, my lord, the waste lands, excepting those in the states, that were original parties to the national compact, belong to the national government, and are placed under the control of the national legislature. I admit, my lord, that the new states make a grievance of that arrangement; but I beg your lordship to observe, that the old states refuse to surrender the broad lands, purchased in the revolutionary war and subsequently by their treasure and their blood. Will the British government make a similar stand against the

French demagogues, and point to the Plains of Abraham? But the cases, my lord, are not parallel. To make them so, the public lands of the Union should be claimed not by the new states but by the vanquished proprietors, the King of England and the red lords of the primeval forest.

But, my lord, even if the system, for which the demagogues clamour, did exist in the United States, it would not necessarily be proved to be proper for Lower Canada, for if republican institutions were, as a matter of course, to be taken as a model without reference to their theoretical accuracy or to their practical results, there would be little either of room or of necessity for political discussion and political action. But, my lord, in the special instance supposed, the cases could easily be shewn to be by no means analogical. In every state or almost every state of the Union, in every country, in short, where the population is homogeneous, political parties fluctuate and mingle to such a degree, as alternately to meet defeat and victory, and thus bear the one with hope and use the other with prudence. Hence unequal laws are almost unknown, not merely because the majority for the time being has a selfish motive for moderation but because it cannot draw any well defined boundary between itself and the existing minority. In Lower Canada, my lord, the case is alarmingly different. A man's accent decides his politics; and the majority is so firmly knit together and numerically so independent of the minority, that the former, even if the latter in a body were to join it and apparently extinguish all political differences, would be just as much a domineering and exclusive faction as it is. To such a faction, my lord, could the wastelands of the crown be entrusted?

The demagogues, my lord, claim the control of these lands not merely on abstract principle, but on the ground of abuses in the existing mode of management. That such abuses exist, I am not prepared to deny; but they may be remedied. That the waste lands have yielded but little revenue, I admit; but they have been as productive of revenue as the public lands of the American states. As much misconception exists on the productiveness of these public lands, permit me to call your lordship's attention to the following extract from a recently published pamphlet.

"On 30th September, 1831, the public lands thus stood in the ledger of the United States. They had cost $48,077,551.40 cents, and had yielded $37,273,713.31 cents, leaving a *clear loss* of $10,803,838. 9 cents. I now come to consider the proceeds of the public lands, not of the whole union, but of the separate states, as I find them stated in the American almanac for 1833.

Proceeds of Lands.   *Total Revenues*

State	Dollars	Cents	Dollars	Cents
Maine	2 452	16	256 401	78
Massachusetts	17 980	81	1 032 082	71
New York	72 047	80	174 0531	16
Pennsyvania	102 229	18	3 033 978	57
Total	195 809	95	6 062 994	22

I have the honour to be,
My Lord,
Your Lordship's most obedient humble servant,

CAMILLUS.

***

No. XVIII.

Montreal, 20th October, 1835.

My Lord,

I shall now attempt to point out the consequences, that must result from the French faction's possession of executive or judicial power.

It is, my lord, a fundamental maxim of the British constitution, that the legislature, the executive and the judiciary should be so far independent of each other, as that not one of the three should either control the other or be controlled by them.[64] Such, in fact, must be the fundamental maxim of the constitution of every free state, for the concentration of all the powers of the state in the hands of an individual or of a party is the very essence of despotism. But, my lord, though the poverty of language compels me to apply the same term to the tyranny of an individual and to that of a party, yet the despotism of one man is far less terrible than the despotism of a multitude An individual may be actuated by fear or pity or compunction; party, as, according to the proverb, it has neither a body to be kicked nor a soul to be damned, is never known to temper its selfishness by any better feeling. *Defendit numerus, juuctaeque umbone phalanges* (Unity in a phalanx creates a shield).[65]

A party, my lord, will take every thing and give nothing but— promises meant to be broken. It will bless its open or secret enemies at the hazard of doing evil to those that love it. It will celebrate the accession of one deserter from the enemy's camp, not by the slaughter of a fatted calf but by the sacrifice of ninety and nine able and zealous supporters. The despotism of a party, my lord, will obviously be more terrible in proportion as that party is well defined and permanently united; and there can hardly be imagined a party better defined or more permanently united than the French faction of Lower Canada.[66] On these grounds, my lord, I maintain, that the surrender of any portion of executive or judicial power to that faction is entirely inconsistent with the principles of constitutional freedom and utterly subversive of the rights of the English inhabitants of the province. Permit me, my lord, to make a single instance the subject of my observations. Your lordship has, doubtless, heard of the riots of 21st May, and of the assembly's infamously dishonest and slanderous persecution of the magistrates, the military and the judges.[67] What, my lord, would have been the fate of the victims of the

Assembly's slander, had Papineaus been the law officers of the crown and Lafontaines controlled the judicial bench? The victims would have been condemned to death as murderers, and could have been saved only by the royal mercy or, if that had been intercepted by a conciliatory cabinet, by the desperate spirit of English outlaws. Similar occasions may occur again;[68] and your lordship may, by bartering offices and emoluments for the sake of a civil list, be instrumental in perpetrating the most appalling enormities under the sacred names of law and justice. An insignificant member of the faction has said that "Camillus" should be prosecuted for sedition and treason and all that kind of thing. What chance, my lord, would "Camillus" have of a fair trial, if arraigned by a French attorney-general before French judges and French jurors?[69]

Your lordship has heard of Lynch law.[70] According to that law, my lord, the same individuals are law-makers, witnesses, jurors, judges and executioners. According to your lordship's system of conciliation, also, the same individuals would virtually be law-makers, witnesses, jurors, judges and executioners. Your lordship's system, therefore, will be doubly conciliatory. It will, of course, conciliate the French faction by gratifying at once its avarice, its ambition and its revenge; and it will, most probably, tickle the vanity of our American neighbours by adopting one of their practical deductions from "the elective principle".

In this age of innovation, my lord, it may be useless to recommend the preference of that system, which has been recently superseded in the United States by Judge Lynch's code. That system, my lord, went perhaps too far in attempting to establish and maintain the mutual independence of the judiciary, the legislature and the executive; but it certainly did not form a precedent for your lordship's conciliatory scheme of concentrating the judicial, the executive and the legislative powers of the province in the hands of the French faction.

I have the honour to be,
My Lord,
Your Lordship's most obedient humble servant,

CAMILLUS.

***

No. XIX.

Montreal, 21st October, 1835.

My Lord,

It was on the 21st day of October, 1805, that Horatio Nelson,[71] the pride of Britain and the dread of Gaul, breathed his own patriotic and indomitable spirit into the humblest seaman in his fleet by the electric exhortation, 'England expects every man to do his duty'. Why not, my lord? Could an English eye in vain see the proud legend streaming from England's noblest emblem, a living ship of war, over England's ancient throne, the broad breast of the ocean, before England's hereditary enemies, the combined forces of France and Spain? What, my lord, was the duty, that England expected every man to do? Let the event answer. The combined fleets were swept from the ocean; the naval power of France and Spain was annihilated; and Horatio Nelson, having thus fulfilled his destiny and left no more fleets to be destroyed, met the envied death of a warrior in the full blaze of what must have been his last and was certainly his most glorious triumph.

A lapse of twenty or thirty years, my lord, works many changes. The narrow spirit of patriotism has given place to the diffusive principle of philanthropy. England still expects every son to do his duty; but—oh the march of liberal principle! — she no longer expects her sons to do that duty to herself—she has taken her enemies under her protection[72]—she instructs her children to fight the battles of republican robbers and murderers in Spain. In the harbour of Navarino, she tarnished her honour, squandered her treasure and shed her blood to make Turkey a Russian province and to wipe off the disgrace of uninterrupted defeat from the Gallic navy.[73] How narrowly, my lord, did the truly national day of Trafalgar escape the pollution of anti-national Navarino. There is, my lord, a fate in days. Cromwell[74] had his lucky third of September; Protestant England has her twice honoured fifth of November;[75] Republican America has the almost miraculous coincidences of the fourth of July; and every true patriot must rejoice, that fate, by an anticipation of twenty-four hours, reserved the twenty-first of October for some nobler counterpart than the conciliatory piracy of Navarino.

A true Englishman's motto,[76] my lord, is 'Trafalgar'; if there be a secret compromise, your lordship's is 'Navarino'. A true Englishman's day, my lord, is the twenty-first of October; if there be a secret compromise, your lordship's is the twentieth. There must, my lord, be some error in the reasoning or in the premises. May I flatter myself, that there is an error in the premises, that your lordship has not entered into a secret compromise with the avowed enemies of English interests, English power and English honour?

Does your lordship doubt, that the French demagogues are so? I solemnly adjure your lordship to answer the question not to me but to your own conscience. Be not deceived, my lord, by the Jesuitical attempt of the mendacious hireling of the *Vindicator* to convince your lordship—for it it to your lordship's presumed ignorance of local matters that the falsehood is specially addressed—of the perfect novelty of the absurdly exclusive doctrine of French nationality. The mendacious hireling refers the origin of that doctrine to 'the commencement of the month of September', just as if your lordship's French organ and the *Minerve*[77] and the *Echo du Pays*[78] had never before your lordship's arrival held up Britons, as such, to the suspicion and the hatred and the indignation of the illiterate habitans, as if the hymns of Napoleon's triumphs had never made Austerlitz and Jena and Wagram[79] familiar to the recollection and dear to the pride of many a one of 'His Majesty's Canadian subjects', as if the appearance of a French squadron in the waters of Quebec, during the revolutionary war, had not been alone wanting to inflame the disaffected neutrality of the Canadians into rebellious violence.[80]

I have the honour to be,
My Lord,
Tour Lordship's most obedient humble servant,

CAMILLUS.

***

No. XX.

Montreal, 22nd October, 1835.

My Lord,

Permit me now to draw your lordship's attention to a more minute analysis of the Jesuitical article of the *Vindicator.*

The miserable hireling confesses, that his liberal disquisition was extorted by the *Minerve's* 'direct mention' of the *Vindicator.* May not one, therefore, justifiably suspect a collusive understanding between the *Vindicator* and the *Minerve,* founded on a desire of continuing to blind the English readers of the former journal to the exclusive nationality of the French faction,[81] as advocated in the latter print.

The miserable hireling attempts to prove that the exclusive doctrine is peculiar to the editor of the *Minerve,* who is said to be a native French man.

I shall give your lordship a few examples, somewhat older than 'the commencement of the month of September'. The first example is extracted from the *Minerve* of the 16th February, 1832. *Ab uno disce onnes* (From one learn to know all).[82]

"*Il existe ici deux partis entièrement opposés d'intérêts et de mœurs, les Canadiens et les Anglais. Ces premiers nés français, en ont les habitudes et le caractère, et ont hérité de leurs pères de la haine pour les Anglais qui à leur tour voyant en eux des fils de la France, les détestent. Ces deux partis ne pourront jamais se réunir, et ne resteront pas toujours tranquilles; c'est un mauvais amalgame d'intérêts, de mœurs, de langue et de religion, qui tôt ou tard produira une collision. On croit assez à la possibilité d'une révolution, mais on la croit éloignée, moi je pense qu'elle ne tardera pas. Qu'on médite bien ces paroles d'un grand écrivain,[83] et l'on ne traitera plus de chimères une révolution et une séparation de la mère patrie. Le plus grand malheur pour l'homme politique, dit-il, c'est d'obéir à une puissance étrangère, aucune humiliation, aucun tourment de cœur ne peut être comparé à celui-là—Je le répète une séparation immédiate d'avec la mère-patrie c'est le seul moyen de conserver notre nationalité.*"

Permit me to select another example from the writings of a monster, whom the blessed principle of conciliation made a legislative councillor. Your lordship has seen the monster. His name is Debart[z]ch.

"*Naguère on a versé le sang Canadien, et nos ennemis* [sic] *se réjouiraient de voir le dernier des Canadiens à son dernier soupir, et VOUDRAIENT DANS LEUR DELIRE BARBARE NE FAIRE DE TOUS LES CANADIENS QU'UNE SEULE TETE, POUR AVOIR LE PLAISIR FEROCE DE L'ABATTRE D'UN SEUL COUP.* Mais il faut jeter le voile sur ces sujets d'horreur et nous opposer sans relâche à l'ambition de ces monstres avides de place et d'honneur[84] et qui tous en maltraitant les Canadiens ne vivent que de leurs sueurs et de leurs travaux. Oui, nous avons à nous plaindre d'une infinité de maux dont on veut nous accabler. Vous connaissez les tentatives des Bureaucrates[85] *qui tentent de s'emparer de vos terres et de vos biens. Témoins cet agiotage injuste, et des efforts de cette société fameuse que la Mère-Patrie vient d'autoriser à l'achat de vos terres.*[86] CETTE

SOCIETE COMPOSEE DE PROPRIETAIRES AVIDES, ET AVARES, MEDITE LA RUINE DES CANADIENS EN VOULANT LES CHASSER DU SOL QUI LES A VUS NAITRE.[87] Quoi, chers compatriotes souffrirez-vous que vos terres qui viennent de vos pères; que vous avez cultivées avec tant de soin, et que votre courage vous a fait arroser si souvent de vos sueurs, souffrirez[-] vous, dis[-] je qu'elles passent entre des mains étrangères? et que vos enfans, objets de votre tendresse, aillent honteusement mendier dans un pays lointain, du pain que vous leur promettiez de manger dans le leur?"

In justice to the bloodthirsty slanderer, I must say, that, inveterate babbler as he is, he had the good taste to absent himself during the session, that followed, from the legislative council. Time, however, extinguishes shame, as well as sorrow; and the man, accordingly, recently had the effrontery to present himself to the King's representative at the Chateau of St. Louis.

The miserable hireling quotes a portion of Mr. Papineau's 'opening speech' at the recent election for the west ward of Montreal[88] apparently in order to prove, that Mr. Papineau did not then entertain the absurdly exclusive tenet of French nationality. Mr. Papineau's remarks, even if sincere, are not very conclusive; but a light consideration of the circumstances, under which they were uttered, and of Mr. Papineau's public character and previously expressed opinions, is sufficient to inspire doubt of their sincerity. The place was the hustings; the auditors were chiefly men of English blood; the speaker was a being, who had previously made a public boast of his own jesuitical hypocrisy. In one word, Mr. Papineau found it convenient to cover his *Minerve*-face with a *Vindicator*-mask.

But, my lord, the basest part of the miserable hireling's dishonesty has not yet been noticed. He will not permit his exclusive readers to know the full enormity of the faction's hatred of the British name. No, my lord; he talks only of 'aliens', and forgets to add, that, according to the standing rule of the *Minerve*, every 'Briton' is an 'alien'. The hired tool's version is, in fact, falsified by his own admission, that the editor of the *Minerve* is 'himself an alien', for nothing could well be more improbable than that any public writer should wilfully and systematically attack himself.

I have, my lord, quoted the extracts, as common fairness required, in the original French; but if this letter does seem to have been written *Canusini more bilinguis* (that of the bilingual people of Canusium)[89] I beg to offer as an apology, that I did not know, whether a French or an English uniformity would be more acceptable in the vice regal halls. Should your lordship make the French the court-language of Lower Canada, your English subjects may, perhaps, strive to become Frenchmen; but they are likely, my lord, to pick up, if I may refer to Condorcet's satirical analysis of his own countrymen, more of the tiger than of the monkey.[90]

I shall to-morrow close this series of letters with a general recapitulation of my somewhat desultory remarks, receiving the discussion of 'the elective principle' for another series to be addressed to the Royal Commissioners

I have the honour to be,
My Lord,
Your Lordship's most obedient humble servant,

CAMILLUS.

***

No. XXI.

Montreal, 23rd October, 1835.

My Lord,

My first eight letters attempted to demonstrate the injustice and the impolicy of your lordship's suspected compromise with the leader of the French faction; the twelve others were drawn forth by a radical journal's factious and illiterate objection to the epithet 'Anti-Gallic' as applied to the letters of 'Camillus'. I shall recapitulate these two sections of the series in their natural order.

I presumed, my lord, to impeach the justice of the secret compromise on several grounds.

Any compact with a part of a legislature perverts, so far as it goes, the constitutional privileges of the remaining part; so that, if your instrument negotiated even with the whole of the French faction, your lordship stood in the unenviable light of a conspirator against the independence of the minority of the assembly, and of the majority of the legislative council. This conclusion, my lord, inevitably springs from my premises; but it is so utterly inconsistent with the character of an English nobleman, as to make any man almost believe, that my premises are false.

But the special nature of the secret compromise is still more repugnant to justice, and renders your lordship's position still more unenviable. The minority of the assembly and the majority of the legislative council are chiefly composed of men of English blood, and are compelled by the exclusive nationality of the French faction to consider themselves as the sole representatives of the English inhabitants. Keep this in view, my lord, and reflect that the revenue, which your lordship and the French faction are said to have divided between the assembly and the provincial government, is chiefly paid by the English constituents of the disfranchised portions of the legislature. Is not the secret compromise, therefore, inconsistent with the assumed principles of all liberals, whether French or English or Anglo-Gallic, that those, who pay the public revenue, should control the public expenditure? Thus, my lord, the strongest argument of the enemy conveys the strongest condemnation of the secret compromise. How long does your lordship imagine, that freeborn Englishmen will patiently dig in the mines for the benefit of French taskmasters?[91] Conciliation, my lord, is at least a new principle in policy, for it compels the conquerors to pay tribute to the conquered. If your lordship can pardon a bitter jest, I may compare the conquest of Canada to a donkey-organ, in which the most ignoble animal carries off the prize. If your lordship can pardon another, I may consider a conciliatory government as giving vindictive damages against the heroic Wolfe, for having assaulted, with intent to murder, the hereditary haters of the English name on the Plains of Abraham, and as entailing the original sin of the dead warrior with its result of vindictive damages on the successive generations of those, who may have the misfortune of being his countrymen.[92] If your lordship can pardon another, I may say that every cabinet, that has ruled England since the conquest of Canada, has, like a conclave of quakers ashamed of a temporary display of pugnacity, attempted to bury in oblivion General Wolfe's ungentlemanly violence, by not having allowed any one regiment of the conquering army to emblazon 'Quebec' on its banners.

But, my lord, I am forestalling the discussion of the impolicy of the secret compromise. My arguments on this head were of two kinds — I warned your lordship, that the ultimate result of any compromise, that might place the English population under the hoofs of the French faction, would be the independence of British America, and that the immediate result of the suspected compromise would be a systematic attempt on the part of your lordship's countrymen in both provinces, to deprive the French assembly and the Frenchified government of Lower Canada, of the means of mutual corruption. I need not again detail the modes of carrying such an attempt into operation; but I must cursorily allude to the frivolous and vexatious objections of treacherous dastards. My proposals, my lord, were based on the presumed necessity of choosing between French domination and some strong measure or other, and were intended as mild substitutes for physical resistance;[93] and the officious assailant of my positions should have shewn, not merely that my proposals were objectionable, but that they were more objectionable than either a Gallic yoke or a civil war. In answer to the mathematical calculations of the insurrectionary republican, I subjoin a few editorial remarks from the *Upper Canada Herald*.

"A writer in the *Montreal Courier* questions the accuracy of the statements contained in the *Montreal Herald*, and copied into this paper, respecting the right of this province to more than one third of the duties levied at Quebec. The writer in the *Courier* says, that the Lower Province is entitled to more than two thirds of the duties, because she consumes by far the largest proportion of the imported articles on which the highest duties are paid, particularly "teas, coffee, high priced, wines, brandy, &c." besides the rum, of which all admit that Lower Canada consumes the greatest part. Some other articles are mentioned, but they are of less moment. From these statements we entirely dissent. Indeed it is obvious that some of them are contradictory; for the fact that Lower Canada consumes large quantities of rum, gives of itself presumptive evidence that she does not use much wine or brandy, unless we mean to say that the Canadians[94] are the greatest drunkards on the earth. And any person who is acquainted with the Canadians knows that they very seldom use either wine, brandy or tea. To speak of them as a tea drinking people argues great ignorance of their domestic habits and manners. We spent upwards of two years among the people of Lower Canada, and from our own observation and experience we can state that, with the exception of rum, and, perhaps of salt and tobacco, the people of this province consume in the proportion of three to one of all other imported articles, more than the Lower Canadians. If the statements of the writer in the *Courier* apply at all to any part of the population of the lower province, it is only to the better part of the inhabitants of Montreal and Quebec that they can apply. A man who has never been out of those cities may suppose that all the Canadians live as the best part of the citizens around him do; but let him visit the *habitans* who form the great bulk of the population, and he will meet with very little brandy, wine or tea throughout the entire province. No man who is acquainted with the respective habits and manners of the people in both provinces would think of denying that the consumption of all imported articles, except rum, is much greater in this province than in Lower Canada."

I now come, my lord, to the second section of the series, which, as I have already mentioned, was drawn forth by a factious and illiterate objection to the epithet 'Anti-Gallic', as applied to the letters of 'Camillus'.

Before I proceed to recapitulate any of my arguments, permit me to demonstrate the propriety of the epithet by the disinterested testimony of the *Vindicator*, which has been driven by the exclusive nationality of the French faction, to range itself beside 'Camillus' under the 'Anti-Gallic' standard.

I assured your lordship, that the English inhabitants of Lower Canada desire only to be placed on a footing of political equality with their French Canadian brethren, and have in view merely such objects, as must be beneficial to the whole province. I attempted to convince your lordship, that the English inhabitants, so far from being able to submit to an increase of the power of the French faction, feel, that, even under existing circumstances, they have not the slightest reason to expect peaceable redress of really oppressive grievances, whether personal or agricultural or commercial.

Your lordship remembers the strikingly brief and expressive epitaph on Sir Christopher Wren within St. Paul's Cathedral, which he had erected, *Circumspice, Look around*. I cannot close these letters more appropriately, than by solemnly impressing that motto on your lordship's heart, both as a maxim of cautious prudence and as a mode of ascertaining the comparative value to the province of the two races of the population. —Look around, my lord

I have the honour to be,
My Lord,
Your Lordship's most obedient humble servant,

CAMILLUS.

* * *

(…)

No. XXIII.

Montreal, 31st October, 1835.

My lord,

I must again throw together a few general observations on your lordship's speech, before 1 enter on the special discussion of the separate paragraphs.[95]

In my letter of yesterday's date, I strove to give your lordship credit for the most impartial spirit of conciliation; and I am now somewhat disappointed to find in a journal, which most generally espouses your lordship's cause, a most serious charge of partiality against your lordship's speech.

> "But to what party does his excellency's speech concedes the most of what was demanded? Some foolishly imagine to the revolutionists. We say, no; but to the constitutional reformers.[96] The 'contingencies' is a boon which is involved in considerable mystery, and which we shall not, therefore, take into our present calculation. — *Morning Courier.*

The acute and perspicuous writer prefers against your lordship the somewhat original charge of partiality to "the Constitutional Reformers."— Against such charge be it my task to defend your lordship.

In your lordship's justification, therefore, I am able to state, that the only boon, which your lordship's speech can be said actually to 'concede', has been conferred not on 'the constitutional reformers' but on 'the revolutionists'. So far, my lord, my refutation of the *Morning Courier*'s imputation of partiality against your lordship is triumphantly unanswerable. If my refutation of one charge should subject your lordship to the graver imputation of partiality to 'the revolutionists', your lordship will be pleased to reflect, that an honest advocate, however zealous, must take facts, as he finds them.—-I may, farther, add, that I have acted on the homoeopathic principle of the German doctors, who remove any disease by engendering it, on the homoeopathic principle of modern liberals, who remedy the evils of one concession by the evils of another.

Having thus discussed the question of your lordship's surrender of the 'mysterious' boon of the contingencies, I now proceed to demonstrate, that the *Courier*'s charge of partiality to 'the constitutional reformers' in regard to the potential concessions of the speech is altogether groundless. Before I enter fully into details, permit me, my lord, to fortify my position by the following observations of the *Quebec Mercury*.[97]

> "Nevertheless, on a second and more attentive perusal of that document, than we were enabled to give it on the day of our last publication, that on which it was delivered, we still hold it to be one of 'concession on almost all the material points which have been demanded by the popular party'—and we will now add, to an extent that ought to satisfy all reasonable men, and far beyond, we believe, what even the most sanguine of that party expected."

The editor of the *Mercury*, my lord, seems also to act on the homoeopathic principle of removing one charge by another; but then, my lord, he, as well as 'Camillus', must take facts, as he finds them.

Your lordship's first paragraph alludes to the various remedies of the various grievances in the following words: —

> "There are some cases in which the executive power of the governor will of itself be sufficient to apply a remedy; in others, though he cannot act by himself, yet, with the help of one or both branches of the provincial legislature, he may effectually accomplish what is required. There are others in which the laws and institutions of the United Kingdom make it impossible for us, without the enactments or sanction of the authorities in England, to effect what is asked; so that if we were to act, we should be acting unlawfully, if we were to make laws, they would be binding on no one."

The 'cases', which the 'executive power of the governor will of itself be sufficient to remedy, may be reduced to two, the 'mysterious' question of the contingencies and the disposal of offices of honour or emolument.

The manner, in which your lordship has already disposed of the first of these 'cases', as I have already shewn, does not at all tend to support the *Courier*'s charge of partiality to 'the constitutional reformers', unless I am to believe with your lordship, that the unconstitutional seizure of the public funds for revolutionary purposes promotes 'the happiness and welfare of all classes of his Majesty's Canadian[98] subjects'. But, if I did believe this, I should still find in your lordship's surrender of the contingencies an evidence of absolute impartiality.

In regard to the second of the two 'cases', I am able to make your lordship your own interpreter; Your fifth paragraph contains the following intimation of the principles, on which 'the executive power of the governor' is to fill 'public stations'.

> "Fitness for the trust is the criterion to which mainly, it not entirely, I am to look, and do not hesitate to avow the opinion, that, *in every country, to be acceptable to the great body[99] of the people is one of the most essential elements of fitness for public stations.*"

Do the words, which I have printed in italics, justify the *Courier*'s charge? No, my lord; they display a partiality not to 'the constitutional reformers' but to 'the revolutionists'. Here, again, I must apologise for the homoeopathic nature of my defence, on the ground, that I must take facts, as I find them. By 'the great body of the people' your lordship, of course, means the French Canadians; so that henceforward the provincial patronage of the crown is virtually to be vested in the French demagogues, as the organs of 'the great body of the people'. Who can hesitate to acquit your lordship of partiality to 'the constitutional reformers'? Permit me to dissect your lordship's language with critical minuteness. Any quality, my lord, if said to be 'essential' to any substance, when without it that substance cannot exist. The precise meaning of 'most essential' I do not understand; but the adverb, if it adds nothing to the adjective, cannot take anything from it. Your lordship, therefore, clearly declares, that the favour of 'the great body of the people', or, in other words, the favour of the French demagogues is an indispensable requisite in every candidate for any public station of honour or emolument. Hereafter, therefore, your lordship is, by your own declaration, bound to place 'the revolutionists', and 'the revolutionists' only, in executive offices, on the judicial bench and in the legislative council. In one of my latest letters, I pointed out to your lordship, that any addition to the judicial or the executive or the legislative power of the French faction would tend to vest a concentrated despotism in that revolutionary body. Little did I imagine, little did the French demagogues themselves expect, that your lordship would so soon enunciate a principle, which not only tends to produce that result, but does actually produce it. Your lordship has, by 'the executive power of the governor', introduced 'the elective principle' not merely into the legislative council but into all the departments of the judiciary and the executive. In regard to the judiciary and the executive, the French demagogues themselves, my lord, never demanded more than a division of judicial and executive offices, proportioned to the respective numbers of the two races. Your lordship, however, has most liberally established the democratic principle, that the majority is everything and the minority nothing, that 'the great body of the people' is omnipotent and the small body of the people powerless. May I anticipate from your lordship's patronage of 'the elective principle', that the inquiry into the 'constitution' of the legislative council, into which, according to the twenty-seventh paragraph, 'the commissioners are not precluded from entering', is to end in the warm recommendation of an elective council? Hereafter, my lord, no Englishman, with the exception of two renegades[100] in a certain assembly, is to hold office in an English colony. The English are still to pay taxes; but the French are to enjoy them. The English are to be permitted by law to speak and write their vernacular language; but that vernacular language is to make them tributaries and outlaws. Your lordship may have heard, that Pope, in his prologue to Cato, softened 'Britons arise' into 'Britons attend'. Your lordship compels me to prefer the original reading.[101]

I now come, my lord, to the second class of 'cases', in which your lordship requires 'the help of one or both branches of the provincial legislature.' I am utterly at a loss to discover any 'case', which your lordship can remedy 'with the help of one' branch of the provincial legislature, with the exception of the 'case' of the contingencies, which your lordship did remedy 'with the help' of the assembly alone. Your lordship surely cannot mean, that, in the settlement of the financial difficulties, the legislative council is to have no voice; and yet, at the close of the nineteenth paragraph, addressed exclusively to 'gentlemen of the house of assembly', your lordship does seem to consider 'your assent' as alone sufficient in regard to the temporary disposal of the hereditary revenue. But let me now enumerate the 'cases' of the second class. These 'cases' may also be reduced to two. The surrender of the hereditary revenue and the granting of a civil list. The surrender of the hereditary revenue to those, who have already so grossly abused their control of the crown duties, can hardly be considered as a concession to 'the constitutional reformers'; and the granting of a civil list is not a boon either to 'the constitutional reformers' or to 'the revolutionists', unless in so far as members of either of these parties may hold offices of emolument under the provincial government. If 'the constitutional reformers' have, what I do not admit that they have, a majority of offices at present, your lordship's respect for 'the great body of the people' will turn the opposite scale in favour of 'the revolutionists'. Thus far, my lord. I have been able triumphantly to acquit you of the *Morning Courier*'s charge of 'partiality to the constitutional reformers'; and I doubt not, that my review of the third class of

'cases' will equally tend to establish your lordship's entire inno-
cence-—at least of that imputation.

I come, therefore, to the 'cases' of the third class, which require
'the enactments or sanction of the authorities in England'. These are
the 'cases' on which the commissioners are to report; and they comprehend, as I learn from the twenty-sixth paragraph and the thirty-
second, all the demands of 'the constitutional reformers'. But as the
twenty-seventh paragraph brings also the constitution of the legislative council within the review of the commissioners, such 'constitutional reformers', as consider inquiry as concession, are in consistency
bound to believe that an elective council is conceded to 'the revolutionists' as well as that register offices and the abolition of the feudal
tenure are conceded to 'constitutional reformers'. But the argument
may be stated much more strongly against the *Morning Courier*'s
imputation. The twenty ninth paragraph, by promising the perpetuity
of the feudal system, shews that the inquiry 'respecting the tenures
of land and the registry of titles', will, as I yesterday mentioned, not
lead to any practical result. The results, on the contrary, of the inquiry
into the constitution of the legislative council must be favourable to
'the revolutionists' on the ground of their being 'acceptable to the
great body of the people'. Will your lordship permit me to repeat my
conviction, that the promised inquiry into the feudal system, and the
other real grievances of the constitutionalists will end in smoke?

Have I not triumphantly refuted the *Courier*'s charge against
your lordship? Has not my general review of your lordship's speech
satisfactorily proved the truth of my oft repeated assertion, that the
main object of all the successive cabinets of England has been to
relieve the provincial executive from financial embarrassments by
any piece of temporary patchwork? If, my lord, they had done it
without any sacrifice of principle, they might still have been accused
of weakness; but by a sacrifice of principle they have added dishonesty to weakness, and have, without even the plea of necessity, acted
on the damnable maxim of doing evil that good may come.

I have the honour to be,
My Lord,
Your lordship's most obedient humble servant,

CAMILLUS.

***

No. XXIV.

Montreal, 2nd November, 1835.

My Lord,

The first paragraph of your lordship's speech opens with the following sentence:—

"It is in no ordinary circumstances, that I meet you; and consequences of vast importance depend on the impression you may receive from my words."

The last paragraph of your lordship's speech closes with the following sentence: —

"There are two paths open to you: by the one you may advance to the enjoyment of all the advantages which lie in prospect before you; by the other, I will not say more than that you will stop short of these and will engage yourselves and those who have no other object than your prosperity, in darker and more difficult courses."

The alpha and the omega of your lordship's speech are very counterparts of each other; and, if there be a difference between them, it is merely that the omega is more particularly worthy of the elegant criticism of the *Minerve*. They are both founded on two fatal misapprehensions, a dread of a French insurrection and a hope of conciliating the contending parties.

Your lordship must have derived your dread of a French insurrection, not from your own powers of observation, but from your 'precise instructions'. Your lordship, in fact, had been told by the *Canadien*, a common organ of your lordship and the assembly, that 'the great body of the people' entertained no opinions, knew no abuses, felt no oppression; but then, my lord, you were in duty bound to obey your 'precise instructions' in defiance of any and every practical reason to the contrary. You had found, that every individual, acquainted with the character and temper of the Canadian habitans, reckoned a French insurrection not only improbable but morally impossible; but then, my lord, you were in duty bound to obey your 'precise instructions' in defiance of any and every practical reason to the contrary. You had perceived, that every Englishman wasted on the absurd supposition no other feeling than that of contemptuous scorn; but then, my lord, you were in duty bound to obey your 'precise instructions' in defiance of any and every practical reason to the contrary.

I must now offer a few remarks on your lordship's hope of conciliating the contending parties. Whatever I may think of the reasonableness of such a hope, I rejoice, that an imperial cabinet has at last discovered, that "Lower Canada is divided by two parties', comprising not the government and the assembly but 'the great body of the people' and the little body of the people. Yes, my lord, this discovery is equally new and important. It is new, for Sir Robert Peel,[102] when prime minister, spoke as if Lower Canada contained only the British government and the French faction. It is important, for it cannot fail to have weight with the slaves of public expediency and political cowardice. May I presume to hope, that your lordship and his Majesty's ministers will strive to remember a discovery, which, if ever forgotten in Downing-Street,[103] will be recalled to the most treacherous memory in a Transatlantic voice of thunder. But this is a digression. Your lordship's hope of conciliating the 'two parties' I must ascribe to your comparative ignorance of the real feelings and real objects of the respective races. Were any individual, who had long resided in the province, to express a similar hope, he would be generally considered either as insane or as dishonest; and I, therefore, feel confident, that your lordship will see the value of your amiable hope before the close of the impending winter. If your lordship has any relish for a comparatively easy task, try to effect a permanent mixture of oil and water, rather than to produce a social union of two races of different languages. Such a union, my lord, is impossible; and, that it may always be so, your lordship proposes to make both languages 'flourish in immortal youth' under the nursing hand of a conciliatory law. The contradictory character of your lordship's views does not surprise me. It is the natural fruit of the conciliatory system of promising everything to everybody; and the present instance is quite in keeping with your conflicting declarations, that the feudal system may be abolished for the gratification of the little body of the people but that it shall be retained for the benefit of 'the great body of the people'. The only mode, in which your lordship can conciliate the two races, is to assimilate the one of them to the other.[104] In my next letter I shall offer a few remarks on the subject of assimilation, and shall also endeavour to shew from reason and experience, that no other mode will ever he effectual.

I have the honour to be,
My Lord,
Tour Lordship's most obedient humble servant,

CAMILLUS.

***

XXV.

Montreal, 3rd November, 1835.

My Lord,

Since I yesterday had the honour of addressing your lordship on the discrepancy between your hope of conciliating the 'two parties' and your design of perpetuating the French language, I have been credibly informed, that the Assembly will forthwith pass a bill to declare the French language the dominant language of this province. It would hardly be prudent strictly to interpret the very words even of an authentic rumour; but such a measure, as the most strict interpretation of 'dominant' could render the proposed bill, would be quite in keeping with the general character of the French demagogues and would not go far beyond the gracious views of your lordship's twelfth paragraph. The difference, in truth, between the assembly's bill and your lordship's views would be rather apparent than real, for, as every public servant must hereafter be 'acceptable to the great body of the people', all 'official acts' will very soon emanate from 'The French inhabitants of this province' and will, of course, be written in the French language. An apparently equal law, therefore, would, 'by the executive power of the governor', become as unequal as possible and render the French Canadian *patois* the 'dominant' language of the province. Permit me, my lord, to predict the practical working of the system. As it is the opinion both of your lordship, and of the French demagogues, that 'the great body' is every thing and that the small body is nothing, the language of the majority, whether in the assembly or in the legislative council or in the executive council or on the judicial bench, will be the language of all 'official acts'. Thus, my lord, would the French language already be the 'official' language of the assembly; while, under your lordship's dispensation of your official patronage, it would speedily gain a similar footing in both councils and on the bench. But one fact, my lord, is more powerful than ten arguments; and it is, my lord, a fact, that the French demagogues, long before they had been emboldened to adopt anti-national courses by the anti-national concessions of conciliatory cabinets, obstinately struggled for the recognition of their own patois as the enacting language, or, in other words, as the language of legislation. That attempt, my lord, even exceeded in audacity the results, which the preceding observations anticipated from the rumoured measure, inasmuch as, if successful, it would have made the legislative councillors and the governor so many French lawgivers. That attempt, my lord, neither led nor professed to lead to the removal of any real grievance of the French population. It sprang, as almost every measure of the French faction has sprung, from the discontented ambition of a few unprincipled leaders. But the attempt, my lord, involved either a ridiculous absurdity or a flagrant contempt of the British parliament. The preamble of every provincial law recapitulates, as the authority under which the provincial legislature exists and acts, the title of the constitutional act of 1791. One of two things, therefore, must have resulted from the success of the attempt. Either a British statute must have submitted to wear a French title or every provincial statute must have been disfigured by a mixture of two languages. The French demagogues, however, might have ordered the imperial parliament to array the constitutional act in a French dress; and past experience, my lord, entitles me to infer, that such an order would have been obeyed. The weakness of almost every English cabinet has imprinted on the hearts of the French demagogues, 'Ask and ye shall receive', and has done so too in the vain, the foolish, the insane hope of lulling avarice and · ambition by gratification. What, my lord, will be the condition of every Englishman in Lower Canada, if the legislative council and your lordship sanction the proposed measure of the assembly. The situation of every Englishman, my lord, would become (I use the words advisedly) ABSOLUTELY INTOLERABLE.[105] What, my lord? Shall the Earl of Gosford and thirty or forty traitorous demagogues achieve over Englishmen of the nineteenth century a victory, which the Duke of

Normandy and forty thousand of the first warriors of Europe failed to achieve over Englishmen of the eleventh?[106] No, my lord, the Earl of Gosford and the French demagogues SHALL not make Norman-French the 'official' language of this province. Breathes there a wretch of English blood in Lower Canada that would submit to the insulting oppression for a single day? No, my lord; your lordship and the assembly will find it safer, if not more honourable, to violate a principle by putting your conjoined hands, without the sanction of law, into the public chest than to inflict a personal injury of daily occurrence on every Englishman by tying his tongue and proscribing the language of his fathers. I cannot, my lord, envy your lordship the very dubious honour of arresting the progress of a language, which has a fairer prospect, than had ever the language of Greece or of Rome,[107] of becoming universal in every region accessible to an English ship.

I have the honour to be,
My Lord,
Your Lordship's most obedient humble servant,

CAMILLUS.

***

No. XXVI.

Montreal, 4th November, 1835.

My Lord,

I shall postpone my remarks on the necessity of assimilating the 'two parties' to each other, till I shall come to the formal discussion of the twelfth paragraph of your lordship's speech;— and I shall, therefore, immediately proceed with the review of your lordship's opening paragraph.

"Dissensions have almost arrested the course of Government."

Yes, my lord, 'dissensions' have done so, just as daggers assassinated Caesar, and bullets felled Marshal Ney like an ox.[108] What, my lord, enabled the 'dissensions' to arrest 'the course of Government'? What, my lord, but the government itself. The 'dissensions', to which your lordship alludes, are the 'dissensions' not of the 'two parties' but of the government and the assembly, and have affected merely the question of the civil list. For twenty-five years, my lord, these 'dissensions' have existed; but, until the crown-duties were surrendered to the provincial legislature, they had not much more practical effect on 'the course of government' than the 'good laws' of the best of all possible republics have on the peace of society. The surrendering, however, of those crown-duties by the conciliatory statute of William the Fourth,[109] enabled the 'dissensions' to arrest 'the course of government', and placed the administration of 'the laws by which society is held together' at the mercy of the French faction.[110] Place the saddle, my lord, on the right horse, and say, 'The act of 1st and 2nd of His present Majesty has almost arrested the course of government'. Such a confession, my lord, would have literally justified the predictions of the Duke of Wellington's sagacious protest against the fatal bill.[111] What, my lord, was the motive for surrendering the crown-duties? The hope of relieving the government from partial embarrassment, by enabling the assembly to render that embarrassment almost universal. Well may I say with Oxenstiern, *Quam parva sapientia regitur mundus.*[112] That the 'dissensions' may still more fatally arrest 'the course of government', your lordship, with equal wisdom, proposes to render the aforesaid embarrassment altogether universal, by surrendering also the hereditary revenues. Should your lordship's conciliatory measure be carried into effect, your lordship's successor will be able to substitute altogether for almost, and to say, 'Dissensions have altogether arrested the course of government'. The proposed mode, too, of surrendering the hereditary revenue is peculiarly objectionable. The crown duties were surrendered by an imperial statute; the hereditary revenue is to be surrendered by a provincial act. The imperial statute might be repealed by the imperial parliament without the violation of any constitutional principle, sound or unsound; the provincial act, on the contrary, could not be repealed without raising up the eternal bug-bear about the unconstitutionality of any interference of the imperial parliament with the provincial legislature.[113] In fine, my lord, 'the course of government', has been 'arrested' not by 'dissensions' but by absurd and pernicious conciliation. The 'dissensions' may be a viper; but it is conciliation that warms the viper into life.

But conciliation, my lord, has not only cherished the viper but even engendered it. Yes, my lord, conciliation is the parent as well as the nurse of the special 'dissensions', which have almost arrested 'the course of government'. These 'dissensions', as the French demagogues have themselves avowed, have not an exclusive reference to the merits or the demerits of 'the supplies required for carrying into execution the laws'. The avowed object of the 'dissensions' is to coerce the government into a compliance with demands, which, whether reasonable or unreasonable, have at least nothing to do with the civil list. In the twentieth paragraph, your lordship seems to be most amiably ignorant of this important fact. That paragraph speaks of the advance of £31,000 out of the imperial funds of the military chest. To that advance the French demagogues objected on the ground of its indirectly defeating the intended coercion of the provincial authorities: while your lordship's amiable misapprehension of the real policy of the faction assigned the very crime as its own apology by confessing that the advance had been 'designed for no other purpose than to prevent a highly inconvenient interruption of the general business of the province'. The imperial parliament might have reasonably complained, that 'British funds' had been misappropriated 'for the purpose of avoiding any undue interference' with the house of assembly of Lower Canada. But the imperial parliament, my lord, did no such thing. It bears its dignities much more meekly than their high mightinesses of the provincial assembly bear theirs.

Under these circumstances, my lord, you must clearly perceive, that, unless you have determined to grant all the demands of the French faction, the surrender of the hereditary revenue will only arm the assembly with additional means of arresting 'the course of government' through coercive views. But even if you did, my lord, grant all the present demands of the French faction, you would soon be required to grant other demands still more extravagant, such as the abolition of the legislative veto of the executive and the transfer of the appointment of governor from his Majesty to 'the great body of the people'. But my memory fails me, for your lordship has already anticipated the latter demand. You have declared, that 'public stations', without exception, should be filled only by men 'acceptable to the great body of the people'. Your lordship was too impartial even to except the highest of all the 'public stations' of the colony from the operation of your own republican rule. It is, my lord, the general opinion of those, who have studied human nature, that your lordship's own rule will very soon press heavily on your lordship.

I have the honour to be,
My Lord,
Your Lordship's most obedient humble servant,

CAMILLUS.

***

No. XXVII.

Montreal, 5th Nov. 1835.

My Lord,

I quote the fourth sentence and the fifth of your lordship's first paragraph.

"The most urgent and conflicting statements of numerous grievances by adverse parties have been borne to the throne of His
Majesty; but accompanied with expressions of an apprehension, that
the ministers of the crown might not have that practical knowledge
of the province which is necessary for the discernment of the most
appropriate remedies. I am amongst you, therefore, not only as your
governor, but as the head of a commission upon which the task is
imposed of inquiring fully, and on the spot, into the complaints
which have been made, and of offering to the King and to the councils, by which the throne is surrounded, the deliberate conclusions
of the commissioners."

The 'adverse parties', to which your lordship refers, are the assembly and 'the great body of the people' on the one hand, and the legislative council and the little body of the people on the other. The
second member of the first of the quoted sentences implies an erroneous belief on the part of your lordship, that all the 'adverse parties'
were equally anxious for a thorough investigation into the 'numerous
grievances'. Such a belief is directly opposed to the facts. The French
demagogues, so far from courting inquiry, have uniformly spoken
and written of the royal commission in the most contemptuous terms;
whereas the constitutionalists, even such of them as do not deem any
inquiry absolutely necessary, have uniformly admitted, that an
inquiry, if impartially conducted, would be rather beneficial than
injurious to the constitutional cause. The second of the quoted sentences, my lord, implies, that the commission was appointed through

an impartial desire of meeting the desire for inquiry of every one of the 'adverse parties.' There are two tests by which one may judge, whether or not the commission was actually appointed through such a motive. The first of these tests is to be found in the general character of the Commissioners; the second, in their special proceedings as gathered from your lordship's speech and from other sources.

The first test, my lord, involves some considerations of delicacy; but the personal feelings of a public officer must not be allowed to stifle inquiry into his public character or public conduct.

His Majesty's ministers, my lord, would, of course, prefer the adherents of their own party with the double view of rewarding friends and of carrying their liberal principles into effect as well in the colonial as in the domestic empire. They were, also, specially bound by their own doctrine, as developed in your lordship's fifth paragraph, to appoint to 'public stations' only such commissioners, as might be deemed 'acceptable to the great body of the people' of Lower Canada, or, in other words, only such commissioners, as might be known to be favorable to the propagation of democratic principles. As a majority, however, binds a minority, his Majesty's ministers could afford to be contented with two such commissioners.

Having thus endeavored to dissect the motives of the cabinet on the general principles of human nature and the avowed feelings of the ministers, I must now consider, whether or not the special appointments justify the result of my dissections of those motives.

Your lordship, having been favorably known in Ireland as a staunch supporter of 'the great body of the people' against the little body of the people, was of course predisposed to display similar sympathies in Lower Canada; and every individual, who has studied the London correspondence of the Montreal *Vindicator*, must be convinced, that your lordship's known attachment to 'the great body of the people', as certified by Mr. Daniel O'Connell,[114] was reckoned the main qualification of your lordship for heading the commission. The annals of the country do not bear testimony to your lordship's experience in civil affairs of momentous import. Where civil power and military command are conjoined in the same functionary, it may be unreasonable to expect the highest qualifications, whether military or civil; but where a purely civil governor is appointed in the most important and the most turbulent of all the English colonies, the cabinet, that does not regard civil experience in the selection, incurs a very heavy responsibility. I do not, my lord, mean to insinuate, that your lordship does not possess political talents; I mean, merely, that your lordship had not, previously to your appointment, displayed them in any conspicuous or eminent degree, and that his Majesty's ministers preferred your lordship rather for a known bias than for known capacity. I beg, my lord, again to assure you, that this language, if it should seem rude, is directed not against the qualifications of your lordship but against the motives of the cabinet.

In the appointment of Sir Charles Grey, a man of learning, of legal habits, of well tried judgment and of moderate views in politics, the cabinet seems to have displayed real impartiality—on the probable ground, that, as a minority, he would be overpowered by the skilfully selected majority.

In regard to your lordship's other colleague, I need not say much. If report does not very much belie him, he must have been known to the cabinet, as a man too violently democratic to give any chance of a report unfavorable 'to the great body of the people'; — while, at the same time, his comparative obscurity rendered his fatally objectionable bias comparatively unknown. His Majesty's ministers, my lord, could not have the testimony of experience in favor of that individual's capacity for discharging a delicate and difficult trust; while the peculiar nature of his professional pursuits eminently disqualified him for political investigations. The literary standard for entering Woolwich academy,[115] where that individual must have received his professional education, has always been so low, and the established course of education so exclusively mathematical, as to entitle me to assert, that every diligent and distinguished student, as your colleague confessedly was, must almost unfit himself for probable reasoning by the contemplation of necessary truths. A mathematician, as such, is bound to believe that every assertion, for which any irrefragable reason can be urged, is necessarily true, and, in proportion to the extent of his mathematical knowledge, virtually smothers the natural talent for weighing fact against fact, argument against argument, testimony against testimony. Hence, my lord, a mathematician, as such, is liable to be the slave of first political impressions, which, as almost every man's own youthful experience tells him, are those of democratic liberality. This disquisition, my lord, may appear finely spun, ill-timed and absurd; but my views are supported by the fact, that the distinguished men of Oxford are generally conservatives and those of Cambridge mostly liberal innovators. So much, my lord, as to the first test.

I have the honour to be,
My Lord,
Your Lordship's most obedient humble servant,

CAMILLUS.

***

No. XXVIII.

Montreal. 6th November, 1835.

My Lord,

Permit me now to examine the second test of the cabinet's honesty in the selection of the Royal Commissioners for Lower Canada, by considering their special proceedings, as gathered from your lordship's speech or from other sources. For these special proceedings, my lord, the cabinet is not less responsible than are the commissioners themselves, inasmuch as your lordship professes to have been guided by full and precise instructions.

The second sentence of my yesterday's quotation from the first paragraph, my lord, distinctly stated, that the commissioners were to enquire 'fully, and upon the spot, into the complaints' of the adverse parties. How can this statement, my lord, be reconciled with the admitted fact, that your lordship had 'precise instructions' to decide on certain points without inquiry 'fully, and upon the spot', such as the payment of illegal and unconstitutional contingencies, the surrender of the hereditary revenue, and the proscription of the English language? Your lordship distinctly confesses, that these points were conceded not in consequence of a full inquiry on the spot, but in compliance with 'precise instructions'. How can these contradictions, my lord, be reconciled with each other? A plain man, my lord, cannot pretend to reconcile them, but by supposing, that the 'instructions', on which your lordship has founded the general expression of your first paragraph about 'inquiry' into 'the complaints', were meant merely to delude the intended victims of 'the great body of the people'. Such a supposition, my lord, is amply justified by the conduct of the same cabinet in regard to other commissions of inquiry.[116] Whig-radical commissioners, too my lord, are not judges but advocates. The municipal commissioners, for instance, were appointed nominally to inquire into the proceedings of municipal corporations, but really to condemn those obnoxious bodies.[117] The words of the commission, my lord, were that 'you or any one of you may be allowed to transmit your report'. Now what happened? One commissioner of the name of Hogg transmitted a report unfavorable to the democratic views of the ministers, and was informed, 'that Lord John Russell[118] entertained some doubts, whether he should be justified in presenting such a document to his Majesty as a report in connexion with the municipal corporation commission'.[119] Permit me to lay a detailed statement of the disgraceful and ominous facts before your lordship and 'the English inhabitants of this province'.

"Mr. Hogg was less fortunate, 'not being prepared', like Sir Francis Palgrave, 'to concur in the general conclusions'. It did appear to be a most extraordinary thing, that the very same authority under which the other commissioners acted, founded upon these words in the commission, that 'you or any one of you may be allowed to transmit your report', &c., was peremptorily denied to Mr. Hogg. The correspondence which had consequently taken place between that gentleman and the home office had been printed, and the first was a letter which he wrote to the home office on the 23rd of March last, stating the time he had been occupied in visiting the different boroughs which had been assigned to him, and that he had not been able to arrive at the same general conclusions adopted by some of the other commissioners. That letter remained unanswered until, on the 13th of April, he wrote another, which, in its turn, remained unanswered, until on the 11th of May, he wrote another, stating that he had not been consulted in the preparation of the report by certain commissioners, and that, if it should seem necessary, he would make a separate report. On the 15th of May, the only answer he received from the home office was to the effect, that his letter of the 11th had been received. He wrote again on the 23rd of May, enclosing his 'first separate general report', and although the commissioners were divided, and sat in different places, for the avowed purpose of receiving information, being authorised to transmit a separate report, if necessary, the only answer he received, was that lord John Russell entertained some doubt whether he should be justified in presenting such a document to His Majesty as a report in connexion with the municipal corporation commission."

Does not this, my lord, look very like chicanery and wilful suppression of dreaded truth on the part of your lordship's noble and right honorable employers? Yet your lordship will be equally surprised and glad to learn, that there breathe in this colony wretches blind or dishonest enough to censure as ultra-toryish and illiberal an honest man's contempt and scorn of the existing administration. For the sake of those noble and right honorable individuals, I am sorry, that neither the talents nor the attainments of their apologists can affect the opinion of any man, whose opinion has any value.

Such persons, my lord, are the plague-spots of the political world. They are the beings, whom Solon's sagacious law against the cowardly or the dishonest babblers about neutrality would have hanged in the forum of Athens or driven into the gulph of Salamis at the point of the 'red pursuing spear'.[120] But such persons, my lord, will considerably moderate their admiration of whigs and radicals, if they do find by experience, which can alone teach a certain class of human beings, that the commissioners are not destined to lie judges between 'two parties' but advocates of 'the great body of the people'. But even then, when too late, they will know nothing more, than what an intelligent and honest man can confidently predict from the uniform discrepancy between the general and the special expressions of your lordship's speech, from the known selfishness and irresoluteness of his Majesty's liberal advisers, and more particularly from the analogous case of the municipal corporation commission.

In regard to the commission, of which your lordship is the head, lord Glenelg[121] will not be troubled, as was lord John Russell, with the anti-democratic report of a minority, not that a minority of the commission may not be disposed to make such a report, but because a minority is not entitled so to do. The report must emanate from the commissioners as a body,—not from 'any one of you' but from 'you' only.

But even if the commissioners, my lord, were to make an unanimous report, unfavourable to 'the great body of the people'— a supposition, which shocks me from its very absurdity, and which I make merely for the sake of argument—would his Majesty's present ministers act on such a report. Your lordship's admiration of their 'magnanimity and wisdom' must be powerful indeed, if you can answer my question in the affirmative. Yes, my lord, that short question puts the fact in the strongest possible light, for the puppets of two democratic factions dare not propose any thing offensive to 'the great body' of any people on earth, British or Irish or Canadian or Spanish or Portuguese, or even to 'the great body' of the Homines

Vespertilion[i]s of the moon.[122] Permit me again to refer to the municipal commission. *Out of one hundred and eight five* corporations, that were comprised in the ministerial bill, no fewer than *ninety-six* had not been censured in the slightest degree even by the commissioners, that had been appointed to condemn them. Thus, my lord, the report even of salaried enemies was favourable to more than half of the obnoxious corporations; but instead of punishing only the guilty, or pardoning the guilty minority for the sake of the innocent majority, his Majesty's ministers sacrificed the whole of them on the altar of 'the great body of the people'. Is not this, my lord, ominous? I fervently trust, my lord, that my anticipations may not be realised; but I cannot close my senses and my mind against either facts or analogies, that may cast the shadows of coming events before them.[123]

I have the honour to be,
My Lord,
Your Lordship's most obedient humble servant,

CAMILLUS.

***

No. XXIX.

Montreal, 7th November, 1835.

My Lord, I must again quote the closing sentence of the first paragraph of your lordship's speech:—

> "There are other cases, in which the laws and institutions of the United Kingdom make it impossible for us, without the enactments or sanction of the authorities in England, to effect what is asked; so that if we were to act, we should be acting unlawfully; if we were to make laws, they would be binding on no one."

The doctrine, which your lordship here laid down, is unquestionably sound; but I would seriously draw the attention of your lordship and of the commissioners to the fact, that there exists no mode of enforcing so sound a doctrine.

I need not prove, that the provincial legislature has ever passed an unconstitutional act. It is sufficient for my present purpose to state, that it may pass such an act; and, though I agree with your lordship, that it 'would be binding on no one' in theory, yet I am unable to see any well defined mode of evading its obligations in practice. The provincial courts would recognise the validity of even the most unconstitutional act, until it might be repealed either by the provincial legislature or by the imperial parliament. Now neither of these bodies, my lord, could pronounce a judicial decision against any provincial statute as unconstitutional, so as to have a retrospective effect on real or personal rights—without, at least, rendering the remedy worse than the disease, by opening the door to the enactment of retrospective laws. I am not aware, my lord, that the court of king's bench or the court of chancery or the privy council or the house of lords is competent to enter on any such judicial investigation.

It is, therefore, evident, my lord, that the only really preventive check to unconstitutional acts of the provincial legislature is to be found in the provincial legislature itself—consisting of the assembly, the legislative council and the governor or the king. Permit me to submit two special contingencies to your lordship. The British statute of 14th Geo. III., c 83, enacts, that the religious communities shall not hold estates; and a bill, proposed during the last session of the assembly by Mr. Bédard,[124] recognised the right of the seminary of St. Sulpice to the seigniory of the island of Montreal, if, my lord, the various branches of the provincial legislature had sanctioned Mr. Bédard's bill, it would have been considered as good law by the provincial courts, though theoretically unconstitutional and 'binding on no one'. Again, my lord, the constitutional act secures to either house of the imperial parliament a negative on any provincial act, that may affect ecclesiastical affairs or the waste lands of the crown; and yet, my lord, if his Majesty took on himself the responsibility of not consulting the houses of parliament on the subject, any such provincial act would be fully recognised, at least for a time, by the provincial courts.

It would, my lord, be well worthy of the attention of the commissioners to recommend, that some tribunal should be armed with a judicial control over every act of every colonial legislature, in order to protect at once the constitutional rights of the colonists and the undoubted prerogatives of the imperial authorities.

Without such a tribunal, my lord, the imperial parliament may be trampled under foot by the provincial legislature; and, though it may subsequently vindicate its own prerogatives, it cannot, without establishing a most dangerous precedent, retrospectively cancel any past injuries of the colonists.

Such a tribunal, my lord, is not the creature of my imagination. It exists in some of the neighbouring states; and, during last winter, the supreme court of the state of Missouri, denounced as unconstitutional a certain enactment of the local legislature.[125]

Such a tribunal, my lord, is demanded by the fundamental principle, that all formally delegated power should be carefully watched and strictly checked.

Thus at last, my lord, I have closed the discussion of the first paragraph of your lordship's speech; and

I have the honour to be,

My Lord,

Your Lordship's most obedient humble servant,

CAMILLUS.

***

No. XXX.

Montreal, 10th November, 1885.

My Lord,

The second, third and fourth paragraphs of your lordship's speech contain merely barren generalities. The fifth paragraph, however, is sufficiently special on the subject of your lordship's official patronage.

After having alluded to the complaint, 'that the French origin of the majority of the inhabitants of Lower Canada has been made a pretext for excluding them from office and employment, and for retaining them in a state of political inferiority', your lordship truly states, that 'The circumstances, which first united this country with the British Empire, must necessarily have occasioned for some time afterwards an exclusion of its prior inhabitants from offices of government'. This statement, my lord, clearly admits, that 'offices of Government' should be filled only by men of well-tried and well known fidelity, and that the public safety may sometimes be justifiably preferred to the momentary caprice of 'the great body of the people'. The real question, therefore, between your lordship and 'the English inhabitants of this province' is, whether equally powerful 'circumstances' do not still exist for 'an exclusion of its prior inhabitants from offices of government'; and I can easily prove to the satisfaction of every unprejudiced person, that 'circumstances' actually more powerful now exist for such 'exclusion'. The French demagogues, my lord, have long professed the most rebellious repugnance to British authority and the most deadly hatred of the British name; and, within the last two years, they have repeatedly threatened to throw themselves into the arms of France or of the United States, unless the imperial parliament should formally relinquish its supremacy and establish a French republic in Lower

Canada[126] by the extension of the elective principle. The ungrateful traitors have substantially said to the imperial authorities, 'If you do not by law render us independent of Great Britain, we shall render ourselves so by force'. Your lordship knows, the cabinet knows, the King knows, that my statement of the feelings of the miserable and despicable wretches is correct. Are such beings, my lord, to be trusted with 'offices of government'?[127] Certainly not, my lord, unless by those, who are themselves ready to sacrifice the empire on the accursed altar of their own avarice and ambition. Are not your lordship's noble and right honourable employers ready to do so? Is not one of your lordship's colleagues, according to the petty measure of his ability, ready to do so? Are you not, my lord of Gosford, ready to do something of a very similar kind? Undoubtedly, my lord, you are so,—and I entreat your lordship solemnly to weigh my words—if you obey 'precise instructions', which were, confessedly, founded on the grossest misapprehensions of the real feelings of the French-Canadian people. Do, my lord, do ask your conscience, why do you not rather resign your honours and your emoluments than obey so absurd, so pernicious instructions.

But, my lord, a more general reason, than that founded on an avowal of disloyalty and treason, would justify the 'exclusion of its prior inhabitants from offices of government'. This reason is, that the concentration of executive power and legislative authority in the hands of the same faction is an absolute despotism. Before I attempt to portray the inevitable tyranny of the uncontrolled French majority of this province, I shall lay before your lordship the opinions of one of the fathers of the American republic in regard to the headlong recklessness of uncontrolled majorities in general.[128] John Adams, my lord, says:

Marchamont Needham[129] lays it down as a fundamental principle, and undeniable rule,

'*That the people, that is, such as shall be successively chosen to represent the people, are the best keepers of their own liberties, and that for many reasons: First, because they never think of usurping over other men's rights, but mind which way to preserve their own.*'

"Our first attention should be turned to the proposition of '*The people are the best keepers of their own liberties*'.

But who are the people? 'Such as shall be successfully chosen to represent them'. Here is a confusion both of words and ideas, which, though it may pass with the generality of readers in a figurative pamphlet, or with a majority of auditors in a popular harangue, ought, for that very reason, to be as carefully avoided in politics as it is in philosophy or mathematics. If by the people is meant the whole body of a great nation, it should never be forgotten, that they can never act, consult, or reason together, because they cannot march five hundred miles, nor spare the time, nor find a space to meet; and, therefore, the proposition, that they are the best keepers of their own liberties, is not true. They are the worst conceivable; they are no keepers at all; they can neither act, judge, think nor will, as a body politic or corporation. If by the people is meant all the inhabitants of a single city, they are not in a general assembly, the best keepers of their own liberties, nor perhaps at any time, unless you separate from them the executive and judicial power, and tamper their authority in legislation with the maturer councils of the one and the few. If it is meant by the people, as our author explains himself, a representative assembly, 'such as shall be successively chosen to represent the people", they are not still the best keepers of the people's liberties, or their own, if you give them all the power, legislative, executive and judicial; they would invade the liberties of the people, at least the majority of them would invade the liberties of the minority, sooner and oftener than an absolute monarchy, such as that of France, Spain, or Russia, or than a well checked aristocracy, like Venice, Bern, or Holland. An excellent writer has said, incautiously, that '*a people will never oppress themselves, or invade their own rights*'.[130] This compliment, if applied to human nature, or to mankind, or to any nation or people in being or in memory, is more than has been merited.

"If it should be admitted, that a people will not unanimously agree to oppress themselves, it is as much as is ever, and more than is always true. All kinds of experience shew, that great numbers of individuals do oppress great numbers of other individuals; that partita often, if not always, oppress other partita; and majorities almost universally minorities. All that this observation can mean, then, consistently with any colour of fact, is, that the people will not unanimously agree to oppress themselves; but if one party agrees to oppress another, or the majority the minority, the people still oppress themselves, for one part of them oppress another. '*The people never think of usurping over other men's rights*', what can this mean? Does it mean that the people never *unanimously* think of usurping over other men's rights? This would be trifling, for there would, by the supposition, be no other men's rights to usurp. But if the people never, jointly or severally, think of usurping the rights of others, what occasion can there to for any government at all? [A]re there no robberies, burglaries, murder, adulteries, thefts nor cheats? Is not a great part, I will not say the greatest part, of men detected every day in some disposition or other, stronger or weaker, more or less, to usurp other men's rights? There are some few, indeed, whose whole lives and conversation show, that, in every thought, word and action, they conscientiously respect the rights of others; there is a larger body still, who, in the general tenor of their thoughts and actions, discover similar principles and feelings, yet frequently err. If we should extend our candour so far as to own that the majority of men are generally under the dominion of benevolence and good intentions, yet it must be confessed that a vast majority frequently transgress; and what is more directly to the point, not only a majority, but almost all confine their benevolence to their families, relations, personal friends, parish, village, city, county, province, and that very few indeed extend to the whole community. Now grant but this truth, and the question is decided: if a majority are capable of preferring their own private interest, or that of their families, countries and party, to that of the nation collectively, some provision must be made in the constitution, in favour of justice, to compel all to respect the Common right, the public good, the universal law, in preference to all private and partial considerations."[131]

"The proposition of our author then should be revised, and it should have been said that they mind so much their own, that they never think enough of others. Suppose a nation, rich and poor, high and low, ten millions in number, all assembled together; not more than one or two millions will have lands, houses, or any personal property; if we take into account the women and children, or even if we leave them out of the question, a great majority of every nation is wholly destitute of property, except a small quantity of clothes, and a few trifles of other moveables. Would Mr. Needham be responsible, that, if all were to be decided by a vote of the majority, the eight or nine millions who have no property, would not think of usurping over the rights of the one or two millions who have? Property is surely a right of mankind as really as liberty.[132] Perhaps, at first, prejudice, habit, shame or fear, principle or religion, would restrain the poor from attacking the rich, and the idle from usurping on the industrious; but the time would not be long before courage and enterprise would come, and pretexts be invented by degrees to countenance the majority in dividing all the property among them, or at least in sharing it equally with the present possessors. Debts would be abolished first; taxes laid heavy on the rich, and not at all on the others; and at last a downright equal division of every thing be demanded, and voted. What would be the consequence of this? The idle, the vicious, the intemperate, would rush into the utmost extravagance of debauchery, sell and spend all their share, and then demand a new division of those who purchased from them.

"The moment the idea is admitted into society, that property is not as sacred as the laws of God, and that there is not a force of law and public justice to protect it, anarchy and tyranny commence. If 'Thou shall not covet', and 'Thou shall not steal', were not commandments of Heaven, they must be made inviolable precepts in every society before it can be civilised or made free.

"If the first part of the proposition, viz: that '*The people never think of usurping over other men's rights*' cannot be admitted, is the second, viz: '*they mind which way to preserve their own*' better founded? There is in every nation and people under Heaven, a large proportion of persons who take no rational and prudent precautions to preserve what they have, much less to acquire more. Indolence is the natural character of man, to such a degree, that nothing but the necessities of hunger, thirst and other wants equally pressing, can stimulate him to action, until education is introduced in civilised societies, and that the strongest motives of ambition to excel in arts, trades and professions, are established in the minds of men; until this emulation is introduced, the lazy savage holds property in too little estimation to give himself trouble for the preservation or acquisition of it. In societies the most cultivated and polished, vanity, fashion and folly, prevail over every thought of ways to preserve their own; they seem rather chiefly to study what means of luxury, dissipation and extravagance, they can invent to get rid of it.

" '*The case is far otherwise among Kings and Grandees*', says our author, '*as all nations in the world have felt to some purpose*'; that is, in other words, Kings and grandees think of usurping other men's rights, but do not mind which way to preserve their own. It is very easy to flatter the democratical portion of society by making such distinctions between them and the monarchical and aristocratical; but flattery is as base an artifice, and as pernicious a vice, when offered to the people, as when given to the others. There is no reason for believing the one much honester or wiser than the other; they are all of the same clay, their minds and bodies are alike. The two latter have more knowledge and sagacity derived from education, and more advantages for acquiring wisdom and virtue. As to usurping others' rights, they are all three equally guilty, when unlimited in power; no wise man will trust either with an opportunity; and every judicious legislator will set all three to watch and control each other.

"We may appeal to every page of history, we have hitherto turned over for proofs irrefragable, that the people, when they have been unchecked, have been as unjust, tyrannical, brutal, barbarous and cruel, as any King or Senate possessed of uncontrollable power. The majority has eternally, and without one exception, usurped over the rights of the minority."

I have the honour to be,
My Lord,
Your Lordship's most obedient humble servant,

CAMILLUS.

***

No. XXXI

Montreal, 11th November, 1835.

My Lord,

Your lordship's fifth paragraph affords a striking instance of the contradictions, which the spirit of liberal conciliation never fails to produce. After having stated, that, 'in the distribution of political offices, my instructions enjoin upon me the utmost impartiality, and an entire disregard of distinctions derived from difference of origin', your lordship states 'that, in every country, to be acceptable to the great body of the people, is one of the most essential elements of fitness for public stations'. How ingeniously your lordship flatters your French allies—firstly, you sympathise with the previous 'exclusion of its prior inhabitants from offices of government' on account of their national origin; secondly, you assure the hungry expectants of office, that a Frenchman will stand on the same footing as an Englishman; thirdly, you place the former's hoof on the latter's neck, by intimating that, though an Englishman, as such, is not to be doomed to 'a state of political inferiority', yet he must be doomed to such a state, unless he be 'acceptable to the great body of the people', or, in other words, unless he becomes a traitor to his name and to his country.[133] To which of the contradictory statements does your lordship adhere? Without any great boast of sagacity, I may reply for your lordship, that the special statement about 'the great body of the people' was sincere, and that the general flourish about 'impartiality' was meant merely to deceive 'the English inhabitants of this province'. Were this equivocation a solitary one of the kind, I might ascribe it to 'inadvertence,' the standing apology of liberal blunders and liberal crimes; but I cannot, my lord, refrain from classing it with your lordship's similar equivocations in regard to the feudal system. One swallow does not make summer; but farther the proverb saith not. What, my lord, are 'the English inhabitants of this province' to think of your lordship's language, whether as it affects their opinion of your lordship's sincerity or as it indicates your lordship's opinion of their understandings? Do, my lord, do, for the sake of your own honour—which ought to be dearer to every man than any thing else—throw off the mask and surrender the ship to the Gallic shark without throwing a tub to the English whale. Uniformity, my lord, is the great aim of your lordship's noble and right honourable employers; and I must congratulate them on the uniform character of their viceroys. Lord Mulgrave[134] and Lord Gosford respectively govern Ireland and Lower Canada with 'impartiality' on their lips, and on their lips only. Head, my lord, the following sketch of Lord Mulgrave, and say, whether I might not say to your lordship, as Nathan said to David, 'Thou art the man'.[135]

> "For when the country witnessed his lordship's countenance of illegal processions favourable to the views of one party, and his denouncement and persecution of the legal assemblies of another— when they behold him proceeding on a tour of ill-dissembled agitation, receiving the homage, and courting the society, and flattering the prejudices of those who have been the chief disturbers of the public peace—when they behold his vice-regal throne surrounded by the creatures and partisans of agitation, and the favours and rewards of his government bestowed exclusively on the leaders of the movement

party—and when, moreover, this partisan exhibition of preference was not balanced by a single word or act of justice, not to say of favour, towards those whose loyalty to the throne and attachment to the British connexion have never been called in question; when the whole country, we say, witnessed those things, was not the favoured party justified in claiming him as their own? and was not the discountenanced portion of the community fully warranted in the distrust which they so unqualifiedly maintained?"

Your lordship has not literally countenanced 'illegal processions' of one party; but you have countenanced its 'illegal' agents, you have countenanced its 'illegal' compromises, you have countenanced its 'illegal' conventions. Your lordship has not denounced and persecuted the 'legal assemblies' of another party; but you did, in spirit if not in letter, absent yourself from one 'legal' assembly at the instigation of an officious place-hunter—you did, in violation of established custom and of common courtesy, refuse to accompany your predecessor[136] and a 'legal' assemblage of constitutionalists to the place of your predecessor's embarkation — you did slight the legislative council, which is still a 'legal assembly', by omitting to name it, as well as 'the representatives of the people,' in your fourth paragraph, and by withholding the customary epithet of 'honourable' from 'gentlemen of the legislative council' in the opening of your speech. Your lordship has not proceeded on 'a tour of ill dissembled agitation', but your lordship has been eagerly 'receiving the homage, and courting the society, and flattering the prejudices of those, who have been the chief disturbers of the public peace', you have surrounded your vice-regal throne with 'the creatures and partisans of agitation', and, if you are not 'bestowed exclusively on the leaders of the movement party' the favours and rewards' of government, you have publicly and solemnly promised to do so. I leave the completion of the parallel to your lordship's own conscience; but I must, in candour, add, that your lordship has balanced 'this partisan exhibition of preference' by more than 'a single word of justice'—words of justice being very much at your lordship's command.

Permit me now to resume the consideration of your lordship's democratic doctrine about the executive power of 'the great body of the people'. Suppose for a moment, my lord, your doctrine to be sound, and apply it to the case of the royal commissioners. Has not Mr. Papineau, as the recognised organ of 'the great body of the people', declared, that the appointment of a royal commission of inquiry is an insult to 'the great body of the people'?[137] Are not the commissioners, therefore, bound to retire from their 'public stations', and to save John Bull their monthly draft for £2,000 sterling? Under these circumstances, your lordship's double capacity, as commissioner and as governor, compels your lordship to draw some very fine distinctions in your intercourse with your French allies. As governor, your lordship thanks the assembly for 'the flattering and kind manner in which you have spoken of myself'. As commissioner, your lordship would display a vast deal either of forbearance or of perspicacity, if you discovered in the assembly's proceedings much either of flattery or of kindness. These very fine distinctions, however, concern nobody but your lordship.

If your lordship will condescend to borrow an argument from a private individual, I can satisfy your lordship, that even your admissions as to 'the great body of the people' do not necessarily compel the royal commissioners to retire from their 'public stations' What does your lordship mean by 'country'. If you mean Lower Canada, you virtually proclaim, that Great Britain is not to have a single representative in the executive government of this colony— that Lower Canada is practically independent—that 'the French inhabitants of this province' are 'La Grande Nation Canadienne'.[138] But these absurd conclusions prove, that by 'country', your lordship must have meant, not Lower Canada but the British Empire or the United Kingdom and Canada taken together. This interpretation, if more absurd than the other, has at least the merit of being less treasonable; and, if it be the true one, it may still permit the royal commission to exist. If, my lord, the democratic absurdity about the 'great body of the people' be set aside, the more extensive meaning of 'country' furnishes the true test of fitness for 'public stations' and presents the executive functionaries not merely as provincial but as imperial officers.

I have the honour to be,
My Lord,
Your Lordship's most obedient humble servant,

CAMILLUS.

***

No. XXXII

Montreal, 12th November, 1835.

My Lord,

I yesterday attempted to prove, that your lordship's democratic doctrine about 'the great body of the people' was utterly incompatible with the necessary subordination of a colony; and I shall now attempt to prove, that it is essentially inconsistent with monarchical institutions. Such a doctrine virtually invests the majority of the representative body with all the powers of the executive government and of the judiciary. It, therefore, tends to establish, not merely a despotism, but a democratic despotism, or, in other words, the uncontrolled domination of 'the great body of the people'. Such a doctrine, my lord, may be cherished by His Majesty's ministers and His Majesty's viceroys; but it is more easily reconciled with their interest than with their honour or their duty. Yes, my lord, your 'precise instructions' seem to plant Mr. Roebuck's 'pure democracy'; and a majority of the commissioners will doubtless nurture it into maturity. Why not, my lord? Is it not their interest to recommend themselves to a democratic cabinet by the propagation of democratic doctrines? One member of that majority,[139] though placed above the temptations of avarice, may still be misled by ambition; the other, my lord, is known to be the selfish slave of the meaner as well as of the nobler vice, is known to have exchanged an honourable profession, for which his country educated him, for a place-hunting subserviency to the ruling powers of the day. To place on a commission of inquiry a man, who neither can nor will afford to be impartial, was indeed an insult to this colony, an insult to his colleague, and an insult to common justice. That man—his name, my lord, shall never pollute the letters of Camillus— has been so indiscreet as to express, with all the dogmatism of self-sufficient vanity, preconceived opinions on the very subjects, on which he is bound to inquire. Though I will not name the man in either of your lordship's languages, yet, to give your lordship an instance of the connexion between names and things, I beg to add, that, in the language of ancient Greece, his name is VULTURE. This translation, my lord, supersedes the necessity of introducing a third language into a province, which has already one too many. In the last clause, my lord, you will cordially concur; but you may not adopt my interpretation of it. It is the French language, that I deem superfluous; it is the English, that is the object of your lordship's proscription. Has not your lordship, as I have already shewn, threatened virtually to banish the English language from every public department by law? Has not your lordship, so far as 'the executive power of the governor' can go, already banished that language by answering the assembly's 'flattering and kind' address in a French original and an English translation? The force of weakness can no further go. Would your lordship deem it a compliment or an insult, were 'the English inhabitants of this province' to speak only the French language within the vice-regal halls? If a compliment, who would not pity your weakness? If an insult, who would regret your chastisement? But this, my lord, is a digression from a digression. The original digression was intended to call your lordship's most serious attention to the almost universal suspicion, that the bird of prey has rooted his talons in your lordship's mind, and draws it hither and thither with every flap of his ominous wings—or, in plain terms, that one of your colleagues exerts over your lordship an influence, equally dishonourable and unconstitutional. Such a suspicion, my lord, must materially diminish your usefulness, whether as governor or as commissioner; and your lordship cannot too speedily refute the suspicion by resolutely casting off the living incubus. Your lordship cannot prevent the bird of prey from continuing a commissioner; but your lordship will incur a heavy responsibility, if your too easy reliance on his superior wisdom virtually renders him the commission.

In regard to the practical result of jour lordship's democratic doctrine as to 'the great body of the people,' I need not say much. It would manifestly enable the French demagogues to oppress 'the English inhabitants of this province'; and any individual, who doubts that they would be willing to do so, possesses much more of charity than of knowledge.

The latter part of the fifth paragraph, my lord, suggests some important considerations. It seems to reserve the more important share of the official patronage to the imperial cabinet, and is quite in keeping with the proverbially grasping selfishness of modern liberals. This view of the case, my lord, enables me to reconcile the apparently contradictory promises of the preceding part of the paragraph. Your lordship promised 'an entire disregard of distinctions derived from the difference of origin'; and your lordship promised also to appoint only men 'acceptable to the great body of the people'. The promised reference to the imperial cabinet reconciles those apparent contradictions in a manner not very gratifying to 'the English inhabitants of this province'. The imperial cabinet will dispense the official patronage with 'the utmost impartiality' amongst Englishmen and Frenchmen; but that it may not violate your lordship's second promise, it will select the Englishmen not from 'the English inhabitants of this province', who want the 'most essential' qualification, but from the place-hunting dependants on Downing street, who, for the sake of office and emoluments, would make themselves 'acceptable to the great body' of the Esquimaux or the Hottentots.[140] Thus, my lord, will 'the English inhabitants of this province' be doomed to 'a state of political inferiority,' be branded as unworthy of serving his Majesty in any capacity, be oppressed as the common victims of Frenchmen and Frenchified Englishmen.

I have the honour to be,
My Lord,
Your lordship's most obedient humble servant,

CAMILLUS.

***

No. XXXIII.

Montreal, 13th November, 1835,

My Lord,

Instead of proceeding with the consideration of the sixth paragraph of your lordship's speech, I must, like the Roman Emperor Titus, lose a day in noticing this morning's effusion of your old champion Coz, in regard to the fifth paragraph. Coz, my lord, has a wonderful versatility of talent. He writes one thing to-day and another to-morrow. But he has at last surpassed himself by pouring out both the one thing and the other tiling on the same day. That Cos is dishonest as well as versatile, I will not venture to assert, for there is not the slightest reason to believe, that, while he says one thing, he means another or any thing at all. Again, my lord, as if to multiply elegant varieties, while Coz writes one thing in chambers, Coz's associate says another thing in the streets. I shall take the liberty, my lord, of proving these assertions with the view of enabling your lordship justly to appreciate the opinions of a certain radical journal[141]. Firstly that journal gave your lordship's speech the credit of 'apparent temper, manliness and impartiality' and, under the double screen of an if and a yet, passed a kind of negative censure on 'the granting of the Assembly's contingencies'.[142] Secondly, that journal threw the contingencies, as being awfully mysterious, entirely out of its calculation and lauded your lordship for your partiality to 'the constitutional reformers'. Thirdly, that journal has discovered, that in addition to the mysterious contingencies, your lordship's democratic doctrine about 'the great body of the people', though 'as a general principle', 'incontestably correct', will yet, 'if applied without extreme caution to Canada in her present circumstances', 'be productive of lamentable consequences'.[143] Fourthly, that journal quotes as 'sensible remarks' an article from the *New York Albion*, in which the demagogues are termed your lordship's 'French allies', and the constitutionalists are advised to 'Let Lord Gosford make his concessions and try his system of palliations'.[144] Have I not, my lord, sufficiently proved the versatility of your old champion Coz? While Coz, my lord, was writing all these silly contradictions, Coz's associate was declaiming almost in the very language of Camillus, against your lordship's democratic subserviency to 'the great body of the people' and was honest enough to praise the letter of Camillus on the French language. I have, my lord, treated this matter in a jocular strain because the actors in the cunningly managed farce are unworthy of serious indignation. I now proceed to discuss the special merits of this morning's effusion.

Coz tries to be fearfully sarcastic on all toryish persons, while he praises your lordship's 'monstrous innovation' about the indispensable test of 'fitness' in holders of 'public stations'. Coz has most unaccountably made a disinterested mistake in praising a test, which dooms himself for ever to an exclusion 'from office and employment'. Coz might have been of some use in ancient times, for according to Horace, any useless log was then good raw material for a god; but, under the reign of the new principle of 'fitness', he is competent only to damn your lordship with false, faint and fluctuating praise.

Coz then proceeds to say, that 'Not the least powerful *arguments* against the policy of an Elective Legislative Council *is* drawn from a glaring want of 'fitness' in the mass of electors, to make a proper choice of members for such a body, &c.'[145] *Arguments is*, my lord, is not a grammatical blunder but a democratic imitation of Andrew Jackson's *Statements is*.[146] The same argument, my lord, may be urged with the same force 'against the policy of an Elective' Assembly on the ground 'of the extreme probability that those so chosen would be very unfit for fulfilling the necessary duties of their trust'.[147] This, my lord, is a pretty severe character of those, whom the 'sensible remarks' of the *Albion* style your lordship's 'French allies', and with whom you are trying 'a system of palliation' at the expense of the obsolete parchment of the constitution, at the expense of sound principles, at the expense of the *corpus vile* of 'the English inhabitants of this province'. Your lordship may well pray to be saved from your friends.

Your old champion Coz must know more even than Camillus of your lordship's personal feelings, for he has discovered, that the democratic doctrine about 'the great body of the people' 'has evidently been uttered with considerable effort on the part of his Excellency'. What Coz seemed to himself to mean, I cannot say; and, however dignified maybe an interpreter of nature, I must beg to elude the task of interpreting a natural. Coz, after having pronounced your lordship's doctrine, 'as a general principle' 'incontestably correct', endeavours to prove by a sneer at 'some persons', that it is not necessarily an emanation of pure democracy. These 'some persons' are, in a subsequent article, stated to be 'Mr. Viger and the majority party' on theone tide and 'Messrs. Moffatt and M'Gill' on the other.[148] 'Some persons' have again to endure the 'unendurable' sarcasm of Coz as 'these people' in the following sentence,

> "We know not which to lament the more, the horrifying picture which these people draw of the future, or their vanity in detailing to others their sinister and morbid feelings."

Finding that 'some persons' and 'these people' comprehended the Honourable George Moffatt and the Honourable Peter McGill, who have nobly done their duty in the Council against a majority of Frenchmen and trucklers, Coz impertinently and gratuitously frames an impertinent and gratuitous apology for these two gentlemen in answer to his own impertinent and gratuitous charge.

> "Messrs. Moffatt and M'Gill appear to have combatted the doctrine more in consequence of the interpretation which may be given to it by the Democrats, than of that which it legitimately bears in the connexion in which it stands in the speech."

Coz displays a most plentiful lack of knowledge as well of words as of things. He seems to be very much puzzled as to the meaning of 'one of the most essential elements of fitness' and tries to shew that 'some persons' and 'these people' consider 'one of the most essential elements' as 'the sole element' of 'fitness'. The fact, that that qualification is 'essential' or indispensable, is quite sufficient to justify 'the horrifying picture' in the eyes of all but those, who pay your lordship the questionable compliment of waiting to gather the meaning of your lordship's 'vague and general language' from 'deeds done'. Coz, my lord, will find it difficult to reconcile this compliment with his declaration, that he feels 'quite at liberty to canvass freely the principles by which the head or other members of that commission may profess to be guided'.

When Coz says, that 'some persons' and 'these people' styled your lordship a 'wretch', your lordship must be rather vexed than surprised at your old champion's falsehood.

I have the honour to be,
My Lord,
Your Lordship's most obedient humble servant,

CAMILLUS.

***

No. XXXIV.

Montreal, 14th November, 1835.

My Lord,

I must once more recur to the fifth paragraph of your lordship's speech.

It is credibly reported, my lord, that an indiscreet member of the royal commission recently stated, that every demand of the French faction, which would not interfere with the constitution, would be granted, but that every other demand would be resisted by an appeal to the sword.[149] The rumour may be false; but commissioners of inquiry should shield themselves against false reports of their language by a religious silence. Though the rumour may be false, yet the indiscreet individual's general habits justify the supposition, that it may be true. The rumour, supported as it is both by external and by internal evidence, is at least worthy of a brief discussion.

So, my lord, the 'two parties', which your lordship is commanded by your 'precise instructions' to recognise, are 'the great body of the people' and the musty parchment of the constitutional act— 'the English inhabitants of this province' being as nothing in the eyes of liberal ministers and liberal viceroys. Every demand of the French demagogues is to be discussed by the powers, that be, not in reference to its practical influence on either 'the great' or the little 'body of the people', but in reference to the inanimate words of a British statute. If these inanimate words present *yes* to your lordship's eye, the demand is to be granted; if *no*, the demand is to be rejected. Do these inanimate words permit his Majesty to invest the French demagogues with all executive and judicial appointments?

Your lordship will be able to read *yes*, even without the aid of a liberal microscope. When, therefore, the French demagogues shall demand all executive and judicial appointments, your lordship will, of course, receive 'precise instructions' to make Mr. Papineau your successor, as the last in a scale descending from Dalhousie[150] downwards, to make Mr. Viger Speaker of the legislative council, to make Mr. Lafontaine chief justice of the province, to make Mr. Debartzch deputy post-master general. In the dismissal of lord Gosford, in the degradation of Mr. Sewell, in the punishment of Mr. Stayner,[151] there is not the slightest violation of the constitutional act.[152]

Your lordship will excuse me for not recommending to your notice 'fit' successors for all the other executive or judicial officers, who hold office merely during pleasure. Could your indiscreet colleague have reflected on the meaning of his own words? So much, my lord, as to executive and judicial offices. But there is something more, my lord, that you may, so far as the government is concerned, surrender without any violation of the constitutional act. You may feed the hungry demagogues with the waste lands of the crown, provided you can obtain the sanction of the provincial legislature and the imperial parliament. Of the former —shame to a few trucklers— you may obtain the sanction with a nod; with the latter you may be equally successful, provided Mr. O'Connell continues to patronise the ministry in the lower house, and lord Melbourne stoutly threaten the refractory members of the upper with the fearful vengeance of 'his Majesty's faithful and loyal subjects, the commons of Lower Canada'.[153] So much, my lord, on the granting of every constitutional demand of the French faction. Permit me now to consider the indiscreet individual's assertion, that every unconstitutional demand would be resisted, if necessary, by an appeal to the sword. Why that individual, unless on the ground of his being indiscreet, should at all allude to the tools of a forsaken profession, I cannot comprehend; but I most respectfully beg to point out the entire discrepancy between that individual's solitary sample of conservative feeling and your lordship's clearly implied admission, that the constitution of the legislative council falls within the range of the inquiry of the royal commissioners. Whether did your indiscreet colleague become partially a conservative on his own responsibility, or did your lordship throw out your clearly implied admission merely as a sop to Cerberus[154]? The former supposition is untenable in regard to a confirmed radical; the latter must, therefore, be the true one. If, my lord, the promised inquiry is to be a delusion even in regard to the expectations of the dreaded assembly, it is much more likely to be so in regard to the just demands of those despised associations, characterised by your indiscreet colleague as 'self-constituted bodies of paltry merchants'—Yes, my lord, the inquiry will be a mere mockery; and the monthly draft of £2000 sterling may, with comparatively good consequences, be thrown into the River St. Lawrence. Your 'precise instructions' have determined, that the French majority shall be every thing and the English minority nothing. I draw aside the veil of futurity, and see through not a very long vista the inevitable workings of an awful retribution. That such a retribution will have ample justification, the following picture of the uncontrolled domination of an ignorant majority will abundantly prove.[155]

> "'Every political object in America is effected by art and duplicity. Politicians proceed upon the principle that the people are fools, that they are a great huge mass of ignorance and stupidity, and can be moulded to any purpose, however weak or wicked, that is calculated to promote their selfish views; and it is a melancholy reflection that there is too much truth in the estimate they have put upon the intelligence of this people. For the illustration of the foregoing, let Mr. Van Buren's acceptance of the Baltimore nomination be duly considered.[156] Weak indeed must be that mind—lost to every thing like common discernment—destitute of the slightest sense of self-respect, if it does not discover, in the very commencement of the article, the most shallow-witted, servile and contemptible dissimulation that ever passed the lips of man.

"I put it to the candour of the best friend Van Buren has, whether he believes that nomination of him by a convention of the democratic republicans of the Union was the only contingency upon which he would consent to become a candidate for the high office of President? Such a barefaced instance of insincerity, to call it by no worse name, admits of no argument. It strikes the senses, without the aid of reason; and yet the weak and deluded portion of this great community, who never think for themselves, but are entirely directed by the cry of 'Huzza for Jackson'—will gulp it down and march up to the polls and vote for Van Buren, as if he were as sincere as Washington, and as virtuous as Wirt. Every man that can read will perceive that Van Buren relies upon no merit of his own, but is vaulting upon the back of Jackson's popularity, full well knowing that among a blind and unthinking people this is enough for his purpose; and hence he so meanly talks about his being the 'honoured instrument selected by the friends of the present administration, to carry out its principles and policy; and that, as well from inclination as from duty. I shall, if honoured with the choice of the American people, *endeavour to tread generally in the footsteps of General Jackson*; happy if I shall be able to perfect the work which he has so gloriously begun'. Can language be more degrading—can sentiments be more menial?

"Would Washington, Jefferson, Madison or Monroe, have been guilty of such humiliating sycophancy for the sake of an office? Would any high-minded man, especially for the office of President of the United States, which implies every thing that is noble, magnanimous and virtuous? Mean, low and abject, however, as he is, with shame be it spoken, it is addressed to the people, a great portion of whom will swallow the whole of it, and therefore subject the morality and discernment of themselves and country to the worst of imputations. Depend upon it, that government is approaching a crisis of fearful portent, when such open and flagrant duplicity on the part of politicians, is not considered too gross for either the credulity or integrity of the people. If they are too ignorant to discover that they are the dupes of a crafty 'ambition, that they are the daily subjects of imposition, bad indeed is their condition; but infinitely worse, if possible, if understanding the vile discipline, they are nevertheless willing to become the instruments of its hollow-hearted purposes.'"

I have the honour to be,
My Lord,
Your Lordship's most obedient humble servant,

CAMILLUS.

***

No. XXXV.

Montreal, 16th November, 1835.

My Lord,

I must still defer for a day the consideration of the sixth paragraph of your lordship's speech.

The envious blunderers, who have nothing else to say against Camillus, accuse him of precipitate haste in inferring your future deeds from your past expressions. Such fawning time-servers, my lord, pay a very bad compliment either to your head or to your heart or to both. They must mean that your language, if intelligible, is dishonest, or that, if honest, it is unintelligible. Your lordship may well pray to be protected against such flatterers: and yet your lordship's discovery of a 'flattering and kind manner' in the assembly's address may lead one to suspect, that your lordship may hail with pleasure the gross insults of the fawning timeservers. My mode of criticism, my lord, is widely different. 1 first endeavour to understand your words; and I then believe that your lordship will second your words by your actions. Common sense enables me to do the former; common charity compels me to do the latter. I trust, my lord, that you are not yet so far corrupted by foolish 'instructions' or by your intercourse with bigotted demagogues as to consider either common sense or common charity as a crime.

Permit me, my lord, to select a few instances, in which the fawning time-servers seem to have been determined neither to believe nor to understand your lordship's language. Firstly, there was your lordship's declaration, not less 'precise' than your remarkably 'precise instructions', which, till it should be justified by 'deeds done', the fawning time servers were determined to consider as ambiguous or false. Secondly, there was your lordship's beautifully laconic promise of the contingencies.

"To both branches of the legislature, I am authorised to offer my warrants for the payment of their contingent expenses."

This, my lord, was sufficiently 'precise'; but yet the fattening time servers either could not understand it, or would not believe it. Understanding it and believing it, I considered the 'mysterious' question of the contingencies settled, and anticipated the actual robbery of the treasury as a mere matter of course; but the fawning time-servers exalt your lordship's actual grant into a 'most important piece of intelligence'. I subjoin your lordship's words:—

"Gentlemen—In conformity with what I stated in my speech at the opening of the session, on the subject of the contingencies, I cheerfully accede to the prayer of this address."

Your lordship's first clause, by proving that you sometimes act 'in conformity' with what you state, must be a severe blow to the fawning time-servers, who had resolved not to give your lordship credit for so vulgar, so plebeian a virtue as veracity. But your lordship's brief reply does contain one 'piece of intelligence', certainly 'most important' to your lordship, as an English nobleman, as a prudent governor, as a man of honour. For the sake of argument (shall admit, that your 'precise instructions' compelled you to 'accede to the prayer of this address'; but surely, my lord, your noble and right honorable masters were not so unreasonably cruel as to command

144 · The Prophetic *Anti-Gallic Letters*

you, 'cheerfully' to put your hand into the public chest, 'cheerfully' to violate the very constitution, which your gallant colleague is to defend with the sword, 'cheerfully' to become the accomplice of Roebuck and the patron of revolutionary conventions. Good heavens, my lord of Gosford, are you mad enough to glory in your shame, hardened enough to rejoice in a delegated opportunity of doing evil, degraded enough to be 'cheerful' under the double lash of a Frenchified cabinet and a French faction? Do not, my lord, suppose, that 1 have lost my temper. No, my lord; with the pen as with the knife, it is temper that cuts keenly, deeply, fatally. It is not, my lord, for a humble individual, who has neither hereditary title to disgrace nor official dignity to prostitute, to expect, that your lordship will answer these letters; but I do expect, that your lordship, as a commissioner of inquiry, will either yield to my arguments or elude their force to the satisfaction of your own intellect, your own conscience, your own honour.

'Cheerfully', my lord! That accursed word, which almost concentrates in itself the whole force of 'Smile and smile and be, &c.',[157] shall be handed down, if Camillus should write a history of Canada for the purpose, to an indignant, a contemptuous, a scornful posterity. Whether Camillus may or may not write such a history, your lordship may rest assured, that, notwithstanding your lordship's attempt to make the French at once the official and the fashionable language of this colony, any future history of Lower Canada will be written only in the English language, only with an English pen, only with English feelings. If your lordship's ambition extends to posthumous reputation, I sincerely pity your lordship. But this, my lord, is a digression.

If, my lord, the fawning time-servers were contented with patiently and silently waiting for 'deeds done', I should not condescend to notice their treacherous imbecility; but when I find them calling upon 'all loyal men' to 'give him their support, because he comes in the king's name, clothed with royal authority and with good intentions', and in the same 'sensible remarks' admitting, that the French demagogues are 'his French allies', I must, my lord, boldly expose their ignorance, their weakness, their dishonesty. Have the fawning timeservers the audacity to advise 'all loyal men' to support the executive ally of the demagogues, because, forsooth, he is 'clothed with royal authority and with good intentions'? The language may be critically correct, for the 'royal authority' and the 'good intentions' are fully as superficial, and fully as easily laid aside as an unbuttoned cloak. No, my lord, so long as the French demagogues are your lordship's 'French allies', I shall consider it the solemn duty of myself and every man of English blood to oppose, to obstruct, to embarrass every movement of the unholy coalition.

Your lordship is said to be a classical scholar; and I present you with a passage from Demosthenes's oration *De Corona*[158], which will convince your lordship, that the precipitate haste of Camillus, if censured by the fawning time-servers, has at least the warm approbation of the prince of orators.

> "The adviser and the sycophant, though they do not resemble each other in any one reaped, differ chiefly in this. The former anticipates probable results from actual appearances, and renders himself morally responsible to the believers in his anticipations. The latter, after having been silent, when he ought, like the former, to have spoken, brawls away furiously, when he sees 'deeds done". * * * The end, indeed, when the Deity shall have determined it, is within the knowledge of every sycophant; but the anticipation itself displays the wisdom of the adviser."

In Montreal, my lord, who is the adviser and who if the sycophant?

I have the honour to be,
My Lord,
Your Lordship's most obedient humble servant,

CAMILLUS.

***

No. XXXVI.

Montreal, 18th Nov. 1835.

My Lord,

The first two sentences of your lordship's sixth paragraph are 'Complaint is also made that incompatible offices are, in some cases, held by the same persons. In whatever degree this grievance may be found to exist, his Majesty has signified to me his expectation, that it should be completely remedied.' How naturally, my lord, the 'complaint' of the just sentence slides into the 'grievance' of the lordship, doubtless, believing with the most liberal good nature, that every complaint of the revolutionary faction is well grounded.— Whether this amiable doctrine be sound or not, your lordship, as an impartial functionary, is bound to give the benefit of it to the constitutionalists as well as to the revolutionists; and I must, therefore, congratulate the good fortune of both parties as well as compliment your lordship's ingenuity on 'the resolution which has been taken to redress every grievance under which any class of his Majesty's Canadian subjects may labour.' Oh happy day, my lord, when the redress of every 'grievance' shall have extinguished every 'complaint'. Oh happier Baron of Worlingham,[159] the conciliatory harbinger of so auspicious a period. Oh the golden age of Lower Canada. Oh the Saturn of modern times. *Redeunt Saturnia regna*.[160] What a contrast between your lordship's scythe and your gallant colleague's sword. Between the old and the new era, however, there will most probably be one point of distinction. Under your lordship's prototype, the rivers rolled tides of milk and nectar; under your lordship, they are far more likely to roll tides of blood *Cerno ipsum spumantem sanguine Thybrim* (I see the Tiber foaming with much blood).[161] In another respect, also, the modern copy resembles the ancient original. Saturn devoured his own off-spring; the Earl of Gosford insults, oppresses and pillages his own countrymen. But this, my lord, is a digression.

What does your lordship mean by 'incompatible offices'? 'Offices' may be 'incompatible' in two ways. They are 'incompatible', if they require the labour of 'the same person' at the same time; and they are 'incompatible', if the possession of the one enables 'the same person' to be negligent or faithless in the discharge of the other. Under the former head might come the chief justiceship of the province and the speakership of the legislative council; and if so, your lordship is bound to leave the present incumbent of these two appointment the choice of resigning one or both of them. Under the second head certainly come our mayoralty and our surveyorship of roads;[162] and your lordship, therefore, is imperatively bound to give Mr. Jacques Viger the hint to secure the richer appointment by the resignation of the poorer one. Remember, my lord, that it is not Camillus but 'his Majesty', that 'has signified to me his expectation, that it should be completely remedied'. Your lordship is unlucky in your adverbs. 'Completely' has been almost as rashly enunciated as 'cheerfully', because it prevents your lordship from displaying a liberal impartiality by carrying the rule into operation only against the little body of the people. The ill-timed adverb will compel you to mete out the same measure either of justice or of indulgence to the English chief justice of the province and the French mayor of Montreal. 'Completely', my lord, is a two edged sword.

Why 'his Majesty' should have presumed to denounce 'incompatible offices' in the face of a whiggish cabinet, and in the ear of your lordship, I cannot understand. Was not the whiggish cabinet of 'all the talents', in 1806, headed by lord Grenville, who at once controlled the financial expenditure and audited the financial accounts? Is not your lordship at once bound to inquire into every 'complaint' as Commissioner, and authorised to decide on many a 'complaint' as Governor? Did not lord Grenville hold, does not lord Gosford hold, 'incompatible offices'? The utter incapacity of 'all the talents' to sustain either the political reputation or the military renown of the British Empire very soon 'completely remedied' lord Grenville's 'grievance';[163] and, if like causes always produce like effects, lord Gosford's 'grievance' will be 'completely remedied' in a few short months. When it is so, my lord, your lordship will have a more honorable train, than your predecessor had, to the place of embarkation. Baron Aylmer was accompanied only by your gallant colleague's 'paltry merchants'; but Baron Worlingham will be closely attended by a coroneted earl. To make the contrast more "flattering and kind', the 'paltry merchants' will not obtrude their plebeian attendance on a fallen victim's solitary grandeur. At Point Levi, my lord, your last look will rest on Cape Diamond; and when your glance crosses the monument erected by the Earl of Dalhousie to one English conqueror of Lower Canada,[164] you may safely give the Earl of Gosford credit for having opened an equally brilliant career to another. Permit me to assure your lordship, that the second conquest shall not be characterized, like the shock of nations at Friedland,[165] as a battle won but a victory lost. The dearly bought lesson of conciliatory experience will not be thrown away.[166]

But on perusing the third sentence of the sixth paragraph, my lord, I find that your lordship's definition of 'incompatible offices', according to the favourite fashion of liberals, is not practical but theoretical. I subjoin the sentence.

> "Commencing with the highest, I have formed the opinion that it is neither right nor consistent with the wholesome separation and independence of the principal bodies of the government, and with the dignity of their members, that out of the limited number of executive councillors[167] in this province, several hold offices under the Legislative Council and House of Assembly."

It is to me, my lord, a matter of perfect indifference, whether these gentlemen resign their seats in the executive council or their 'offices under the legislative council and house of assembly'; but I confess, my lord, that the governor, who can 'cheerfully' violate the constitution and feel shocked by an imaginary evil, does strain at a gnat and swallow a camel. What does your lordship mean by 'right' as distinguished from 'consistent, &c.'? Your lordship must answer the question yourself, for I cannot attempt to do so. I cordially agree with your lordship that there should be a 'wholesome separation and independence of the principal bodies of the government'; but 'separation and independence' may be 'wholesome' without being complete. This not only may be, but actually is, the case, for the more intelligent Americans have discovered, that the complete 'separation' is not 'wholesome' and regret that a partial mixture is prevented by that theoretical obstacle 'the genius of their government.' As to the phrase 'dignity of their members,' I do not profess to understand it. I shall resume this subject tomorrow.

I have the honour to be,
My Lord
Your Lordship's most obedient humble servant

CAMILLUS.

***

No. XXXVII.

Montreal, 19th November, 1835.

My Lord,

At the close of my yesterday's letter, I stated to your lordship, that intelligent Americans do not consider the complete separation of all the departments of government as wholesome; and I now beg to lay before your lordship the opinion of one of the most distinguished jurists of the union on the subject.[168]

"If, then, occasional or periodical appeals would not afford an effectual barrier against the inroads of the legislature upon the other departments of the government, it is manifest that resort must be had to some contrivances, in the interior structure of the government itself, which shall exert a constant check, and preserve the mutual relations with each other. Upon a thorough examination of the subject, it will be found that this can be best accomplished by an occasional mixture of the powers of each department with those of the others, while the separate existence and constitutional independence of each are fully provided for. Each department should have a will of its own, and the members of each should have but a limited agency in the acts and appointments of the others. Each should have its own independence secured beyond the power of being taken away by either, or both of the others. But, at the same time, the relations of each to the other should be so strong that there should be a mutual interest to sustain and protect each other. There should not only be constitutional means, but personal motives, to resist encroachments of one on either of the others.

"Thus ambition would be made to counteract ambition; the desire of power to check power; and the pressure of interest to balance an opposing interest.

"There seems no adequate method of producing this result, but by a partial participation of each in the powers of the others; and by introducing into every operation of the government in all its branches a system of checks and balances, on which the safety of free institutions has ever been found essentially to depend. Thus, for instance, a guard against rashness and violence in legislation has often been found by distributing the power among different branches, and each having a negative upon the other. A guard against the inroads of the legislative power upon the executive, has been in like manner applied by giving the latter a qualified negative upon the former; and a guard against executive influence and patronage or unlawful exercise of authority by requiring the concurrence of a select council or a branch of the legislature in appointments to office and in the discharge of other high functions, as well as by placing the command of the revenue in other hands.

"The usual guard, applied for the security of the judicial department has been in the tenure of office of the judges, who commonly are to hold office during good behaviour. But this is obviously an inadequate provision, while the legislature is entrusted with a complete power over the salaries of the judges and over the jurisdiction of the courts, so that they can alter or diminish them at pleasure. Indeed the judiciary is naturally and almost necessarily (as has been already said) the weakest department. It can have no means of influence by patronage. Its powers can never be wielded for itself, it has no command over the purse or the sword of the nation. It can neither lay taxes nor appropriate money, nor command armies, nor appoint to offices. It is never brought into contact with the people by the constant appeals and solicitations and private intercourse, which belong to all the other departments of government. It is seen only in controversies or in trials and punishment. Its rigid justice and impartiality give it no claims to favour, however they may to respect. It stands solitary and unsupported, except by that portion of public opinion which is interested only in the strict administration of justice. It, can rarely secure the sympathy or zealous support either of the executive or the legislature. If they are not (as is not unfrequently the case) jealous of its prerogatives, the constant necessity of scrutinizing the act of each, upon the application of any private person and the painful duty of pronouncing judgment, that their acts are a departure from the law or constitution, can have no tendency to conciliate kindness or nourish influence.

"It would seem, therefore, that some additional guards would, under such circumstances, be necessary to protect this department from the absolute dominion of the others. Yet rarely have such guards been applied; and every attempt to introduce them has been resisted with pertinacity, which demonstrates how slow popular leaders are to introduce checks upon their own power; and how slow the people are to believe, that the judiciary is the real bulwark of their liberties.

"In some of the states the judicial department is partially combined with some branches of the executive and legislative departments; and it is believed that in those cases it has been found no unimportant auxiliary in preserving a wholesome vigour in the laws, as well as a wholesome administration of public justice."

I cannot, my lord, prosecute the discussion more appropriately than in the closing remarks of Anti-bureaucrat's fifth letter.

"It is not as the advocate of the government, but as the supporter of my own conscientious opinions, that I argue for the practical intermixture of the three great branches of the civil government, the executive, the legislature and the judiciary; and I do so with the more diffidence, as some gentlemen, of whose friendship any one may be proud, are decidedly opposed to such an intermixture.

"Such an intermixture exists in England according to the ordinary forms of the constitution. It exists in France by an anomalous violation of constitutional principles. It exists, to a certain extent, even in the American republic—the vice-president, the second member of the executive government, being president of the senate; and the senate a whole, being I as well of the executive government as of the legislature.

"If a digression may be pardoned, I must take tail opportunity of suggesting, in reference to my yesterday's communication, that, in the neighbouring republic, exists the perfect identity of the legislative and executive council, which is falsely stated by Messrs. Nelson and Chapman to exist in Lower Canada.[169] Such an identity does not exist in any other free country, so that the offensive identity is part and parcel of the very institution envied and coveted by the consistent and intelligent revolutionist of Lower Canada. It may be necessary to apprise some of my readers, that the senate is a council of control as to the appointment of public officers. In other words, the legislative council is an executive council, armed, too, with higher powers than those of the executive council of Lower Canada.[170] Let me now pass from analogy to reason.

"The absolute separation of the three great department of civil government must have the unfortunate effect of excluding the ablest men of the country from the most powerful and most dangerous department, the legislature. Who ought to be appointed judges? The most learned and most upright lawyers. Who ought to hold political or diplomatic offices? The most enlightened and most consistent statesmen. The system of absolute separation, therefore, necessarily commits the fearful power of making laws for the regulation of property, liberty and life, to second-rate professors of law and politics. Exclude his Majesty's ministers from the two houses of the imperial parliament; and, by taking away a tithe of the members, you must take away a full half of the talent. But that is not the whole mischief. The talent that is left is all on one side; so that the system of absolute separation would inevitably make an opposition morally and intellectually overwhelming, and produce a succession of administrations, as rapid as that of the scenes in a puppet show."

I have the honour to be,
My Lord,
Your Lordship's most obedient humble servant,

CAMILLUS.

* * *

No. XXXVIII

Montreal, 20th November, 1835.

My Lord,

Permit me now, my lord, to offer a few special remarks on your lordship's declaration, that it is improper 'that out of the limited number of Executive Councillors in this Province, several should hold offices under the legislative council and the house of assembly'.[171] In this declaration, my lord, there is a good deal of vagueness. If the possession of 'office' alleged to be 'incompatible' be inconsistent 'with the dignity of the members' of the principal bodies of the Government, I cannot understand, why the limited, or the unlimited number of executive councillors has even the most remote bearing on the question. Does your lordship mean, that every one of 'the principal bodies' has a fixed amount of 'dignity' and that every one of 'their members' has a share of 'dignity' inversely proportioned to the number of his colleagues? If so, my lord, your 'dignity' as governor must far exceed your 'dignity' as commissioner; and this mathematical theory explains and justifies the different degrees of respect paid by the 'flattering and kind' assembly to your lordship in your different capacities.

Felix, qui potuit rerum cognoscere causas (Blessed is he who has succeeded in learning the laws of nature's working).[172]

If, my lord, 'the limited number' were the only circumstance, that rendered 'incompatible offices' inconsistent 'with the dignity' of executive councillors, your lordship might have remedied the alleged evil by enlarging the number of executive councillors without adopting the absurdly republican doctrine of a complete separation of 'the principal bodies of the government'. If the executive councillors be incompetent to discharge their duties, supersede them, my lord, without fear and without compassion; but do not, my lord, act on a merely theoretical principle of a very questionable application. The best way, my lord, of testing the propriety of the merely theoretical principle, as such, is to apply it in its fullest extent to every possible object, and thus to give an indirect demonstration of its practical falsehood. Now, my lord, the principle of complete separation of the principal bodies of the government is inconsistent with your lordship's tenure of two 'offices'— more particularly as they are 'incompatible'— is inconsistent with any governor's possession both of legislative authority and executive power, is inconsistent with your lordship's tenure of office 'under the house of assembly' as Mr. Papineau's viceroy. If, however, one may judge from certain discrepancies between words and actions, your lordship does not consider your lordship bound by your lordship's own rules. Some people, my lord, make rules, as bees make honey and Frenchmen build ships, not for themselves but for others, but your lordship seems determined to punish the whole of 'the limited number' for even the theoretical fault of only 'several' of them. Am I to suspect your lordship of condescending to assign an untrue motive for your dismissal of the executive councillors or am I to give your lordship credit for being candid enough, on your present footing with regard to the anti-national demagogues, to admit, that 'Evil communications corrupt good manners'?[173] How classical, how pious, how humble to pay a 'flattering and kind' compliment to Menander and St. Paul, at the expense of your own reputation for loyalty and honor.

But, my lord, does any one of the 'executive councillors in this province' hold an office 'under the house of assembly'? The honorable Mr. Heney,[174] my lord, holds the office of law clerk in the house of assembly, but under his Majesty. The verbal inaccuracy might have been excusable, my lord, had it not tended literally to justify the assembly's presumption of last session, in having cancelled his Majesty's commission by the dismissal of Mr. Heney, on the ground of his being an executive councillor. During the present session, 'the commons of Lower Canada' have taken the same means of shewing themselves 'his Majesty's faithful and loyal subjects' by nominating the revolutionary editor of the *Canadien*[175] in Mr. Heney's stead. It is difficult, my lord, to say, whether the dismissal of the one or the nomination of the other be the grosser insult to the majesty of the English sovereign, of the English people and of the English name. Your lordship is reported to have expressed or rather muttered your disapprobation of' the assembly's conduct in this matter. Why should you do so, my lord? Did not Mr. Heney hold office 'under the house of assembly'? Has not your lordship, by permitting the assembly to define its own contingencies, enabled it to pay any hireling, whether in Canada or in England, in violation of the law? Has not your lordship, in spirit if not in letter, justified any encroachment on the part of 'the great body of the people'? But it is, my lord, consolatory to all 'the English inhabitants of this province', with the exception of a few blind or dishonest advocates of fair play, that your lordship begins to be galled by the chains of your faction. A worm, my lord, when trampled under foot, will turn upon its oppressor. Will your lordship do less? No, my lord; and I venture to predict, that you will soon be shielded by Camillus according to his feeble power, from the envenomed darts of cowardly, ungrateful and disloyal traitors.

But to return to Mr. Heney's case, my lord, your lordship dismisses him from the Executive Council because he is law clerk of the assembly, and the assembly dismisses him from the office of law clerk because he is an executive councillor. Can any thing, my lord, be more marvellously absurd? Your lordship pulls out the grey hairs, because they do not match the black; the assembly pulls out the black hairs, because they do not match the grey. Ludicrous as is the proceeding, there is, I trust, at least one individual in the province, that cannot 'cheerfully' smile at it.

Your lordship, however, may still permit Mr. Heney to retain his commission, and may include his salary in the civil list to be submitted to the house of assembly. The demagogues, my lord, will not grant his salary; and your lordship will not dare 'cheerfully' to pay, in defiance of the law, one, who is, merely a legal servant of William the Fourth and not an illegal servant of your lord ship's faction.

I have the honour to be,
My Lord,
Your Lordship's most obedient humble servant,

CAMILLUS.

***

No. XXXIX.

Montreal, 21st November, 1835.

My Lord,

In the third sentence of your sixth paragraph, your lordship states, that you 'desire however that it may be understood, that no dissatisfaction with the conduct of the members of the executive council, nor any mark whatever of his Majesty's displeasure is intended to be conveyed.'— I have, my lord, already shewn, that your doctrine about 'dignity' and 'separation' and 'independence' and all that kind of claptrap does not justify your meditated degradation of the executive councillors; and your lordship's own words, which I have quoted above, admit, that there does not exist any practical justification of your lordship's intended course. Would it not have been more manly, my lord, to confess, that you wished to make room for men 'acceptable to the great body of the people'?

Your lordship's appeal to your 'precise instructions' shared the infamy of robbing the provincial treasury between your lordship and your lordship's noble and right honorable masters; but your lordship's contemplated surrender of all executive authority to 'Excellency's faction' emanates from the liberal justice and the impartial wisdom of yourself alone. You say, 'I felt it my duty to impart to them the conclusion to which my mind had come' and 'I shall communicate the same opinion to the proper authorities at home'. When your lordship wrote these passages you must have forgotten, that you were a commissioner of inquiry as well as a governor-in-chief. 'My mind', forsooth! So your lordship presumes to inquire and decide on your own responsibility, in a matter of the very highest importance. Might not your lordship send your colleagues and their standing army home and save John Bull the monthly draft of £2000 sterling? Should the executive councillors, whom your lordship will select as being 'acceptable to the great body of the people', be invested, as is likely, with an extensive control of the governor, your lordship must perceive, that the factious leaders of 'the great body of the people' will become an uncontrolled oligarchy. How long would your lordship's despicable allies abstain from an abuse of power? How long would your lordship's insulted countrymen submit to it? Suppose, my lord, for the sake of argument, that 'the English inhabitants of this province' were to vindicate their right by an appeal to arms?[176] Whom would your lordship employ to shed the blood of your countrymen? The British soldiers and the militia of 'the great body of the people'. The latter, my lord, would either remain at home or speedily return home with their swiftest heels. The former, my lord, are not cannibals;[177] they have eyes to read, hearts to feel and heads to understand; and what must be unaccountable to your lordship, they are more disposed to sympathise with Englishmen than with Frenchmen. Does your lordship imagine, that 'the English inhabitants of this province' know not the influence of pen, ink and paper? But this is a digression.[178]

Your lordship subsequently adds insult to injury by speaking of 'the wish they have expressed to relinquish their seats'. Richly, my lord, does such an expression deserve the elegant criticism of the *Minerve*. It is true, my lord, that you merely imparted to the executive councillors 'the conclusion to which my mind had come' in regard to 'incompatible offices' and left them to choose between 'their seats' and their 'offices under the legislative council and house of assembly'. Their very natural preference of the more lucrative appointments, your lordship somewhat oddly represents as 'the wish they have expressed to relinquish their seats'. But let me test your lordship's sincerity by asking, whether 'these gentlemen', if they had preferred 'their seats' to their 'offices' would have been permitted to remain in the executive council. This, my lord, is a question, which your own conscience will not permit you to elude; and your lordship's future proceedings in regard to Mr. Heney will be a practical answer from your lordship to the public. You will stand convicted of an evasive statement on your own testimony, if you do not either compel the assembly to receive Mr. Heney as law clerk or retain him in the executive council.

Your lordship proceeds to say, 'My views are not limited to those cases; no union of incompatible or incongruous offices will be willingly acquiesced in by me'. Your lordship's distinction of 'incompatible' and 'incongruous' I do not precisely apprehend; nor do I fully understand the force of 'willingly'. If you at all acquiesce in a 'union of incompatible or incongruous offices', it cannot materially affect the interests of the public, whether you do so 'willingly' or not. What consolation, for instance, can any place-hunter derive from your lordship's unwilling acquiescence in a 'union of incompatible or incongruous offices' in the person of Mr. Mayor Viger or of Mr. Chief Justice Sewell or of my lord Gosford? So far from deriving consolation, he would be distressed by the violence done to your lordship's feelings. 'Willingly', my lord, is a far more convenient adverb than 'cheerfully', because it will enable your lordship to enforce or suspend the rule against 'incompatible offices' according to the convenience of yourself and your 'flattering and kind' friends. Really, my lord, the writer of your speech must have been labouring under Bacon's 'first distemper of learning', which 'is when men study words and not matter'.[179]

I have the honour to be,
My Lord,
Your Lordship's most obedient humble servant,

CAMILLUS.

***

No. XL.

Montreal, 23rd November, 1835.

My Lord,

Permit me, my lord, to close my analysis of your lordship's sixth paragraph with a few general remarks. Your lordship's argument against the same person's tenure of 'incompatible offices', in so far as your lordship has condescended to illustrate your views by the instances of certain members of the executive council, assumes the necessity of 'the wholesome separation and independence of the principal bodies of the government' and the propriety of consulting 'the dignity of their members.'— The latter foundation of your lordship's argument is too shadowy for a logician's grasp; and the former, though undeniably sound in itself, receives a fatal shake from your lordship's ingeniously assumed identity of *wholesome* and *complete*. But, my lord, I shall take the foundations of your lordship's argument, as I find them, and shall attempt to prove, that they are more competent to support an argument against your lordship's new reign of professed liberality than against the established system of alleged corruption. Your lordship's fifth paragraph pledges your lordship to confer 'office and employment' only on men 'acceptable to the great body of the people,' or, in other words, only on the members or the tools of 'excellency's faction'. What will then, my lord, become of the 'wholesome separation and independence of the principal bodies of the government'? Instead of *wholesome separation and independence*, my lord, your new system will establish *complete connexion and dependence, a perfect identity of purpose, an undivided unity of action*. In this conclusion, your lordship must inevitably concur, unless your lordship is so singular as to doubt, that your French allies, in the strictest sense of language, constitute a regularly organized faction. On any individual, who may doubt that they are so, reasoning may be lost;

and yet duty, my lord, may sometimes compel a public writer to offer even fruitless reasoning. Has not the majority of the assembly repeatedly formed conventions of a virtually legislative character? Did not the edict of the despot force on the electors of Yamaska a representative, of whom they had never heard? Did not he literally and practically force his half-learned tool on his unlettered dupes? If your lordship cannot answer these questions in regard to Dr. O'Callaghan's election, the honorable member for L'Assomption,[180] who has the reputation of being honest and candid, can answer them for you. But, my lord, I can prove from a more recent fact, that your French allies are a faction. Your lordship may have observed in the public journals the names of three candidates for the representation of the county of Montreal,—Mr. Brown, Mr. Evans, and Mr. Jobin. In Great Britain or Ireland, my lord, such a show of candidates for a vacant seat would certainly produce a most glorious contest; but, in Lower Canada, electioneering matters are very differently managed. The election took place not in the county of Montreal but in the county of Quebec. The sealed tenders of the three aspirants were forwarded to head-quarters, and submitted to the honorable conclave; and a verdict was given, as your lordship ought to expect, in favor of the French name and to the prejudice of the English names.— The only duty of the free and independent electors was to register the decree of the demagogues. Do not these instances, my lord, prove, that your lordship's French allies are a banded faction, not representing but ruling 'the great body of the people'? Does your lordship, then, require farther demonstration, that, by surrendering 'office and employment' only to men 'acceptable to the great body of the people', you would absolutely prevent 'the wholesome separation and independence of the principal bodies of the government'. Neither a sense of duty nor a feeling of shame would restrain the factious disposition of a revolutionary councillor or a revolutionary judge.[181]

Then as to 'dignity', my lord, would it be quite consistent with the 'dignity' of a judge or of an executive councillor to be the slave of a majority even of his own faction? Certainly not, your lordship replies; and I now, confidently, ask your lordship, whether your own argument against 'incompatible offices' is not more repugnant to the new reign of professed liberality than to the established system of alleged corruption.

Your lordship, moreover, seems to forget, that place-hunters are fully more likely than place holders to be influenced by interested motives in the discharge of public duties. Has your lordship, for instance, ever heard, that Mr. Vanfelson[182] exchanged the loyal for the revolutionary ranks, that he might punish the government for not having appreciated and rewarded his superior merit? If you have not heard so, I must ascribe your lack of knowledge on this interesting subject to your almost exclusive preference of the society of Mr. Vanfelson's honest and gentlemanly friends. The province, my lord, must be revolutionized, because Mr. Vanfelson is not his Majesty's attorney general. The following apposite passage from Hutchinson's history of the colony of Massachusett's Bay[183], will show that Mr. Vanfelson's patriotism has not the merit even of originality.

"The opposition to government which resulted in the loss of the colonies to Great Britain took its rise from the disappointment of an ambitious spirit. Upon the death of Stephen Sewell,[184] Esquire, chief justice of the province of Massachusett's Bay, in September, 1760, James Otis, Esquire, of Barnstable, solicited governor Bernard for the situation; the governor, however, thought fit to confer it, without solicitation, upon Mr. Hutchinson, the deputy governor of the province; and from that time Mr. Otis and his son (author of the first political pamphlet upon the rights of Americans,) were at the head of every measure in opposition, not merely in those points which concerned the governor in his administration, but in such as concerned the authority of Parliament, the opposition to which first began in this colony, and was moved and conducted by one of them, both in the assembly and town of Boston. The younger Otis was the ostensible, whilst the elder, being speaker of the assembly, was the actual leader of the opposition".

The sequel of the story may be interesting and useful to your lordship. It will, I trust, be well digested by your lordship.

"The governor flattered himself that he should be able to reconcile to him both father and son. By the demise of the king, all civil as well as military commissions must be renewed. This was the only opportunity which a Massachusetts governor could have of nominating persons to office, at pleasure. When he came to settle the county of Barnstable, where the speaker lived, he made him an offer of taking to himself the principal offices in the county, and of naming many of his relations and friends to other offices: and the whole county was settled to his mind. He took for himself the place of first justice of the county court of common pleas, and also that of judge of probate, which gives him much weight and influence in the county'.

"Mr. Otis, the son, soon after appeared in favour of a grant, made by the assembly to the governor, of the island of Mount Desert; and then was the appearance of reconciliation. It lasted but a short lime.'

But why, my lord, should your lordship be at all anxious to be surrounded by executive councillors? If rumour tell truth, your lordship already has a sufficient body-guard of tolerably ready advisers, which, in the vulgar but expressive language of American writers, would be styled your lordship's "Kitchen Cabinet'. Had your lordship ever displayed any practical regard for constitutional principles, I might say something about the unconstitutional character of secret and irresponsible advisers; but the special fact, that your officious friends are not less ignorant, than is your lordship, of the true state of provincial affairs, is a practical objection to any interference on their part with your lordship's public conduct; and your lordship's polite refusal to accompany your noble predecessor to the place of embarkation has shewn that your lordship brings even the ordinary courtesies of life within the limits of your official sphere. Shake off your 'Kitchen Cabinet', my lord. If you do not, I shall, notwithstanding Mr. O'Connell's testimonial of your firmness, be obliged to make the voice of history declare, that inflexible obstinacy in all intercourse with the world is quite compatible with the feeblest and most dependent spirit of favouritism in the petty circle of petty courtiers.

That I may at once finish so disagreeable a subject, I implore your lordship, if you have any regard for the dignity of a vice-regal earl, strictly to prohibit any of your officious parasites from again writing such productions as 'Another Loyalist' and 'A Fair Trial'.

I have the honour to be,
My Lord,
Your Lordship's most obedient humble servant

CAMILLUS.

***

No. XLI.

Montreal, 25th November, 1835.

My Lord,

The seventh paragraph of your lordship's speech opens with the following remarks.

> 'It is stated as a grievance, that the government has, at various times, refused to give the legislature access to accounts and other documents which were necessary for the prosecution of its inquiries; and that the executive has not, in all cases, communicated, when requested, the despatches which have passed between the colonial department and the local government. His Majesty's government fears, that the assembly may have been exposed to some inconvenience from this source'.

With what a beautiful simplicity does your lordship sweep aside the upper house by identifying 'the legislature' of the first sentence with 'the assembly' of the second. Unless your lordship believes with the satirist, that words are intended to conceal thoughts, I must infer from your lordship's language, that your lordship habitually considers the assembly as the legislature. I must either draw such an inference or suspect your lordship of having, in the first sentence, disingenuously wished to impute the complaint as well to the legislative council as to the assembly, and of having, in your second, been thrown off your guard by the natural and irresistible force of truth. Your lordship has unfortunately furnished too many instances both of unconstitutional feelings and of jesuitical language to enable me to decide between the two explanations of your lordship's obvious confusion of legislature and assembly. A thought strikes me, my lord. May not your lordship, in imitation of the liberal fathers of the reform bill, throw the blame of your own wilful blunder on the 'inadvertence' or the bad taste or the 'first distemper of learning' of your own scribe?

Again, my lord, how ingeniously you contrast 'the government' of Lower Canada in the first sentence, with 'his Majesty's government' of England in the second. You confess, that the provincial 'government' is not 'his Majesty's'. Why did not your lordship complete the antithesis by styling it 'Mr. Papineau's'? How provokingly your scribe's 'first distemper of learning' does reveal the degrading reality of the demagogue's despotism over both 'the government' and the people.

I now proceed to consider the substance of the quoted sentences. The second sentence, my lord, passes a general vote of censure on some of your lordship's predecessors. Would it not, my lord, have been more manly, more candid and more equitable to specify some of the instances, in which 'the assembly may have been exposed to some inconvenience from this source'? Had your lordship at tempted to specify such instances, you would, most probably, have found, that, like your lordship's own exceptions from your own general rule, the required documents could not have been communicated 'without violation of confidence, or a special detriment to the public service'. That your lordship will be less scrupulous, than any of your predecessors ever was, about 'violation of confidence' and 'detriment to the public service', I am reluctantly compelled to believe.

Your lordship seems to labour under an erroneous impression as to the powers of the assembly. You allude to 'accounts and other documents which, were necessary for the prosecution of its inquiries' without deigning to qualify *inquiries* by the epithet *constitutional*. The constitutional power of the assembly is merely to co-operate with the legislative council and the governor in making laws not repugnant to any imperial statute; and your lordship will admit, that the French demagogues overstep the limits of the constitutional act, when they erect themselves into a judicial tribunal. When Colonel Eden,[185] my lord, was required to surrender certain 'documents, which were necessary for the prosecution' of the unconstitutional inquiry into the riots of May, 1832, he was amply justified in refusing such 'documents' without any reference to 'violation of confidence' or 'special detriment to the public service'.[186] When Mr. Collector Jessop[187] was required to exhibit certain 'accounts', 'which were necessary for live prosecution' of a measure intended to take effect in the ports of Great Britain and Ireland, he also was amply justified in refusing such 'accounts' without any reference to 'violation of confidence' or 'special detriment to the public service'. If I am not very much mistaken, it is to those 'accounts' and those 'documents', that your lordship specially refers; and, if by *its inquiries* your lordship means *its constitutional inquiries*, I maintain, that even on your own admission, the assembly had no right of 'access' to such 'accounts' and such 'documents'. Your lordship, moreover, seems to labour under an erroneous impression as to the assembly's mode of proceeding. That illustrious body, when it wishes access to accounts and other documents' does not always request 'the government' strictly so called, to make its subordinate agents give such 'access'. It rather attacks the latter than the former, because it believes that it can imprison the subordinate functionaries and admits that it cannot imprison the governor. The following letter of 'Querist' in Monday's *Quebec Gazette* brings the question home to your lordship's business and bosom.

TO THE EDITOR OF THE QUEBEC GAZETTE.

Much has been said upon the powers vested in the Royal Commissioners, and it is understood that an opinion has been expressed by a leading member in his place, that so far from these gentlemen having the power to inquire into the proceedings of the assembly, it would be competent to that body to cause them to appear at the bar of the house, for the purpose of being examined as to their own proceedings under the commission. I would feel obliged if some of your correspondents, conversant with constitutional law, would instruct us upon the subject; for, if such be the case, the impolicy of the measure must be apparent to all; and it would be well that those who would be disposed to give information should be aware of the paramount power of the assembly over them. This difficulty would seem to arise from the circumstance of three commissioners being named, one of whom was protected by his office of governor-in-chief, and would not have obtained under the commission as originally proposed to be conferred upon the earl of Canterbury or upon lord Amherst. Nor would this difficulty have arisen upon the commission proposed to be given to the duke of York in the year 1766, as mentioned in the communication of your correspondent under the signature of 'A Constitutionalist'. As the question now stands it is one full of importance whether looked at theoretically or in its practical consequences.

Querist.

Suppose the demagogues, my lord, to call the members of your lordship's 'kitchen cabinet' before them, and, in default of attendance or of returning civil answers to civil questions, to send them all to conduct the grand inquiry in the common, gaol, what would your lordship do? Should your lordship dare to thick or say or do any thing at all on the subject, you would be practically divided into two characters, sent to the common gaol as head of the commission, and permitted, if you should feel so inclined, to remain in the Chateau as head of 'the government'. Seriously, my lord, there is nothing so absurd or so audacious, that it will not be attempted by your French allies.

Your lordship has most successfully contrived to place yourself between two fires; and I think that I know, whether of the two you feel to be the hotter. I would recommend to your lordship to forget your English, that you may at once escape the hotter fire and become more 'acceptable to the great body of the people'.

I have the honour to be,
My Lord,
Your Lordship's most obedient humble servant,

CAMILLUS.

***

No. XLII.

Montreal, 26th Nov. 1835.

My Lord,

In my last letter I pointed out to your lordship the necessity of confining the 'inquiries' of the assembly to the objects of constitutional legislation, and of refusing to aid it with 'accounts' and 'documents' for the prosecution of any other 'inquiries'. From the neglect of the maxim *Principiis obsta*,[188] my lord, very much mischief has arisen in this colony. Under the constitutional act, the 'inquiries' of either branch of the legislature are strictly limited to such objects, as come within the legislative power of the whole legislature; and yet the assembly has been quietly permitted to erect itself into a judicial tribunal under the imposing title of the 'grand inquest of the country'.[189] As reasonably, my lord, might the legislative council have erected itself into a high court of impeachments, or the governor have usurped any prerogative of the king of England. But the assembly's usurpation of judicial power is not only unconstitutional but iniquitous— for nothing, my lord, can be more glaringly unjust than to commence an inquiry in regard to any man's public or private character, which, for want of a court of impeachments, can never be brought to any satisfactory conclusion. The usurped power of the demagogues exposes every one of their victims to the certain injury of an accusation without granting them the probable benefit of a trial. Until a high court of impeachments be established, your lordship commits a crime against the constitution and against the sacred laws of justice, as often as you acknowledge the assembly to be the 'grand inquest of the country'. There does, to be sure, exist a tribunal, before which the charges of the assembly can be investigated and decided. The judges or that tribunal, my lord, are his Majesty's colonial secretary and the law-officers of the crown. Of the impartiality, learning and intelligence of such a tribunal, the case of the late attorney general of Lower Canada[190] affords ample proof. That gentleman, my lord, had been suspended by your lordship's predecessor in a bitterly regretted hour of conciliation. He was acquitted by lord Goderich of the assembly's charges, condemned unheard by the same nobleman on new charges invented by Denman and Horne, and subsequently declared innocent both of the charges of the assembly and those of lord Goderich, by Mr. Stanley. But the merits of the tribunal, my lord, are not all told. Mr. Stuart, after having been acquitted, condemned and acquitted again, was virtually punished for crimes, of which he was innocent, by those who acknowledged his innocence. Such, my lord, is the appropriate tribunal for investigating and deciding the charges of the assembly. Permit me, my lord, to state, in brief and undeniable language, that Mr. Stuart was condemned, not because he was guilty but because the assembly was his accuser. Does the recent progress of conciliatory principles, my lord, promise a more equitable decision from my lord Glenelg? No, my lord; your lordship's conscience tells you, that any similar accusation will meet a similar fate. This long digression, my lord, at last brings me to review your conciliatory sanction of the assembly's unconstitutional and iniquitous inquiry into Mr. Judge Gale's appointment.[191] Having already seen your lordship, on untenable ground, dismiss the executive councillors to make room for men 'acceptable to the great body of the people', am I, my lord, uncharitable in suspecting your lordship of the same paltry motive for aiding in the persecution of Mr. Gale [?] But your lordship, as head of the government, is not less interested in defending Mr. Gale, than Mr. Gale himself. In this respect, Mr. Gale's case, my lord, differs very widely from Mr. Stuart's. In prosecuting a public officer for alleged malversation in his office, there may have been much malice, much injustice, and a glaring violation of the constitution; but in persecuting a judge on the score of ante-judicial conduct, which, what ever may be its merits or demerits, was known to the government at the time of appointment, is a direct and daring encroachment on 'the executive power of the governor'. But I forget, my lord, that you have introduced the elective principle into the system of dispensing 'office and employment'. Does not your lordship's suicidal conduct in this matter justify my prediction, that your lordship would even make vacancies for hungry knaves 'acceptable to the great body of the people'? But, in Mr. Gale's case, your lordship may perhaps find it difficult to ascertain the opinion of 'the great body of the people.' If the demagogues, who profess to be the organs of the people, hate and envy Mr. Gale, among the people themselves he is remarkably popular. What 'great body of the people' will your lordship prefer? 'The great body' of course, that recommends a vacancy for some of the hungry and illiterate demagogues.

Your lordship should exhibit your peculiar kind of impartiality with a little more caution, if you wish to escape the pity of your countrymen and the contempt of your French allies.

The demagogues, my lord, begin to be seriously afraid, lest, under the indulgent reign of your lordship's impartiality, some of them may cease to be patriots. Of patriots they entertain nearly the opinion of Sir Robert Walpole.[192]

> "'Patriots', said Sir Robert Walpole 'spring up like mushrooms; I could raise fifty of them within the four-and-twenty hours. I have raised many of them in one night. It is but refusing to gratify an unreasonable and insolent demand, and up starts a patriot!"

I have the honour to be,
My Lord,
Your Lordship's most obedient humble servant,

CAMILLUS.

***

No. XLIII.

Montreal, 1st December, 1835.

My Lord,

The city of Montreal yesterday exhibited a spirit-stirring sight. Your lordship's oppressed and insulted countrymen peaceably and proudly walked in procession through the streets of this city to the sound of martial music. Before I explain the nature and the objects of the procession, permit me to carry your lordship back to a previous procession of 15th November, 1834. On that day, my lord, 'the English inhabitants of this city', in order to testify their sense of the illegal conduct of the returning officer for the West Ward of Montreal—a miserable creature of the name of Lusignan —marched in peaceful triumph through the city, and literally paralysed the more than equally numerous dupes of the French demagogues. Nothing, my lord, but a reliance on the very soldiers, whom the demagogues had repeatedly recommended to the tender mercies of the assassin, and whom they seemingly wished to remove from the scene of every election,[193] prevented the loyal and faithful descendants of the traitors of 1775 from abandoning their homes in the extremity of their terror.[194] Ask Mr. Papineau, my lord, what would have happened— but for the presence of the British troops. Push the iron of the question, my lord, into, the very marrow of the dastard's soul. The coward's red blood, my lord, will become white on his cheek and his brow; and, without giving your lordship a direct answer to your question, he will clasp your knees, lick your feet, promise you a civil list, provided your lordship will reject the bill for the removal of troops from the scenes of parliamentary elections.[195] Your lordship will, of course, reject the bill, not because it is unconstitutional and impracticable, but because it affects the nerves of your greatest and best friend. The appearance of yesterday's band of brothers convinces me, my lord, that the provisions of that bill, if they ever come into operation, will, in less than three years, give your lordship's oppressed and insulted countrymen the exclusive possession of the island of Montreal and of any the communications with Upper Canada both on the Ottawa and on the St. Lawrence.[196] How can your lordship prevent such a result? Your French allies would run without being driven. This my lord, is a course to be strongly deprecated. But of two evils, my lord, the least must be chosen; and on the unhappy author of the greater evil the responsibility must rest. Ask your conscience, while it is yet comparatively unworn and tender, who that author is.

Yesterday's procession, my lord, was composed of all classes of the citizens, with the exception of your French allies. The day, my lord, was sacred to St. Andrew; and your Scotch victims, aided by your English, your Irish and your German victims, had met to revive the tender recollections of their native land, to refresh the proud associations of national glory and to strengthen each other in the resolution of being worthy of their fathers.[197] Against such a band of brothers would your lordship commit the crime, enormous even in its very expression of ordering British troops to point the deadly tube? Could British soldiers withstand the effect of national music? Would the gallant sons of St. George attack 'The Roast Beef of Old England'? Would the gallant sons of St. Patrick direct their aim against 'St. Patrick's day in the Morning'? Would the gallant sons of St. Andrew charge with fixed bayonets the sacred tune of 'Tullochgorum'? No, my lord; 'the English inhabitants of this province' laugh your lordship and your lordship's French myrmidons to scorn.[198] Your oppressed and insulted countrymen despise your allies more heartily than they despise any one, but the miserable trucklers that dread them. In the foregoing remarks, the place-hunting gladiator will doubtless find a justification of his indiscreet charge of Orangeism, against the inhabitants of Montreal.[199] That man, though almost unworthy of notice, is not unworthy of chastisement; and I shall persecute him, wherever he may hide his head, if there the English language is spoken, if there an English newspaper is published. Dishonest enough to come to Canada with his opinions formed on the very subjects of local inquiry and indiscreet enough to avow such dishonesty, he can make no other atonement to the province for his conduct, than by immediately retiring beyond its limits. On these grounds, my lord, 'the English inhabitants of this province' will undoubtedly demand the man's official degradation. The place-hunting gladiator, my lord, knows nothing of the real feelings of the loyal population of Montreal. The societies, which have been here formed, are absolutely necessary for the relief of the poor and the sick 'English inhabitants of this province'. Your lordship's French allies, having the public purse in their hands, can relieve their poor or sick dupes, after the ingenious fashion of the man,

Who, out of his great bounty,
Built a bridge at the expense of the county.[200]

Yes, my lord, the demagogues have granted money to a French hospital and have refused aid to an English one. Thus do they make extremes meet, by promoting the uncongenial union of charity and spoliation. Like Robin Hood, they take money from one class to give it to another. This, my lord, is a true specimen of liberal justice. In the evening, my lord, about one hundred and fifty members of St. Andrew's Society, with the office-bearers of the other societies as guests, sat down to dinner. The tremendous cheers for the first six toasts sufficiently evinced the unshaken loyalty of the party. The seventh toast,[201] my lord, was admirably received. Every glass was empty; every hand was motionless; every tongue was mute. Contrast this, my lord, with the enthusiastic cheering at the name of Lord Dalhousie.

I have the honor to be,
My Lord,
Your Lordship's most obed[ien]t humble servant,

CAMILLUS.

***

No. XLIV.

Montreal, 2nd December, 1835.

My Lord,

After my yesterday's episode, I now resume the consideration of your lordship's speech. Your lordship's seventh paragraph closes with the following sentence:—

"There is scarcely any document within the power of the government which it will not always be willing to lay before you, except those confidential communications with the authorities at home, or with its own officers here, which it is obvious could not be made public in all cases, and at all seasons without extreme inconvenience."

In my minute criticisms on the style of your lordship's speech, my object has been not to act the pedant at your lordship's expense, but to break through the misty veil of your lordship's language into your lordship's breast. With the same view, I now ask your lordship to give a specific interpretation of 'scarcely', which implies a general exception from the rule of submitting 'accounts and other documents' to the assembly in addition to the special exception stated by your lordship. Your lordship either uses unmeaning words or shelters yourself under a general expression against future contingencies. When any document, that does not fail within the range of 'those confidential communications', is demanded by the assembly, it may, if such a course should be convenient, be refused by your lordship on the admirably strong, liberal and honest ground, that you had not promised to submit every other document without qualification or reserve. So far, as your lordship's apparent want of candour may affect the French assembly, I entertain the most callous indifference; but I cannot but feel an honest indignation that your lordship, after having censured the conduct of preceding governors for withholding 'accounts and other documents' from the assembly, has adopted their very rule of action as your own guide. But how can your lordship carry into effect your own special exception? How can you prevent the assembly from having access to 'those confidential communications with the authorities at home or with its own officers here'? Have you not retained Mr. Roebuck as a spy on 'the authorities at home' as a burrowing ferret, for investigating 'those confidential communications with' them?[202] Have you not trusted 'those confidential communications with its own officers here' to the keeping of an indiscreet and unprincipled adventurer, and have you not proclaimed the damnable principle of pure democracy, by which 'its own officers here' will be the delegated creatures of your favourite assembly? After the promulgation of a principle, that must produce the perfect identity of 'the government' and 'the assembly', your lordship does surprise me by your inconsistent simplicity in alluding to the Frenchified government and the French assembly as two different bodies. About the promulgation of that principle, my lord, I have, on good authority, heard an amusing story. Your lordship stated, that you had 'precise instructions'; but few people suspected the extreme degradation of your splendid servitude. Who could have supposed, that a coroneted peer would have submitted to be so far the puppet of others as to read from the vice-regal throne of Lower Canada a speech manufactured in Downing Street? If the story ended here, your lordship would simply appear as the passive and perhaps unconscious tool of your noble and right honorable employers; but your lordship, by having advisedly made certain modifications, such as the democratic doctrine, in the document, identified yourself in reality as well as in appearance, with the anti-national and blundering framers of the speech, and rushed headlong into a participation both of their intellectual weakness and of their moral guilt. Like Philip's soldiers, to wham the editor of the *Herald* lately alluded, I am so vulgar as to call every thing by its right name, to style a tool a tool, a knave a knave, a traitor a traitor. The implied comparison, my lord, is unjust not towards the enemy within, who stabs the constitution in the security of power, but to the enemy without, who has at least the merit of courage in his open and dangerous assaults.

Your lordship's special exception seems to consider that only two parties, the government and the legislature, are interested in the production of 'accounts and other documents'. In this, my lord, you entirely forget, that there are such parties as the law and the people and the sacred principles of justice and other countries besides Lower Canada. Is your lordship prepared to neglect and spurn and trample in the dust all these parties in your intercourse with the French assembly? Oh no, replies your lordship, I shall give these parties the benefit of the general exception of 'scarcely'. Has your lordship done so? Did you respect the law or the people or the sacred principles of justice, when you supplied the assembly with documents for the prosecution of Mr. Gale and the virtual annihilation of executive patronage? Did you respect the rights of Britain or of the neighbouring colonies, when you encouraged the republican demagogues to interfere with an imperial establishment, such as the post office?[203] The post office, my lord, is placed, even in republican America, under the control of the general government?;nor can the entire continuity of the British system be broken into disjointed pieces with impunity. It is the duty of every man to refuse to give the assembly any information on the subject. Whether your lordship do your duty or not, others may do theirs rather than adopt the servile maxim *regis ad exemplar.*[204] Let your French allies, if they dare, send to Montreal for an unwilling witness. Let them try to find a messenger hardy enough to attempt the seizure of a single citizen of English blood.[205]

I have the honour to be,
My Lord,
Your Lordship's most obedient humble servant,

CAMILLUS.

***

No. XLV.

Montreal, 3rd December, 1835.

My Lord,

Your lordship's eighth paragraph, which treats of some 'Blue Book' or other, I pass without remark.

I quote the first sentence of your ninth paragraph.

"The too frequent reservation of bills, for the signification of his Majesty's pleasure, and the delay in communicating the King's decision upon them, is a grievance of which his Majesty's government are solicitous to prevent the recurrence".

This conciliatory passage, my lord, differs so widely from the cabinet's notorious desire of concentrating all power in its own hands, that I must either suspect the cabinet's sincerity or consider such an instance of self-denial as a measure of its entire subserviency to the French faction. Is not my view of the grasping selfishness of the existing administration amply justified by the arrangements, which are mentioned in your fifth paragraph, in regard to the disposal of all offices, 'of which the emoluments shall exceed a stated sum'? Is it not amply justified by the provisions of the municipal bill, which refer almost every thing to Downing Street, as a court of last resort? Is it not consistent with the almost universal proceedings of the bawling liberals—whether of France or of England or of the United States? With the affairs of France and England your lordship ought to be well acquainted; but you may not be aware, that Andrew Jackson, who professes to be more liberally democratic than any former president, has done more than all his predecessors to concentrate all legislative power and all executive authority in the hands of the chief magistrate of the republic. In one word, my lord, the concentration of all power in one and the same point is part and parcel of the pure democracy of your lordship and the imperial cabinet, as it is the only thing that can render the numerical majority of a people wholly independent and altogether uncontrollable.

But, my lord, I can offer a special proof of the insincerity of your lordship's noble and right honorable masters. While my lord Glenelg was actually sketching the very sentence, which I am now considering, he had, for months, been guilty of shameful and fatal 'delay in communicating the King's decision upon' two measures of vital importance to Upper Canada —the bill for establishing a bank in the Gore district, and the bill for enlarging the capital of the commercial bank of Kingston. But, my lord, even after 'communicating the King's decision upon them', the indolent baron was guilty of still farther delay in transmitting the sanctioned bills as authorities for actual operations. It is just possible that the indolent baron's fears of the assembly of Lower Canada may spur him on to more vigilant activity and more 'flattering and kind' courtesy; and, if he entertains your lordship's peculiar admiration of Frenchmen, the circumstance, that that assembly is French, will doubtless enlist his affections on the side of his fears. 'Oh, for Hogarth's magic power',[206] my lord, to represent your lordship and your lordship's noble and right honorable roasters in the attitude of kissing the rod of a despicable demagogue. I will not, my lord, inveigh against such slaves; I shall reserve my searing scorn for those, who can feel shame. I must, how ever, add, that, if the moderate and conciliatory course, which your lordship publicly and privately recommends to the 'two parties', is to be found in your lordship's own conduct, every man of English blood in the colony 'would rather be a dog and bay the moon than adopt a course of such degradation.

I now subjoin the second sentence of the ninth paragraph.

> "I shall consider the power of reserving bills, as a right to be employed not without much caution, nor except on some evident necessity".

In this remark I cordially agree with your lordship; but I must, in candour, add, that I do not consider your lordship remarkably competent to carry your own view into operation. How is your lordship, after having discarded the executive council, to decide on the existence of 'evident necessity'? Will your kitchen cabinet counsel your lordship and realise the picture of 'The lame leading the blind'? Will your lordship rather prefer, as a ground for reserving any bill, the objections of 'the great body of the people'? I have, my lord, hit the truth at last; and your lordship, therefore, will not often have occasion to exert the right of reservation. It is impossible for any bill, that is not 'acceptable to the great body of the people', ever to reach your lordship.

In every thing, that your lordship has either said or done, you have seemed to consider Lower Canada as an independent state; and I am much afraid, that, were your judgment sound and your knowledge of constitutional principles correct, your democratic prejudices in favour of 'the great body of the people' would blind you to any and every encroachment on the supremacy of the imperial parliament. The danger of unconstitutional legislation, which arises from your lordship's weakness of judgment, want of knowledge, and democratic prejudices, is alarmingly increased by the anti-national and republican avowals of the assembly, and the almost entire corruption of a majority of the legislative council. I venture to assert, that, should the two houses pass four unconstitutional bills, your lordship, in your present helpless condition, would sanction three of them.

I have the honour to be,

My Lord,

Your Lordship's most obedient humble servant,

CAMILLUS.

***

No. XLVI.

Montreal, 5th December, 1835.

My Lord,

I subjoin the second sentence of your ninth paragraph.

"His Majesty's government also undertake on their part, to bestow the most prompt attention on every question of this nature which may be brought under their notice, and especially, *that no measure, having for its object the institution in this province of any colleges or schools for the advancement of Christian knowledge or sound learning, shall hereafter be unnecessarily deferred*".

The 'flattering and kind' generality, which I have printed in the ordinary characters, amply merits the elegant criticism of the *Minerve*, more particularly when illustrated by the special boon held out in the remainder of the sentence to your French allies. The passage, as a whole, exhibits your lordship and your lordship's noble and right honorable masters, as unbecomingly eager to propitiate the hungry, ambitious and anti-national demagogues of the assembly. Well might the free and independent republicans of the *Burlington Free Press* say of your lordship's speech,

"While reading this speech, we were amused at and disgusted with the cowardly spirit, which seemed to pervade and characterise the whole of it".

At the hazard of offering an unpleasant digression, I submit the remainder of the article from the *Free Press*, that your lordship may see how far even foreigners of English origin sympathise with your lordship's proscription of 'the English inhabitants of this province'.

"His excellency seems not to be aware of the real state of affairs as they now exist in the province. The position which the earl has assumed we think he will find it difficult to maintain, conjointly with his delegated authority. A candid unbiased mind cannot but come to the conclusion that he has taken for granted, without any investigation, that the French are in the right, and that nothing more is required of him than to comply with their requests, and peace and harmony will be restored. He is careful to say nothing contrary to the wishes of the French part of the population; while those of British origin are spurned in contempt from the fool of the throne. We very much mistake the spirit of Britons, or his lordship will find he has his hands full to effect his unhallowed designs. In his speech the French are the first named in defiance of all precedent, they are held up as the bone and sinew of the nation, as the *intelligence*; and, therefore, as those fit to rule. He says, as governor, he 'will execute with alacrity, *impartiality* and firmness, whatever he is competent to do of himself'. What security, we ask, have the people of British origin that he will execute any thing with impartiality when the whole tenor of his speech shows that he is a partisan. With how much firmness he will act when called upon to oppose a Papineau measure, we leave time to determine".

The latter part of the sentence, which I have printed in italic characters, deserves a more particular discussion. I do not precisely know the meaning which your lordship attached to your words; but I do know, that they must have been generally understood to convey a censure on Lord Aberdeen's rejection of a bill for erecting into corporations the French Canadian institutions 'for the advancement of Christian knowledge or sound learning' and to imply a promise, that my lord Glenelg would 'cheerfully' sanction any similar bill and virtually relinquish his Majesty's claims to the seigniories of the seminary of Montreal in defiance of the British statute of 1774.[207] I am afraid, my lord, that 'the most prompt attention', which the indolent baron promises to pay to all reserved bills, may sometimes interfere with the due consideration of such bills, for Lord Glenelg is notoriously incapable of doing any thing both promptly and well.[208] Thus, my lord, may the most prompt attention' be a sacrifice offered at the shrine of a despicable demagogue, at the expense of 'the English inhabitants, of this province', of the provisions of the constitution, of the just rights of the imperial authorities, Such an evil, if it do occur, will be almost irremediable, for, as I already apprised your lordship, there does not exist any judicial tribunal for reviewing and, if necessary, reversing the acts of colonial legislatures.

But what, my lord, is the tendency of the special promise about 'colleges or schools for the advancement of Christian knowledge, or sound learning'? Its tendency, my lord, is to encourage the assembly to squander such portion of the public revenue, as a greedy faction and a corrupt government may not pillage, on the dissemination of one kind of 'Christian knowledge', and of one kind of 'sound learning', on the propagation of the religion and the language of 'the great body of the people'. Your lordship must be highly delighted to find, that your democratic scheme for pillaging and oppressing your countrymen, because they are few and, on account of their fewness, entitled to your generosity and protection, may be extended as well to religious or literary privileges as to civil and political rights. But the democratic scheme, my lord, not only may be extended, but actually has been so. Inquire, my lord, how much money, within these few years, has been expended on French-Canadian colleges and how little on McGill college or any English institution 'for the advancement of Christian knowledge or sound learning'. The result of such an inquiry will highly delight an impartial champion of 'the great body of t people'. You will find, that the great body has got every thing and the *little body* nothing. Your satisfaction may, also, be enhanced by the consideration, that, the *little body* has paid almost every thing, and the *great body* almost nothing. Your lordship, of course, remembers Horace's opinion, that to admire nothing is almost the only thing which can make and keep a man happy.[209] — Does not your lordship wish, that you had permitted Horace's opinion to prevent your admiration of public robbery? Your admiration of the indiscreet and dishonest place-hunter, however, is justified by the example of the Venusian bard, who was himself a warm admirer of *Vultur*.

But it is not merely by the misappropriation of money, that the French demagogues display an undue partiality towards institutions 'for the advancement' of the religion and the language of 'the great body of the people'. They have, my lord, attempted by unequal legislation to attract pupils, to these institutions at the expense of the interests of English seminaries of safer principles and of higher pretensions. This very day, my lord, I have seen a petition, that is to be presented to the legislative council, against a bill for shortening the period of a law-student's clerkship from five to four years, provided he has attended at a French-Canadian College. To have petitioned the assembly would have been a waste of time and labour. The framers of the petition, my lord, seem to be apprehensive, that the legislative council, in order to remove a theoretical anomaly, may aggravate a practical grievance by extending the invidious privilege to the graduates of any British university. Should the legislative council adopt such an amendment, your lordship may soon have a glorious opportunity of scourging with both handsome class of 'the English inhabitants of this province'. The scheme of the demagogues, my lord, is glaringly iniquitous, for it is not even pretended, that French-Canadian colleges give a better education than the English schools of the province. Seriously and solemnly, my lord, you cannot sanction such a measure whether the bill be vitiated or not by the damning blot of retrospective legislation.

I have the honour to be,
My Lord,
Your Lordship's most obedient humble servant,

CAMILLUS.

***

No. XLVII.

Montreal, 14th December, 1835.

My Lord,

During the past week, which was so cruelly fertile in hostile deeds as to open with the project of a political congress, and to close with the formation of a military brigade, I deemed it charitable and humane to give your lordship a respite from the infliction of hostile words.

Your lordship's tenth paragraph is remarkable only for obsequious senility. The latter part is most amusingly obliging.

"His Majesty takes so deep, and if I may use the expression, so personal an interest in the affairs of this country, that his ministers have received the most unqualified commands to lay before his Majesty, immediately on its arrival in England, every communication which either branch of the legislature may address the Throne, and to see that his Majesty's answer be conveyed to the province with the utmost possible despatch".

How amiable are 'so deep', 'so personal', 'most unqualified', 'immediately', and 'utmost possible despatch'. A simple man would imagine, that all this meant something. Your lordship knows better. Permit me, my lord, in passing, to marvel, that your lordship, after having violated the law of the land, should have hesitated, as your phrase 'if I may use the expression' implies, to violate the rules of language. Is not this, my lord, straining at a gnat after having swallowed a camel?

But how, my lord, could the quoted passage mean what it says? How can his Majesty constitutionally return a personal answer to every communication which either branch of the legislature may address to the Throne? Has not the writer of the speech merely made his sovereign ridiculous, by gravely representing him as the source of the answer and the ministers as his mere instruments. The writer's language, my, lord, may be courtly; but it is not constitutional. These remarks, my lord, will appear trifling to none but the illiterate and the superficial, for I cannot too often repeat to your lordship that words are things. The writer of the despatch, whoever he may be, is manifestly either destitute of constitutional knowledge or ignorant of the meaning of language. He certainly is not both a statesman and a scholar. The following letter of 'Philo-Camillus' your lordship has, of course, 'cheerfully' read; but I must subjoin it as a corroboration of my estimate of the literary merit of your lordship's speech.

TO THE EDITOR OF THE QUEBEC GAZETTE.

Sir,—In the 45th letter of 'Camillus', published in a late number of the *Montreal Herald*, it is surmised that the speech of his excellency lord Gosford, at the opening of the present session of the provincial legislature, was written or sketched by lord Glenelg. The information of this writer must be incorrect; for it is quite impossible that a man so conversant with public affairs and of such acknowledged ability as lord Glenelg, could have been the author of this paper. The great peculiarity of the speech in question is, that it has nothing of the tone and manner which belong to such papers. It is evidently the work of more than one hand. You have, in some parts of it, the short military sentence,—in others, the long, involved parenthesis sentence of the lawyer—and some other sentences that are *sui generis*, and of which may be said what Pope said of moat women, 'they had no character at all.' There is, too, an affectation towards the close of the speech, of fine writing in the circulating library style, which lord Glenelg could not have been guilty of. Let any one compare it with the despatches from the colonial office, of which so many have been lately published—and he will find it separated from these by an immense interval. Lord Glenelg doubtless directed the adoption of a truckling policy here—a sin against good government; but we must not fasten upon him a sin against taste, which this production exhibits.

PHILO-CAMILLUS.

December 9, 1835.

To the best of my recollection I never stated, that your lordship's speech had been 'written or sketched by lord Glenelg'. I merely asserted on very good authority, that it had been manufactured in Downing-street; and my assertion is quite consistent with the supposition of 'Philo-Camillus', for the military man and the lawyer and the individual who writes in 'the circulating library style' may have tried their 'prentice-hands' at the document under the eye of the noble and right honourable secretary. It is certain, however, that the document, as a whole, was imported in the Pique, and that it was slightly altered merely by way of acclimation. The improvements, however, were not very creditable to the discretion or the tact of your lordship and your lordship's colleagues, for one of them was the famous promulgation of 'pure democracy' in virtually surrendering the executive patronage to 'the great body of the people'. Your 'precise instructions', my lord, ordered you to act on so damnable a principle; but they did not authorise you to proclaim it. Your lordship knows, that my statement is true; and you also know that your motive for 'cheerfully' going beyond your 'precise instructions' was the weak desire of courting a temporary popularity. How it must gladden the heart of every true patriot, of every independent Englishman, of every honest man to reflect, that your lordship's indiscreet avowal of a principle, which the more crafty secretary meant, that 'the English inhabitants of this province' should discover only by the painful and tedious process of induction, has signally baffled its practical application.

If your lordship do not now embrace the earliest opportunity of practically disavowing the anti-national principle, your lordship is either something more or something less than man. Your lordship's eleventh paragraph presents an incongruous mixture of petty complaints, on which even your desire of conciliating the demagogues of the self-constituted Assembly should not have induced you to 'make any specific observations'.

The twelfth paragraph, my lord, sets grave discussion at defiance. What a contrast between your lordship's anxiety to reconcile the 'two parties' and your lordship's desire of legally perpetuating the distinction of language! It is to be regretted, that your lordship's dislike of 'incompatible or incongruous offices' does not extend to incompatible or incongruous sentiments. Difference of language must produce difference of feeling. The unity of the former is the only thing that can engender the unity of the latter. Would it not have been more statesmanlike to have advised 'the English inhabitants of this province' to speak French or your Gallic friends to speak English? Either language would politically be preferable to both; and yet I fear that even the influence of your lordship's example would not induce your countrymen 'cheerfully' to confine themselves to a language, which cannot express comfort, which knows not the endearing term home, which requires ever muscle and every limb to act as an interpreter of the tongue, and which, though last not least, is said to harden and distort the features of youth and beauty.

But seriously, my lord, the measure will be as fatal as it is ridiculous. It is a lever, my lord, with which I shall vigorously attempt to raise the national and patriotic feelings of every man of British blood in British America. The French faction's rashness and your lordship's weakness have rendered the struggle no longer political but purely and exclusively national. A French state shall not be permitted to exist on this English continent. Five hundred thousand determined men will speedily repeat that declaration in voices of thunder.

I have the honour to be,
My Lord,
Your Lordship's most obedient humble servant,

CAMILLUS.

***

No. XLVIII.

Montreal, 16th December, 1835.

My Lord,

The next twelve paragraphs of your lordship's speech either require no comment or have already been incidentally considered. The next three, respectively numbered 25, 26 and 27, may perhaps form the subject of a series of didactic letters for the information of the Royal Commissioners. The remaining seven paragraphs are worthy of a brief discussion.

In the commencement of your twenty-eighth paragraph, your lordship says, 'This moment, as it seems to me, is a great opportunity for good or for evil'. I very strongly doubt, whether your lordship attached any definite meaning to the quoted words; and I cannot gather any other meaning from them, than that your lordship's conciliatory course, as it seemed to yourself, was destined either to narrow or to widen the breach between the 'two parties'. So safe a prediction displayed at least as much of a cautious temper as of a prophetic spirit. I do not know, whether your lordship and myself attach the same significance to 'good' and 'evil'.—If your lordship, according to your avowed principle of 'a pure democracy', considers the patient submission of a numerical minority of Englishmen to a numerical majority of Frenchmen as 'good', then, my lord, I tell you in words what thousands will soon tell you in deeds, that 'the English inhabitants of this province' consider such submission as supremely 'evil'. If your lordship considers a fearless and determined resistance to an illegally constituted executive and a self-constituted Assembly as 'evil', then, my lord, I challenge you to name six Englishmen in the colony, who do not consider such resistance as comparatively, if not positively, 'good'. On this subject, my lord, I quote the opinion of a man, whose very name ought to have some weight with a liberal nobleman. In a speech on General Smith's motion relative to barracks, Charles James Fox[210], the idol of your lordship's party, spoke as follows:—

"He has, however, alluded to one general principle, that particularly claims attention; and, in doing so, he has noticed an expression of mine, made use of on a former occasion, when I advanced a general principle, which I have always entertained and ever will entertain, a principle which he himself formerly espoused, and which I believe to be espoused by almost all those with whom I have the honour of acting, I mean the general principle of resistance; the right inherent in freemen to resist arbitrary power, whatever shape it may assume, whether it be exerted by an individual, by a senate or by a king and parliament united. This I proclaim as my opinion; in the support of this principle I will live and die. * * * * I speak of the connexion which ought to subsist between the military and the rest of their countrymen. Upon this point I am indeed proud to differ from the right honourable gentleman. Because, says he, there are bad men and bad principles abroad in the country, the military must be secluded from the society of their fellow-subjects. He then most aptly introduces the language of the Mock Doctor, and says, 'If I cannot make others dumb, I can make them deaf'. I will place them entirely out of reach, where no such doctrine shall assail their ears. What is the full meaning and extent of this doctrine? Can the right honourable gentleman make his troops partially deaf? Can he prevent them from listening to the voice of sedition, without, at the same time, shutting them out from the knowledge of those principles of rational liberty, whose animating influence, I say, ought to inspire the soldiers of a free country? They ought not, says he, to be taught disobedience. God forbid, that they should; but, is it not a plain proposition, that *indiscriminate obedience is not the duty of an Englishman, whether he be a soldier or any other citizen? Where commands are illegal, it is his duty to resist them.* The right honourable gentleman surely does not intend to say, that his troops should be altogether deaf; if he does it will be in vain for him to look for an army in this country, possessed of that physical advantage; he must call in foreign aid; he must at once introduce into the bosom of our island an army of foreign mercenaries'.

Will your lordship condescend to read, mark, learn and inwardly digest the foregoing sentiments of Mr. Fox—with particular reference to the state of affairs in Lower Canada? Will you also condescend to remember the very peculiar circumstance, which extorted Catholic Emancipation[211] from the Duke of Wellington's cabinet? Has not your lordship, has not the Royal Commission, has not the French faction so treated 'the English inhabitants of this province' as to justify their acting on your idol's doctrine of resistance? But let not the coming storm, my lord, be misunderstood. 'The English inhabitants of this province' wage war not with the British people but with the British cabinet, not with his Majesty but with his Majesty's Ministers, not with the law but with its dishonest and 'cheerful' violators. For myself, my lord, and most of 'the English inhabitants of this province', I confidently declare that they would, even after a completely successful resistance to the anti-national measures of temporarily misguided rulers, rather return into the bosom of their mother than attempt the establishment of a precarious independence or become part and parcel of the American republic.[212] Flatter not yourself, my lord, that 'the English inhabitants of this province' will halt between two opinions. Why, my lord, the only English journal, that supports the anti-national faction, boasts a French proprietor, and, during the temporary absence of your privy councillor Dr. O'Callaghan, glories in a French editor. The French gentleman's anti-national lucubrations are translated into the English language; but they are not translated so accurately as to conceal the fraud. What Englishman, my lord, could have used the expression 'in our midst', which adorned an anti-national article in yesterday's *Vindicator*? But I am too hasty, my lord, for the writer, though an Englishman, may yet have been actuated at once by the ambition of following a noble example and by the conciliatory desire of blending the two languages into one harmonious whole.

After this long digression about physical resistance,[213] permit me, my lord, to resume the consideration of the 'good' or 'evil' results of your lordship's conciliatory course. In the first place, my lord, ask your own conscience, whether your course has been impartially conciliatory. Have you not made every one of the 'paltry concessions' to one of the 'two parties'? Have you not, on every possible opportunity, violated the rules of etiquette and the decencies of polished society, that you might shew partiality to 'the great body of the people'? Have you not accompanied your official answers to one of the 'two parties' with private notes to individual demagogues, while the Royal Commission, of which you are the head, suffered an official letter from the other of the 'two parties' to remain for eight or nine days without even an official reply? Whether, my lord, was so partial a mode of carrying your conciliatory principle into effect more likely to produce 'good' or 'evil'? 'Evil', my lord, in the first instance; but if that 'evil' has roused the indignation and stiffened the sinews of 'the English inhabitants of this province', I venture to console your lordship with the assurance, that such 'evil' will be productive of 'good' as well to this colony as to the whole empire. In the foregoing estimate of your lordship's impartiality, I have purposely omitted any mention of those public acts, which flowed from your 'precise instructions', as my main object was to demonstrate the purely personal feelings of your lordship.

Is your lordship happy? The question is a startling one; but it must often force itself on your lordship's mind. In Ireland, my lord, the violent opposition of one party of your countrymen was more than neutralised by the cordial support of another. In Lower Canada, however, the almost universal suspicion of your lordship's motives, and the universal opposition to your lordship's measures, which your countrymen display, cannot be rendered much more palatable to your lordship by the cold applause of a few revolutionary and illiterate Frenchmen.

I have the honour to be,

My Lord,

Your lordship's most obedient humble servant,

CAMILLUS.

***

No. XLIX.

Montreal, 19th December, 1835.

My Lord

Your twenty ninth paragraph opens with the following sentence:

—

"To the Canadians of French origin[214] I would say, do not fear that there is any design to disturb the form of society under which you have so long been contented and prosperous."

In this sentence and in all the succeeding sentences of your speech, your lordship seems to have forgotten, that you were addressing 'Gentlemen of the Legislative Council, Gentlemen of the House of Assembly', and not 'the English and French inhabitants of this province' from Dan to Beersheba.[215] What a melancholy want of that dignified gravity, that ought to characterise diplomatic documents, particularly if appearing 'in no ordinary circumstances' and affording 'a great opportunity for good or for evil'! Did not our lordship's indirect address to the people, as distinguished from the legislature, almost degrade you to the level of an electioneering rhetorician? What would your lordship think, had President Jackson's message to congress apostrophised the lawless murderers of Vicksburgh,[216] or were King William's next speech to apostrophise the white boys of Ireland?[217] What would your lordship, what could your lordship think of such a mixture of bad taste and pusillanimous condescension?

But the quoted sentence, moreover, is not more deficient in manliness and taste than it is in soundness of policy and veracity of assertion. So far, my lord, as I understand the words 'form of society', your lordship gravely recommends to 'the Canadians of French origin' a bigotted and eternal attachment to their peculiar customs, peculiar prejudices and peculiar laws, and solemnly promises, that 'England' has no 'design to disturb' the aforesaid customs, prejudices and laws. I shall not, my lord, be so unreasonable as to repeat my unreasonable request, that your lordship will attempt the impossibility of reconciling this 'design' of 'England' with the royal commission's 'design' of inquiring into the seigniorial tenure of land. But what is any rational politician to think of the policy of your lordship's virtual recommendation to 'the Canadians of French origin'? In the whole range of history, such a man could find a parallel to it only in your lordship's doctrine on language. Your lordship visits Lower Canada for 'the abatement of dissensions and the conciliation of adverse parties'; and your lordship most consistently

194 · The Prophetic Anti-Gallic Letters

proposes to aggravate 'dissensions' and render 'parties' more 'adverse' by perpetuating the distinctions of language, of customs and of laws. Will your lordship graciously extend the system so far as to give each of the 'two parties' a legislature and an executive government of its own?

Your lordship says, that the 'Canadians of French origin have so long been contented and prosperous.' The meaning of 'contented' is sufficiently definite; but I am at a loss to understand what is your lordship's 'precise' interpretation of 'prosperous'. In 'no ordinary' sense can the epithet be applied to 'the Canadians of French origin'. Gradual improvement, my lord, is essential to the very idea of prosperity; and prosperity, therefore, is 'incompatible or incongruous' with the long continued duration of any undisturbed 'form of society'.— The colony, as a whole, may be 'prosperous'; but to speak of the French race as 'prosperous' can only excite the ridicule even of the objects of your lordship's 'flattering and kind' compliment.

But how, my lord, did you so far forget your conciliatory 'instructions' as, in the very presence of the French demagogues, to insinuate, that 'the Canadians of French origin' were 'contented'? Had not those demagogues and Mr. Roebuck, the accomplice of a French faction and a Frenchified government in their conspiracy against the constitutional act, repeatedly declared to the imperial cabinet and the imperial parliament, that 'the Canadians of French origin' were discontented, were miserable, were rebellious? What could have tempted your lordship to contradict your very dear and very true friends? 'The Canadians of French origin' are either contented or discontented? If the latter, your lordship has made a mistake; if the former, your lordship has charged your French allies with a want of veracity and displayed a not very statesmanlike degree of anxious alarm. Why should your lordship, or the noble and right honourable framers of your lordship's 'precise instructions', or your lordship's inquisitorial colleagues, deprive yourselves of the only plausible apology for a truckling course of illegal and unconstitutional concessions? That apology, my lord, was fear; but what Englishman could be so dastardly as to entertain a fear of a 'contented' population? Was it likely, my lord, that a theoretical passion for the elective principle would drive 'contented' people to an armed insurrection? No, my lord; and on this point, I am happy in being able to lay before you the opinion of a well known champion of extremely liberal principles, the editor of the *Leeds Mercury*. Speaking of the impossibility of subverting the constitution of the House of Lords, he says

> "We scarcely need point out to any man of reflection, that the proposed abolition of the House of Peers could not be carried without a revolution. The Peers would, to a man, resist it; and the Constitution affords no means of overcoming that resistance. If overcome at all, therefore, it must be, as in the days of Cromwell, by the arbitrary assumption of the House of Commons. No man can imagine that such an act of revolutionary violence could be effected without a civil war. *And in such a civil war, what would be the grievances to animate and support the democratic party? for a great and industrious people will not cut each other's throats for nothing?* WHAT STRETCH OF PREROGATIVE HAS BEEN COMMITTED? WHAT PATRIOT HAS BEEN BROUGHT TO THE BLOCK? WHAT POPULAR RIGHTS HAVE BEEN OUTRAGED? WHAT GRIEVOUS AND INSULTING TAX HAS BEEN ENFORCED? Why, there is not so much as a single straw of fuel wherewith to kindle popular indignation."

Read this, my lord, and say, whether the love of the elective principle could have roused the 'contented and prosperous' Canadians into open rebellion. Will your lordship condescend carefully to peruse the capitals, which imply the justifiable and sufficient grounds of popular insurrection, and then, my lord of Gosford, ask your conscience, whether your short career in the misgovernment of this colony has not placed all the grounds, but the second, firmly under the feet of 'the English inhabitants of this province.'

Recent events, my lord, tempt your lordship to stigmatize the constitutionalists as rebels. But I tell your lordship, that the essence of rebellion consists rather in 'cheerfully' violating the law than in 'reluctantly' vindicating it with arms and ammunition. Who, my lord, are the rebels? While I can wield a pen, my lord, I shall not cease to proclaim, that Lower Canada is oppressed by the despotism of an illegally constituted executive and a self-constituted Assembly, and ought systematically to resist such despotism by all means, that may be justified by expediency and a regard to the connexion of the mother country and the colony. That I do not stand alone, your lordship may learn from the following remarks of the editor of the *Montreal Gazette*:—

> "We understand from a respectable source, that letters have been transmitted to certain law officers of the Crown, and to certain of the Military authorities, in this city, by orders of his Excellency the Governor in Chief, enquiring into the nature and object of an advertisement which appeared lately in the Constitutional journals of this place, relative to the organization of eight hundred men as a Rifle Corps."

> So says the *Vindicator* of last evening. We certainly hope that Lord Gosford has taken this step, and that he will make every necessary enquiry and examination into the object and nature not only of this Rifle Corps, but of every Association in the province, now forming, or in operation. He will then ascertain the state of public feeling—he will find that he has excited the public mind to a higher pitch than any of his predecessors—that by his open violation of the Constitution, he has rendered resistance to an usurped authority, a necessary step for the preservation of our rights as freemen—that he has enlisted in our cause the sympathies of thousands of Britons throughout the adjoining provinces— that he has rendered his own situation in the province so uncomfortable that his continuation in office here cannot be long.

> His enquiries will satisfy him of the devotion to the Constitution avowed by our party, and of their firm de termination to abide together for mutual assistance and protection,"

I have the honour to be,
My Lord,
Your Lordship's most obedient humble servant,

CAMILLUS.

***

No. L.

Montreal, 21st December, 1835.

My Lord,

Your lordship's twenty-ninth paragraph proceeds as follows: —

"However different from those of her colonies in other parts of the world, England cannot but admire the social arrangements by which a small number of enterprising colonists have grown into a good, religious and happy race of agriculturists, remarkable for the domestic virtues, for a cheerful endurance of labour and privations, and for alertness and bravery in war. There is no thought of endeavouring to break up a system which sustains a dense rural population, without the existence of any class of poor."

Permit me, my lord, to remark, that, for the sake of perspicuity, a pronoun should invariably come after the noun to which it refers, and that, therefore, the preceding quotation ought to have opened with 'England cannot but admire the social arrangements, however different from those of her colonists in other parts of the world, by which, &c.' This, my lord, might have been generally intelligible.

But what, my lord, do you mean by gravely telling 'the Canadians of French origin', that 'England cannot but admire' them? What can your lordship mean, or rather does your lordship mean any thing at all? Why, my lord, not one man of a thousand in 'England' knows as much of Lower Canada as of the moon; and not one of ten thousand has a single definite idea of the 'social arrangements'. Really, my lord, it is painful to witness so melancholy a sacrifice of sober truth, good taste and official dignity on the accursed altar of pusillanimous conciliation. But permit me, my lord, to bring the soundness of your lordship's puerilities to a specific test. Did your lordship, before you arrived in Canada, know any thing of 'the social arrangements', which 'England', whether she will or not, 'cannot but admire'? No. Does your lordship even now, after an amiably familiar intercourse of some months with the fashionables 'of French origin' in Quebec, know much of 'the social arrangements' which 'England', whether she will or not, 'cannot but admire'? But knowledge, as your lordship may reply, is not essential to admiration; and 'England' and your lordship very probably 'admire' 'the social arrangements' in accordance with the maxim— *Omne ignotum pro magnifico.*[218]

If your lordship's knowledge of the past, as it is displayed in the mention of 'a small number of enterprising colonists', is to be taken as a measure of your knowledge of the present, I cannot but marvel at your lordship's self-complacent rashness in habitually dispensing with the advice of your executive council. Had your lordship even superficially read the history of Lower Canada, you would have known, that 'colonists' at the time of the conquest, so far from being 'enterprising', were the torpid victims of feudal tyrants and that the enterprise, which, as the English colonies felt to their cost, confessedly did exist in Canada, animated only the political and the military emissaries of the King of France. 'Enterprising colonists' forsooth! Why, my lord, too indolent to cultivate the ground, they relied on the fishing-rod and the fowling piece, and actually required to be bribed by the government into matrimony.

Your lordship hazards the compliment of 'a cheerful endurance of labour and privation'. Patience, my lord, is undoubtedly a virtue; but one part of your lordship's compliment seems to be 'incompatible or incongruous' with the other. In Lower Canada, my lord, 'a cheerful endurance' of 'labour' renders physical 'privation' almost impossible; and physical 'privation', when it is felt, is generally the result of bodily indolence and mental stupor. While a man of English blood invades and subdues the forest with his axe in his hand, 'the Canadians of French origin' subdivide their patrimonial farms into miserable patches of badly tilled soil, preferring indolence and 'privation' to 'labour' and plenty.— It is true, my lord, that their seigniors sometimes produced this state of things by refusing to concede land on the legal conditions; but it is only 'the Canadians of French origin', that would rather linger out their lives of penury in their native seigniories than try their fortunes in more favourable positions.

As to the 'alertness and bravery in war' of your French allies, the past has contradicted, as the future will contradict, your lordship. Recent articles in the public journals have satisfactorily settled the question as to 'bravery'; and the value of 'alertness', my lord, varies considerably, according as that military virtue is displayed in the retreat or in the advance. When your lordship comes to Montreal, pray don't compliment our first citizen on 'alertness', and all that kind of thing. So much, my lord, for the past.[219] Now, my lord, contemplate the probabilities of the future. About two years ago, the honourable proprietor of *L'Écho du Pays* ferociously and seditiously attempted to make 'the Canadians of French origin' rise and massacre their English brethren.[220] So general and so loud was the burst of indignation, that even the dog-faced impudence of the monster gave way. During the session, that followed, the honourable Mr. Debartzch had not the audacity to take his seat in the Legislative Council. Now, my lord, mark the sincerity of the Hessian mercenary's bravado. He is almost frightened into fits by the organization of the 'British Rifle Corps' and raves not about organizing a Canadian Rifle Corps[221] as a counterpoise but about the necessity of inquiries and proclamations. Is there much reason hereafter to expect 'alertness and bravery in war' from 'the Canadians of French origin'? Does not the paralytic terror, with which the 'British Rifle Corps' has inspired your lordship's French allies, clearly evince the hollowness of all the vaunting threats of insurrection?[222]

How ingeniously the writer of your lordship's speech does ring all the changes on language. In the first sentence of the twenty-ninth paragraph, something or other is styled 'the form of society'; in the second, 'the social arrangements'; in the third 'a system'. You extol 'a system' as something 'which sustains a dense rural population, without the existence of any class of poor.' What your lordship understands by 'poor' I do not know; but surely-land-holders, who annually require seed corn at the expense of the country, cannot but be 'poor' even in your lordship's estimation. There are, my lord, myriads of poor in Lower Canada, myriads of individuals, that do not live so well as the 'class of poor' in England.

I have the honour to be,
My Lord,
Your Lordship's most obedient humble servant,

CAMILLUS.

***

No. LI.

Montreal, 23rd December, 1835.

My Lord,

Your lordship's twenty-ninth paragraph closes with the following mixture of the sublime and the ridiculous.

> "England will protect and foster the benevolent, active and pious Priesthood, under whose care and by whose examples, so much of order, of good conduct and tranquil bliss is created, preserved and handed down from generation to generation."

Tell me, my lord, in what way 'England will protect and foster the benevolent, active and pious priesthood'. Against whom do the French

Canadian priests require to be protected by 'England'? Against their flocks? No, for that would be 'incompatible or incongruous' with 'so much of order, of good conduct and of tranquil bliss.' Against 'the English inhabitants of this province'? No, my lord, for they have no interest in removing or alleviating the burden of the tithes, which sustain 'the benevolent, active and pious priesthood.' Against your lordship's dear friends of the self-constituted Assembly? That, my lord, is not only possible but probable, for the priests themselves will tell your lordship that they dread the unbelieving demagogues as their most virulent and most dangerous enemies.— But would not the self-constituted Assembly's attack on the 'priesthood' place your lordship and 'England' in an awkward dilemma, by compelling you either to offend 'the great body of the people' or to injure 'the benevolent, active and pious priesthood'[?][223]But in sober earnestness, my lord, 'England', that has always been renowned as the hospitable refuge of distressed exiles, will soon be required, if your lordship's hopeful schemes succeed, to 'protect and foster' the French Canadian priests as exiles on her own shores. The priests have already been attacked by the faction, and will soon be attacked again. The whole career of the demagogues, my lord, has been, indirectly, one continued attack on the priesthood; for the influence of the priests on the maintenance 'of order, of good conduct and of tranquil bliss' has diminished, just as the influence of the faction in fomenting anarchy, turbulence and discontent has extended. Ask the rural priests, my lord, whether I have not told you the truth. Ask them, also, whether they have not themselves to blame for the manifest diminution of their influence. Had they, my lord, acted on the sound maxim *Principiis obsta*, had they manfully resisted the propagation of doctrines equally subversive of loyalty and religion, had they warned their flocks to stand aloof from the wolves of the faction, they would have protected their own interests and, in spite of the ignorant sneers against a political clergy, would have merely discharged the duties of good subjects and good christians. It was only by taking an active interest in politics that they would have been able to 'protect and foster' religion. In every country, my lord, radicalism and irreligion go hand in hand; and a christian, whether layman or priest, who tamely opens an unobstructed career to the former, virtually lets loose the fiery and bloody floodgates of the latter. I do not, my lord, mean, that any clergyman should become a brawler at public meetings or a fierce controversialist in public journals; but I do advisedly declare, that every clergyman, who does not, in the discharge of his special duties, warn his flock against every known enemy of religion, is either a traitor or a coward. A governor, who professes to be wonderfully impartial, ought to have displayed some regard as well for the Protestant clergy as for the Romish priesthood; but, in this instance, as in almost every other, your lordship's impartiality is all on one side. The peculiar character of your lordship's impartiality is the more wonderful, as the former stand more in need of fostering protection than the latter. On this point, I cannot do better than quote the following remarks from a pamphlet recently published:[224]

> On the subject of the reserved lands, the Committee remarks, that it 'entertains no doubt that the reservation of these lands in mortmain is a serious obstacle to the improvement of the colony," and subsequently adds, that it is 'fully persuaded that the lands thus reserved ought to be permanently disposed of.' It might be difficult to find any impartial person acquainted with the situation of the colony, who would not concur in these sentiments of the Committee. But if it be right, that these reserved township lands should be withdrawn from mortmain in the hands of a Protestant clergy, can it be right that nearly a seventh of the extent of the seigniories, including the most wealthy city in Canada and numerous villages should remain by sufferance in mortmain in the hands of Romish Ecclesiastical bodies? If while the Committee was making enquiry into the claims of the Protestant clergy in Canada, it had thought proper to examine also into those of the Romish clergy, it might have discovered that, although the Protestant clergy are not entitled to tythes, yet the Romish clergy are by law entitled to dues of that description, while, at the same time, they are nevertheless allowed

by sufferance to retain possession of estates amounting to almost a seventh of all the seigniories, notwithstanding that the British Act of 14th Geo. 3, which confirmed their right to tythes, distinctly stated that the religious communities should not hold estates. This prevision of the law has never been enforced, as the following table, which after all is incomplete, abundantly testifies:

1	Seigniory of Lite island and city of Montreal, about	200
2	Do. of the Lake of Two Mountains and augmentation,	140
3	Do of St. Sulpice,	110
	(These three belong to the Seminary of Montreal.)	
4	Do. of Chateauguay (Grey Sisters)	54
5.	Do. of 6 Do. of isle-Jesus	50
6.	Do. of Cote de Beaupre, (Seminary of Quebec)	900
7	Do. Isle aux Coudres,	10
8	Do. of St. Jean, (Ursul. of Three Rivers)	40
9	Do. of St. Augustin, (Religieuses de l'hop. of Quebec)	34
10	Do. D'Orsanville, (Religieuse)	4
		1632

Besides all the above mentioned estates, amounting to nearly a million of acres, these and other ecclesiastical bodies possess property of great value in Quebec and Montreal and elsewhere.

If it would be proper and beneficial to the community, and it probably would be so, that the Protestant clergy, who have no tythes, should be divested of the lands, to which the law has entitled them, would it not likewise be proper that the Romish clergy, who have tythes, should cease to retain the estates, which the law has declared that they shall not hold? Or while the laws are to be repealed in order to reduce the rights of the former, ought they to be violated to increase the rights of the latter I

I have the honour to be,
My Lord,
Your Lordship's most obedient bumble servant,

CAMILLUS.

***

No. LII.

Montreal 24th December, 1835.

My Lord,

Your lordship's thirtieth paragraph is a most extraordinary production. I subjoin its first sentence.

"Of the British, and especially of the commercial classes, I would ask, is it possible that there should be any design to sacrifice your interests, when it is clear to all the world, that commerce is one of the main supports of the British system of finance, that without it the wonderful fabric of British power and dominion would crumble into dust, and that it is especially the object and purpose, for which, at a vast expense, the mighty colonies of England are maintained in every quarter of the globe."[225]

In the name 'of the British, and especially of the commercial classes', I boldly tell your lordship, that such a 'design', is not only 'possible' but probable; and I do not hesitate to add, that the framers of the sentence must have been actuated rather by a weak love of conciliation than by a strict regard for truth. In enunciating such a tissue of wilful blunders, your lordship must either have been actuated by a singular degree of hardihood or have formed a very humble opinion of the intellectual acuteness of 'the English inhabitants of this province'.

Does your lordship imagine, that the 'commercial classes', have never heard of the crusade of Sir Henry Parnell[226] and other liberal supporters of Lord Melbourne's cabinet against the whole of the colonial empire of Great Britain?[227] Does your lordship imagine, that 'the commercial classes' are ignorant of the liberal party's hostility to the timber trade of British America? Does your lordship imagine, that 'the commercial classes' forget, that your lordship has yourself displayed so strong a feeling against them, as to have 'cheerfully' violated the law in order to retain a gang of unprincipled hirelings at the seat of the imperial government as their bitterest enemies? Does your lordship dare to imagine, that all the sentimental verbiage, that was ever uttered from a vice-regal throne, can overcome the influence of the damning facts, to which I have alluded, even on the weakest members of 'the commercial classes"? Do not, my lord, again insinuate the impossibility of a 'design' which actually exists—Has your lordship dipt so slightly into the profound mysteries of metaphysics as not to know that 'Whatever is, is'? Your lordship has heard the maxim *Credo, quia impossibile est, I believe it, because it is impossible.* Your lordship's doctrine about the 'design' almost realises the paradox, for that, which is impossible, exists, and that, which exists, is impossible. Permit me, my lord, to add, that facts are too stubborn to be denied by words.

But farther, my lord, 'the commercial classes' have a right to expect from 'England' something more than the mere absence of 'any design to sacrifice your interests' by positive acts of the imperial parliament. They call on 'England' to 'foster' them rather than foreigners, and to 'protect' them from the deadening grasp of an anti-commercial faction. Your lordship must know, that every one of the 'paltry concessions' augments the mischievous power of that faction without checking in the slightest degree its mischievous inclination. It is true, my lord, that the faction, which you have laboured to render omnipotent, cannot alone impose pecuniary burdens on the commerce of the colony; but it can, my lord, negatively inflict evils more fatal than the augmentation of a tax. The faction can and does refuse to improve the internal communications in the colony. It has, as your lordship knows, rejected every bill for opening rail roads through the English Townships of the province, and has clogged the solitary measure of internal improvement, which it did sanction, with impracticable conditions. I allude, my lord, to the Quebec and Portland rail road.[228] If the faction has offered aid for the improvement of the Harbour of Montreal, it has placed or at least intended to place that aid under the virtual control of a few petti-fogging members of the self-constituted Assembly. Before you venture to sanction the Montreal Harbour bill, read, mark, learn and inwardly digest the thirtieth paragraph of your own speech, and reflect, that 'the commercial classes' will consider your decision in regard to that bill as a test of that paragraph's truth or falsehood. But the worst, my lord, is still to come. The anti-commercial proceedings of the French faction, my lord, have driven the inhabitants of Upper Canada to contemplate a scheme, which, if successful, must be fatal to 'the commercial classes' of Lower Canada.[229] Our brethren, my lord, have been compelled to think seriously of making New York the seaport of Upper Canada. If they should carry their design into effect, Lower Canada will then contribute very little to the support of 'the British system of Finance' or of 'the wonderful fabric of British power and dominion.' Then too, of course, will 'the English inhabitants of this province' be sacrificed to the petty ambition of a petty faction, inasmuch as the motive, which 'is especially the object and purpose' of holding colonies, will have ceased to influence 'England'. But I suspect, that your lordship libels 'England'. That country, though stigmatized by Napoleon as a country of shop-keepers,[230] feels the noble impulse of ambition as well as the mean hankering of avarice, and does not cherish her colonial empire merely through a grovelling love of money. But is there not some con-fusion in your lordship's remark about 'a vast expense'? If the colonies be profitable to the mother country, the 'vast expense' is no 'expense' at all; if they be unprofitable, either your lordship's doctrine about 'the object and purpose' is so much verbiage or else 'England' is by no means alive to her own interest.

'The mighty colonies of England', my lord, are politically as well as commercially useful. They bind the terrestrial globe in her grasp, and render her, more truly than ever ancient Rome was, the mistress of the world.

England commands every channel of commerce whether ancient or modern.

Gibraltar and Malta on the one hand, Bombay and its dependencies on the other, make her more decidedly the mistress of the ancient routes of Indian traffic than ever was Tyre or Alexandria or Constantinople or Venice. Ceylon and Singapore, respectively situated at the southern extremities of the two peninsulas of India, complete a line of possible or, to speak learnedly, of potential monopoly along the whole of the southern boundary of Europe and Asia. England's domestic territory, reaching in an almost unbroken line from the coast of Brittany to the Shetland Islands, physically blockades all the western outlets from the Loire to the Baltic; while her natural and almost inevitable connexion with Portugal indirectly subjects to her power the more southerly portion of the western coast of Europe, and completes a chain of commercial superiority from the coast of Norway to that of China. Her settlements on the western coast of Africa, the Cape of Good Hope and the Mauritius give her the entire trade of eastern Asia, and bring the whole of Africa within the sphere of her commercial supremacy.

Englishmen, my lord, may well be proud of the use which England has made of her widely ramified and absolutely resistless influence. By clearing the Mediterranean of pirates, who chased from that rich channel of traffic every flag but that of the United Kingdom, she sacrificed a commercial monopoly on the altar of humanity. Her possession of western Africa, which might secure to her the undisturbed monopoly of the slave trade, is considered valuable chiefly as the means of annihilating that odious traffic.[231] Though she be absolute mistress of India, she permits the existence of independent French and Danish settlements in the very heart of her territory, and actually gives more extensive privileges to foreigners than to her native subjects.[232]

On the eastern coast of the New World, England has an almost continuous line of posts from the mouth of the Orinoco to Baffin's Bay. Newfound land, Nova Scotia, the Bermudas and the Bahamas are thorns in the breast of the American republic; while Canada and the West Indies, commanding the two extremities of the basin of the Mississippi are equally sharp thorns in the bock of the republican giant. But the West India Islands have a prospective value, far greater than their present influence. Forming an impenetrable arch in front of the Gulph of Mexico, they command the whole isthmus between the broader masses of the two Americas, and must secure to England the mastery of any canal or any rail-road, that may hereafter connect the Atlantic and the Pacific oceans and as a matter of course, the mastery of the trade of the western coast of America.

I have the honor to be,
My Lord,
Your Lordship's most obedt. humble servant,

CAMILLUS.

***

No. LIII.

Montreal, 30th December, 1835.

My Lord,

The second and last sentence of your thirtieth paragraph is neither less ridiculous nor less sublime than the first.

"Rely upon it, that the great and powerful country from whence you have removed yourselves to these shore will not abandon there the policy, which has established the prosperity of her people in every region, and that a government, of which constancy and good faith are the main elements of power, will not fail to sustain in this portion of the empire, the spirit of that constitution which has been so long held out as a boon to its natives, and an inducement to the settlers who have embarked in it their enterprise, their wealth and their hopes of individual happiness."

However much, my lord, 'the British and especially the commercial classes' may be disposed to shew a 'flattering and kind' deference for the commands of a coronetted representative of Majesty, they cannot, they will not, they must not, they shall not 'rely upon' the assurances of a 'cheerful' violator of the constitution, of a 'cheerful' traitor to the very language of his fathers, of a 'cheerful' builder of French democracy on the ruins of English monarchy. Yes, my lord, the time has come, when 'the English inhabitants of this province' must place reliance only on themselves and on those of their own blood in the Neighbouring provinces.—Would it not, my lord, be a cruel sarcasm to hint the bare possibility of their relying on your lordship, or on the Assembly, or even on the Legislative Council? They have to thank French traitors and Frenchified trucklers for having compelled them to throw their sole reliance on their own moral determination—the only prop that was never known to prove a broken reed. Should they rely on the Legislative Council, they would probably fall victims to the active treachery of present or the passive treachery of absent members. Should they rely on the unholy coalition of your lordship and the self constituted assembly, they would inevitably become the slaves of men, to whom the elegant Chateaubriand's description of some ancient sophists is eminently applicable:[233]

> « *Divises pour le bien, reunis pour le mal, gonfles de vanite, se croyant des genies sublimes, au dessus des doctrines vulgaires, il n'y a point d'insignes folies, d'idees bizarres, de systemes monstrueux que ces sophistes n'enfantent chaque jour————marche a leur tete, et il est digne en effet de conduire un tel bataillon!*

The supplying of a nominative to *marche*, I leave to your lordship's conscience. I am told, my lord, that you do not seem to feel the humiliating nature of your position. Am I to ascribe the almost incredible fact to habitual 'cheerfulness' or to fortitude or to insensibility? Whatever, my lord, be the cause, I am glad, that your lordship does not, by a shew of misery, exchange universal contempt (The expression, my lord, is strong but true) for general compassion. Answer the following question, my lord:—

> Breathes there a man, with soul so dead,
> Who never to himself hath said
> "This is my own, my native land,"
> Whose heart has ne'er within him burned
> As home his footsteps he hath turned,
> From wandering on a foreign strand?[234]

Yes, my lord, there breathes an Englishman, who 'cheerfully' prefers a French republic to an English monarchy. Of that Englishman, my lord, the heart shall quail but the cheeks shall burn,

> As home his footsteps he shall turn
> From truckling on a foreign strand.

Do, my lord, act on the maxim, 'He gives twice, who gives quickly', that you may at once evince some remains of national feeling, and may obey a French ally's modest address to every '*Breton*',

> This land is mine, begone, away.[235]

For the wilful blunders, that have been committed, neither your lordship nor the commissioners ever can atone; and were I to ask any and every constitutionalist whether he believed the emissaries of Lord Melbourne's cabinet *both willing and able* to arrive at sound conclusions on any point of provincial policy, I should receive an unhesitating answer in the negative. Were I then, my lord, to ask any and every constitutionalist, whether he believed them *either able or willing*, I should hear three nays for one aye.

Yes, my lord, 'the English inhabitants of this province' have at last determined not merely to resist the prevailing system of iniquity and oppression, but to resist it at the hazard of their fortunes and their lives,[236] till they have sufficient and irrevocable guarantees for the full and free enjoyment of equal rights,[237] for the inviolability of constitutional principles, for the steady march of commercial and agricultural prosperity. They have determined, that the French faction and its Frenchified abettors shall be prostrate at their feet.

Your lordship speaks of 'the policy which has established the prosperity of her people in every other region', and assures 'the commercial classes', that England 'will not abandon' that policy in Lower Canada. As that policy, my lord, is English, I must agree with your lordship, that England cannot now abandon here, what she abandoned more than sixty years ago. Had 'the policy which has established the prosperity of her people in every other region' been permitted to direct the affairs of Lower Canada, that province, so extensive, so fertile, so advantageously situated for commerce, would not have been at this moment inferior in 'the prosperity of her people' to 'every other region' of the British Empire. In 1774, my lord, 'the policy', which your lordship justly applauds, was solemnly sacrificed by an act of the British Parliament, on the accursed altar of conciliation, which has, however, this redeeming point about it, that, like Nebuchadnezzar's furnace,[238] it invariably burns its ministers.

But even if 'the policy', my lord, does exist, what guarantee does your lordship's general conduct afford, that England 'will not abandon' it? Do not your lordship's overt acts and avowed sentiments justify a suspicion, that such 'policy' would be abandoned *because it would be English*? Your lordship's Frenchified taste goes far beyond the Frenchified taste of the conciliatory act of 1774. 'The policy', which your lordship pursues, is not that 'which has established the prosperity' of the British people, but that which was mainly instrumental in dismembering the British empire. Think of this, my lord, before it be too late.

I have the honour to be,
My Lord,
Your Lordship's most obedient humble servant,

CAMILLUS.

***

No. LiV.

Montreal, 31st December, 1835.

My Lord,

Permit me to repeat a portion of the second sentence of your thirtieth paragraph:—

"Rely upon it that———Government, of which constancy and good faith are the main elements of power, will not fail to sustain, in this portion of the empire, the spirit of that constitution which has so long been held out as a boon to its natives, and an inducement to the settlers, who have embarked in it their enterprise, their wealth and their hopes of individual happiness."

What does your lordship mean by 'a government, of which constancy and good faith are the main elements of power'? The English government, I presume. Why did not your lordship briefly and perspicuously say so? Was it not bad taste, my lord, 'to consider the main elements of power', which are common to every government, peculiar to that of the British empire? Can there be real 'power' in any 'government', which is destitute of 'constancy and good faith', which is true neither to itself nor to others? Without 'constancy and good faith', my lord, 'a government may exist, but cannot be said to possess 'power', however powerful may be the nation, which it professes to rule. But your lordship's language violates historical truth as well as good taste. So far as Lower Canada, my lord, is concerned, the English government has displayed not constancy and good faith but *vacillation and deception.*

Your lordship must know that, in 1763, a royal proclamation invited Englishmen to settle in the newly conquered province of Quebec and there to live under the protection of the laws of England.

In this, my lord, there was no want of 'constancy' or 'good faith', for England, by introducing her own laws, was true to herself without violating a single line of the capitulation of Montreal or of tie definitive treaty of peace.

Your lordship must, also, know, that, in 1774, a British Statute annulled the royal proclamation of 1763, placing 'the settlers' under the feudal law and depriving the 'natives' of the benefits of a trial by jury. In this, my lord, there was a want of 'constancy and good faith' towards both the old subject and the new.

From time to time, my lord, successive cabinets, so far from atoning for the deception practised on 'the settlers', have made con-cession after concession for the exclusive gratification of French ambition at the expense of 'the English inhabitants of this province' and of the imperial authorities. Has so suicidal a course, my lord, savoured of the English government's 'constancy' to itself or of its 'good faith' to the deluded 'settlers'? So flagrant violations of 'con-stancy and good faith' were doubtless justified by that necessity, which acknowledges no law. That they were not so justified, every Englishman must blush to confess. The act of 1774 was confessedly intended to render the French Canadians instrumental in oppressing the English colonies; and I may, without being very uncharitable, suspect, that the subsequent course of conciliation was meant to render the same foreign people a political non-conductor in the chain of English population throughout British America. As surely as the first scheme accelerated the event, which it proposed to retard, so surely will the second produce a similar result. — When the English inhabitants of British America shall be goaded into physical resistance by the undue preference of conquered foreigners, then will the imperial government find, that, m relying on the French Canadians, it has leaned on a broken reed.

The notorious result of all these concessions, my lord, amply proves that 'constancy and good faith are the main elements of power' of any government, for what has Great Britain gained by vacillation and deception? What, but the contempt of her pampered step-children and the distrust of her slighted and deluded sons? As surely as *power* results from *constancy and good faith*, so surely does *weakness* result from *vacillation and deception*. Your lordship will admit, that an English cabinet displays more of weakness than of power, when it fancies itself compelled to prostrate the letter and the spirit of the constitution, its own dignity and the character of its emissaries under the hoofs of a petty faction of illiterate, unprincipled and treacherous Frenchmen. Do, my lord, do, I implore you, say nothing more of 'power' or of 'constancy' or of 'good faith'.

But if, my lord, I descend to more minute in stances of the want of 'constancy and good faith', I must say, that it is the part of infatuation to ascribe 'constancy and good faith' to a perpetually fluctuating government more particularly in regard to the comparatively trifling affairs of a remote colony. Has not every colonial Secretary his own peculiar views? Did not one secretary approve and another disapprove the elevation of Mr. Gale to the judicial bench? Did not Lord Glenelg give your lordship 'precise institutions' to pay the salaries of agents, whom his predecessors had refused to recognize in any official capacity? Did not the same indolent statesman give your lordship 'precise instructions' to violate the very constitution, which Mr. Pitt had 'held out as a boon to its natives, and an inducement to the settlers'?

What a humiliating contrast, my lord, does the inevitable answer to the preceding question present with your lordship's puerile bombast about sustaining, 'in this portion of the empire, the spirit of that constitution, &c.' Really, my lord, I am sometimes compelled by an ignominious compound of dishonesty and weakness in a certain speech to believe, that my perseverance in addressing your lordship is more foolish than St. Anthony's homily to the fishes. Had your lordship regaled the legislature with four or five columns of cross readings from a newspaper or with a few pages of *Johnson's Dictionary*, you would given your hearers some amusement and instruction without sacrificing your own character for judgement, honesty and knowledge.

Your lordship must have given great offence to your French allies in styling the constitution 'a boon to its natives and an inducement to the settlers'—a matter of grace to the former and a matter of right to the latter. The demagogues, my lord, maintain, that the constitution was extorted as a right from the fears of the British authorities.

Does your lordship gravely imagine, that the 'constitution,' which, according to your lordship's liberal interpretation of its 'spirit,' vests all power, executive, judicial and legislative, in the anti-British hands of 'its natives,' either is or can he 'an inducement, to the settlers' to embark in Lower Canada 'their enterprise, their wealth and their hopes of individual happiness'?

I have the honour to be,
My Lord,
Your Lordship's most obedient humble servant,

CAMILLUS.

***

No. LV.

Montreal, 4th January, 1835.

My Lord,

The thirty-first paragraph of your lordship's speech surpasses the twenty-ninth and the thirtieth in the want of dignified gravity. While addressing 'Gentlemen of the Legislative Council, Gentlemen of the House of Assembly,' your lordship condescended to apostrophise 'the Canadians of French origin' in the twenty-ninth paragraph, and 'the British and especially the commercial classes' in the thirtieth; and, by way of capping the climax of indecorous puerility, your lordship graciously directs your attention to 'many among you who inhabit this city' in the thirty-first. Had your lordship made the third of these paragraphs a continuation of the second, the term 'you' would have referred to 'the British and especially the commercial classes'; but the enigmatical pronoun, standing, as it does, in the beginning of a separate paragraph, must, according to all the laws of good taste, refer both to these 'classes' and to 'the Canadians of French origin.' As a correspondent of the *Quebec Mercury*, who, under the signature of 'A Non-Combatant' and 'The Goose that saved the Capitol', seems to espouse your lordship's cause in the most disinterested manner, attacks me for having criticised the '*style*' of your lordship's speech, I must take this opportunity of reminding your lordship and your lordship's truly disinterested champion, that I have studiously abstained from noticing the 'style' of the voluminous document, unless where the inaccuracy of language clearly affected the 'most essential' virtue of perspicuity. Permit me, my lord, to add, that moral honesty and literary taste equally demand a perfect harmony between an invisible idea and its visible symbol. Your lordship's elevated station may enable you to preserve a language by the force of 'a law'; but so obscure an individual as myself must resort to the more humble, though perhaps not less effective, shield of verbal criticism.

I may presume, my lord, that by 'many among you who inhabit this city,' your lordship meant the signers of the Quebec Petitions, which Mr. Neilson carried to London;[239] and I would respectfully ask your lordship whether it was not 'incompatible or incongruous' with politeness and good taste to exclude from the benefit of your condescension 'many among you who inhabit' Montreal.

In short, my lord, I cannot better characterise the puerile blunders, whether of omission or of commission, in your lordship's closing paragraphs, than by repeating the description of a correspondent of the *Quebec Gazette*, that those paragraphs are written 'in the circulating library style.'

Before I can enter on the discussion of the thirty-first paragraph, I must quote it in connexion with the succeeding one.

"In a declaration put forth by many among you who inhabit this city, I have seen the following objects enumerated; first, to obtain for persons of British and Irish-origin, and other, his Majesty's subjects labouring under the same privation of common rights, a fair and reasonable proportion of the representation in the Provincial Assembly; secondly, to obtain such a reform in the system of Judicature and the administration of justice, as may adapt them to the present state of the Province: thirdly, to obtain such a composition of the Executive Council, as may impart to it the efficiency and weight which it ought to possess; fourthly, to resist any appointment of members of the Legislative Council otherwise than by the Crown, but subject to such regulations as may insure the appointment of fit persons; fifthly, to use every effort to maintain the connexion of this colony to the Parent State, and a just subordination to its authority; and sixthly, to assist in preserving and maintaining peace and good order in the province, insuring the equal rights of his Majesty's subjects of all classes."

If these objects are indeed all, that are desired by the whole commercial interest, I trust it will be satisfactory to those, who aim at them to know that there is not one of them which is not strictly within the line of duty of the King's Commissioners to take into consideration, to receive respecting them the fullest evidence and information which may be offered, and finally to submit to our Gracious Sovereign and his Ministers their impartial and well weighed conclusions."

The first clause of the thirty-second paragraph, to say nothing of its uncourteous doubt as to the candor of 'many among you, who inhabit this city,' betrays your lordship's usual degree of logical inaccuracy, for it obviously confounds 'many among you who inhabit this city' with 'the whole commercial interest.' Your lordship ought to have known, that there are 'paltry traders' in Montreal as well as in Quebec; and you ought, also, to have known, that more objects 'are desired' by the 'paltry traders' of the former city. Thus, my lord, to logical inaccuracy is added ignorance of notorious facts.

I have the honour to be,
My Lord,
Your Lordship's most obedient humble servant,

Camillus

***

No. LVI.

Montreal, 6th January, 1836.

My Lord,

The thirty-second paragraph of your lordship's speech promises, that the 'objects enumerated' in the thirty-first shall be investigated by 'the King's Commissioners'. Here again, my lord, I am 'cheerfully' compelled to point out the flagrant partiality of his Majesty's ministers.

While almost all the demands of the French faction are granted, every demand of 'the English in habitants of this province' is met with a promise of inquiry. To the French faction are surrendered the contingencies, the hereditary revenues, and all offices of power and emolument; to 'the English inhabitants of this province' are generously offered the inquisitorial services of the Royal Commissioners.

The partiality of his Majesty's ministers appears to be more flagrant from the fact, that they had distinctly stated to the agents of the constitutional associations, that they would decide nothing, till they should have received the report of the Royal Commissioners. But his Majesty's ministers, my lord, have gone even beyond their own intentions of partiality, for they do not seem to have reflected, that, in granting the demands of the French faction, they were reducing the investigation of many grievances of the English population to a mere matter of theoretical speculation. In other words, my lord, the concessions, which have been made to the self-constituted Assembly, have not only aggravated the grievances of its constitutional opponents but have rendered impracticable any adequate remedy for those grievances.

Permit me, my lord, to corroborate this assertion by considering the 'objects enumerated' in order.

> "First, to obtain for persons of British and Irish origin, and others, his Majesty's subjects labouring trader the same privation 'of common rights, a fair and reasonable proportion of the representation in the House of Assembly".

For the sake of argument, my lord, I shall suppose, that the Royal Commissioners will recommend some scheme as favourable as possible to the little body of the people. In what way can his Majesty's ministers carry such a scheme into effect? Through the instrumentality either of the Imperial Parliament or of the Provincial Legislature. Will those, my lord, who dread to resume the control of the crown-duties by the repeal of the conciliatory act of 1st and 2nd of William the Fourth, dare to recommend to the imperial parliament any direct and fundamental interference with the internal legislation of Lower Canada? The supposition, my lord, can only serve to excite a melancholy smile. The required change in the representative system must, therefore, be effected by the provincial legislature. Will the concessions, which your lordship has made to the self-constituted Assembly not from a sense of justice but from a dastardly spirit of conciliation, render it more willing to listen to the suggestions of a Commission, that it has refused to recognize, or of a cabinet, that it has trampled under foot? But might not the French faction very consistently avail itself of your lordship's democratic doctrine as to the absolute power of 'the great body of the people'? Every French demagogue knows, as well as your lordship, that a majority is every thing and that a minority is nothing, and doubtless thinks that 'the great body of the people' ought to appoint all the legislators as well as all the executive officers and all the judges. Yes, my lord, your French allies might refute your lordship's recommendations, as a Commissioner, by a simple reference to your democratic doctrine, as the Governor-in-Chief.

"Secondly, to obtain such a reform in the system of judicature, and the administration of justice, at may adapt them to the present state of the province.'"

Here again your lordship's democratic doctrine; has rendered inquiry an absurdity and a delusion, for what can 'a reform in the system of judicature' do, for constitutionalists, if all the judges are to be virtually appointed by 'the great body of the people'? The value of machinery, my lord, must depend on the instruments for keeping it in motion. If allowed to stand still, it is useless; if turned in the wrong direction, it is pernicious. But if you do, my lord, wish to convince constitutionalists, that any practical result is meant to flow from the inquiries of the Royal Commissioners, your lordship must unhesitatingly reject the judicature-bill of the self-constituted Assembly. If the inquiries of the Royal Commissioners are to lead to anything, the new system, which that bill proposes to introduce, might endure but for a year.

"Thirdly, to obtain such a composition of the Executive Council, as may impart to it the efficiency and weight which it ought to possess."

Here again, my lord, your democratic doctrine defeats the just desires of constitutionalists, for the Executive Council must be composed of members 'acceptable to the great body of the people' and consequently any tiling but acceptable to 'the English inhabitants- of this province'. But your lordship has assumed the responsibility of carrying on the government without an executive council at all; and if 'the English inhabitants of this province' take this step as an earnest of your lordship's predilections for constitutional principles, they have not much reason to be sanguine as to your future proceedings under this head.

> "Fourthly, to resist any appointment of members of the Legislative Council otherwise than by the Crown, but subject to such regulations as may ensure the appointment of fit persons".

'*Fit* persons', my lord. Aye, there's the rub. What is a 'most essential' element of fitness? To be 'acceptable to the great body of the people'. If your lordship's democratic doctrine is to remain valid, what have 'the English inhabitants of this province' to expect from any inquiries of the Royal Commissioners into the constitution or the composition of the Legislative Council? What is it to them, that a legislative councillor, if the creature of Mr. Papineau, holds his Majesty's commission?

> "Fifthly, to use every effort to maintain the connexion of this colony to the Parent State, and a just subordination to its authority".

Here again, my lord, your conciliatory concessions have tended to weaken the very connexion, which the promised inquiries of the Royal Commissioners are ostensibly meant to strengthen, for they have emboldened its enemies and alienated its friends. But might not I justifiably infer, that the individual, who delights to honour the avowed enemies of monarchical institutions and British supremacy, is himself hostile to 'the connexion of this colony to the Parent State', and to 'a just subordination to its authority'. I must infer that your lordship is either thus hostile or weak, blind and inconsistent. I leave to your lordship to choose between the moral crime and the intellectual misfortune.

> "Sixthly, to assist in preserving and maintaining peace and good order throughout the province, and insuring the equal rights of his Majesty's subjects of all classes".

I am surprised, my lord of Gosford, that the 'cheerful' violator of the law should profess to be friendly to 'good order', which he has disturbed, and to 'equal rights', which he has trodden under foot. But of what avail, my lord, will be the promised inquiries of the Royal Commissioners, in regard to 'peace and good order', after your lordship has attempted to perpetuate the distinctions of language, or in regard to 'equal rights', after your lordship has proclaimed the absolute despotism of 'the great body of the people'?

In fine, my lord, your lordship's special decisions are utterly 'incompatible and incongruous' with your lordship's general promises; and I may, without being very uncharitable, infer, that such promises are meant only to deceive. But, my lord, if I admit the perfect sincerity of the Royal Commissioners and of his Majesty's Ministers, the recommendations of the former cannot, in all cases, be carried into effect by the latter without the consent of third parties, so that, while the French faction has got actual concessions, the English population has got only promises from those, who are not competent to perform them.

I have the honour to be,
My Lord
Your Lordship's most obedient humble servant,

Camillus

***

No. LVII.

Montreal 7th January, 1836.

My Lord,

Your lordship's thirty-second paragraph states that it is 'within the line of duty of the King's Commissioners', 'to receive respecting them (the 'objects enumerated') the fullest evidence and information which may be offered, and finally to submit to our Gracious Sovereign and his Ministers their impartial and well weighed conclusions'.

Permit me, my lord, to inquire, whether 'the King's Commissioners' have, so far as they have hitherto proceeded, adhered to 'the line of duty'. Have they received 'the fullest evidence and information', which have been offered? Have they not refused 'evidence and information' on some of the 'objects enumerated' without condescending to apprise the public of such other 'objects', as they were then carrying forward to 'impartial and well weighed conclusions'? Have they not confessed, that, for the convenience of witnesses, they are to remove their sittings from Montreal to Quebec, and yet have they not sent, or determined to send, a report to Downing Street on a most important point without enabling any inhabitant of Montreal to give evidence, unless at a considerable sacrifice of time and money? They bear a stronger resemblance, my lord, to a Spanish Inquisition, than to an English Commission. If they have surpassed the former body in honesty and mercy, they have fallen equally short of it in tact and ability. So much, my lord, as to the Royal Commission's mode of obtaining 'the fullest evidence and information.'

Does any man of competent knowledge and sound judgment believe, that 'the King's Commissioners' are likely to form 'conclusions' either 'impartial' or 'well weighed'. The former epithet is 'incompatible or incongruous' with the avowed prejudices of at least one of the Commissioners in favour of the democratic faction; the latter is lamentably 'incompatible or incongruous' with everything, that has directly or indirectly emanated from 'the King's Commissioners'. I shall never cease, my lord, to warn 'the English inhabitants of this province' against the probable result of the Royal Commission's inquiries, on the very simple ground, that all the visible and tangible evidence proves it to be equally unwilling to form impartial and unable to form well weighed 'conclusions'.[240]

In your thirty-third paragraph, my lord, you most graciously pour forth your winged words for the benefit of the whole population of the province at once.

"In the meanwhile, to the Canadians, both of French and British origin, and of every class and description, I would say, consider the blessings you might enjoy, and the favoured situation in which, but for your own dissensions, you would find yourselves to be placed. The offspring of the two foremost nations of mankind; you hold a vast and beautiful country, a fertile soil, a healthy climate; and the noblest river in the world makes your most remote city a port for ships of the sea. Your revenue is triple the amount of your expenditure for the ordinary purposes of government; you have no direct taxes, no public debt, no poor who require any other aid than the natural impulses of charity."

Your lordship, while reading this paragraph, doubtless considered yourself as the Saturn and your reign as the golden age of Lower Canada. Let me ask your lordship, whether your anticipations have been realised or blasted.

In the commencement of the paragraph, my lord, you give the usual preference to 'French' over 'British,' in compliance with the conciliatory tenor of your 'precise instructions.' For this I do not severely blame you, as you do not profess to have done it 'cheerfully.' 'The Canadians, both of French and British origin, and of every class and description'! How amiably anxious your lordship appears to let nobody continue ignorant of the commencement of a new and happy era. It is, my lord, very deeply to be regretted, that so many members of 'the great body of the people' are unable to read.

In the first sentence of the paragraph, your lordship rightly infers, that 'dissensions' retard the improvement of the colony; but your lordship is mistaken in imagining, that these 'dissensions' subsist between the Canadians of French and those of British origin. They used to subsist between certain constituted authorities and 'the English inhabit ants of this province' on the one hand, and a few

French demagogues on the other. (Since the commencement of the golden age, certain constituted authorities have changed sides; so that now 'the Canadians' of 'British origin' are arrayed against the French faction and the Frenchified government. Have they, my lord, been weakened by the desertion of their anti-national rulers? No, my lord, the spirit of self-dependence, which that desertion has called forth, has knit your oppressed and insulted countrymen into an unconquerable phalanx.[241]

Your lordship has adopted a singular mode of allaying the 'dissensions', for you have strengthened the physically weaker party, as the French faction undoubtedly was—and attempted to weaken the physically stronger party, as the English population was known to be. Was such a process, unless accompanied by some moral medicine for softening asperities, likely to remove or mitigate the 'dissensions'? Your lordship, however, so far from exhibiting any such moral medicine, has done all in your power to aggravate them by seriously proposing to perpetuate the distinctions of language. But, though 'dissensions' retard the improvement of the colony, yet they do not, my lord, alone retard it. If the whole population of the province should zealously co-operate with your lordship in reviving the golden age on the banks of the St. Lawrence, the feudal law would still blast 'the blessings' and neutralise 'the favoured situation'.

I have the honor to be,
My Lord,
Your Lordship's most obedient humble servant,

CAMILLUS.

***

No. LVIII.

Montreal. 8th January, 1836,

My Lord,

Permit me to repeat the second sentence of your lordship's thirty-third paragraph.

"The offspring of the two foremost nations of mankind, you hold a vast and beautiful country, a fertile soil, a healthy climate; and the noblest river in the world makes your most remote city a port for ships of the sea."

I must, my lord, repeat my regret, that the ignorance of most of the members of 'the great body of the people' must have prevented them from perusing the 'flattering and kind' observations of their noble partisan in regard to their lofty origin, their picturesque scenery, their agricultural advantages and their commercial facilities.

Your lordship's discovery, that both 'nations' are 'foremost', I must ascribe to a conciliatory figure of speech; and, if one may judge from your undisguised predilections, you might have been more 'precise' as to the relative rank of the 'nations', without offending the patriotic prejudices of 'the great body of the people'. But permit me, my lord, seriously to ask you, whether it was consistent with humanity, with sound policy, with your lordship's avowed desire of conciliating 'adverse parties', to flatter the French prejudices of British subjects. But I forget, my lord, that consistency and conciliation are 'incompatible or incongruous'.[242]

As to the 'vast and beautiful country', your lordship's experience of the last few months must have taught you that the most picturesque views in the world have very little influence on human happiness. If they had any such influence, Cape Diamond, my lord, would be the favourite refuge of criminal outcasts. External nature, my lord, may charm innocence, but cannot 'minister to a mind diseased'[243].

What villain from himself can flee?
To zones, though more and more remote,
Still, still pursues, where'er he be,
The blight of life, the demon thought.[244]

But this, my lord, is a digression. What avails it to 'the English inhabitants of this province' that the 'country' is 'vast and beautiful', if it is to be given up to the French faction? Your lordship, perhaps, is not aware, that that faction not only demands the legislative control of all the waste lands of the crown, but has avowed its conviction that, according to the capitulation of 1760 and the treaty of 1763, it ought to reserve these lands exclusively for Canadians of French origin. The following allusion to this modest opinion, your lordship may have observed in the Legislative Council's address to his Majesty in 1833.

> "We respectfully advert * * * * to the claim advanced by the assembly to preserve this extensive and important part of your Majesty's dominions (in which there is room for millions of inhabitants) as a colony to be settled only by Canadians of French origin and descent."

Does not your lordship perceive, that every one of your conciliatory concessions increases the French faction's power to enforce that absurd claim, and to exclude 'the offspring' of one 'of the two foremost nations of mankind' from any and every share of the 'vast and beautiful country.' But, my lord, what avails it even to 'the French inhabitants of this province,' that the 'country' is 'vast and beautiful,' if they are too 'indolent' to occupy it? On this head, my lord, I extract a few apposite remarks from the *Montreal Herald* of 11th June, based on a parliamentary report.

> "While the Americans have covered a continent with the smiling monuments of their agricultural industry, the Canadians have literally squeezed their rapidly and regularly growing numbers almost within the original settlements of 1763. We extract the following

paragraph from the report of a committee of the assembly in 1834. 'The extreme denseness of the population of lower Canada, which appears to your committee to have increased and to continue to increase, in a much higher ratio than that in which the clearings extend into the forest, and the productive powers of the earth are brought forth, rendered it a matter of anxious inquiry', &c.

"We extract a few more minute statements from evidence given before the said committee. 'There is more over a large number of young men who would have taken some lands, and who have been disgusted by the high rent required, and they have thereby been discouraged from taking them. The rent demanded is four dollars for three arpents in front by thirty in depth'. The 'high rate', if we reckon interest at 6 per cent, per annum, would correspond with a price of 3s. 8½d., Halifax currency, per acre; and so paltry a barrier, for the prospective dread of a mutation fine could not have entered in to the heads of the 'young men', 'disgusted' the 'young men' more than the most exquisite miseries of cheap 'indolence' and starvation. The following scraps of the evidence will show, that the 'young men' had not sufficient ingenuity to try their fortunes in another seigniory.

"The 'young men' had too much respect for the decrees of fate. Having been born to be *habitans*, they would not rebel against their destiny by presuming to migrate. On the local patriotism of the 'young men', even hunger and cold exerted no influence. There was not a 'banal mill' in the seigniory, and 'it was necessary to go very far to have our corn ground'. There was a scarcity of fuel, and 'I have been myself obliged to go three quarters of a league off for my fire wood'. The following portion of the evidence speaks volumes for the local patriotism of the 'young men', in defiance of all the foregoing disadvantages.

"Q. How do the young people of this parish proceed in order to obtain settlements?

"A. They are retarded; they wait until the lands shall be conceded; some of them have even grown old while waiting for lands, but they continue to wait, and according to what people say, if the unconceded lands were granted, many persons would take some of them.

"Q. Do the old lands begin to be subdivided?

"A. Some of them do.

"Q. Why do they make those subdivisions?

"A Because they do not find an opportunity of settling their children elsewhere.

"Q. What is the effect of those subdivisions?

"'A. Some of them are much injured thereby, because when the land is old, and no more new land remains for cultivation, the soil is not sufficiently productive to support two families, and they are both reduced to want."

As to 'a fertile soil,' my lord, it is rather a curse than a blessing to confessedly 'indolent' individuals, who, according to the statement of a recent correspondent of the *Quebec Gazette,* do not produce 'more than one third of what other agriculturists do.'

What your lordship means by 'you *hold* * * * a healthy climate,' I really do not know. Your pompous allusion to 'your most remote city' as 'a port for ships of the sea,' betrays your lordship's want of tact in so pointedly alluding to the long gnawed bone of contention between the Canadas.

I have the honor to be,
My Lord,
Your Lordship 's most obedt. humble servant,

CAMILLUS.

***

No. LIX.

Montreal, 9th January, 1836.

My Lord,

In the third sentence of your thirty-third paragraph, you tell the astonished 'Canadians, both of French and British origin', that 'your revenue is triple the amount of your expenditure for the ordinary purposes of Government.' What your lordship means by so vague an expression as 'expenditure for the ordinary purposes of government,' I do not know. I may, however, suppose that you do not comprehend in it the salaries of Messrs. Viger, Roebuck, &c, for services performed beyond the limits of the 'vast and beautiful country' and intended to counteract what plain men understand by 'the ordinary purposes of government'. Now, as your lordship has 'cheerfully' conceded to the self-constituted Assembly the unqualified power of squandering on extra-provincial and anti-constitutional agents such portions of the revenue as are not required for 'the ordinary purposes of government', your lordship's insinuation, that two-thirds of the revenue are reserved for the moral and physical improvement of the 'vast and beautiful country,' must fall to the ground. But your lordship's statement of the proportion, which the whole revenue bears to the 'expenditure for the ordinary purposes of government' might have been known by your lordship to be extravagantly incorrect, for the public chest, even before your lordship 'cheerfully' abstracted from it twenty-two thousand pounds in an illegal manner and for illegal purposes, did not contain the means of paying the arrears of the civil list, though not a single shilling had been appropriated in the previous session of the legislature to any object whatever. Of the wilful misrepresentation of a matter of fact I dare not suspect your lordship; but I must pay the 'flattering and kind' compliment to your lordship's honesty at the expense of your lordship's circumspection. Your lordship, utterly forgetful or ignorant of the claim of Upper Canada to a third of the most productive duties, must have compared the 'expenditure for the ordinary purposes of government' with the amount of duties collected in Lower Canada for both provinces. The blunder, my lord, whether it be ascribed to dishonesty or to rashness, is a very doubtful sample of your lordship's 'fitness' for arriving at 'impartial and well weighed conclusions' in regard to the complicated politics of this 'vast and beautiful country'.

Your lordship adds, 'You have no direct taxes, no public debt, no poor who require any other aid than the natural impulses of charity'.

But to 'the Canadians' of 'British origin,' my lord, a surplus revenue is far from being a subject of congratulation, so long as it is expended by French demagogues either for purely French objects or in purchasing the dishonest neutrality of selfish constitutionalists[245] with a parallelogram of mud as a road, with a hurdle as a bridge or with an uninhabitable dungeon as a gaol. The surplus revenue, which ought to be a general blessing, is a millstone about the necks of constitutionalists.

The absence of 'direct taxes', so far from being a benefit to 'the Canadians' of 'British origin', is a grievance, which burdens them with a disproportionately heavy share of the public expenditure. The existing taxes are almost exclusively levied on British goods and chiefly borne by British consumers; but 'direct taxes', my lord, would necessarily transfer the great body of the burden to 'the great body of the people' and enable 'the English inhabitants of this province' to offer direct and effective resistance to illegal appropriations of the public revenue.

The absence of a 'public debt', my lord, is an equally lame and vulgar subject of congratulation. The policy of contracting a 'public debt' for the prosecution of offensive wars may well be doubted; but on the English portion of this continent, my lord, the expression *public debt* is practically synonymous with *internal improvement*, the *internal improvement* doubtless remains after the public debt has disappeared; but, to say that an American country neither has nor ever had a 'public debt', is to stigmatise her as being behind her neighbours in the march of civilisation and prosperity. What but a 'public debt', my lord, made New York and Pennsylvania the pride of America and the envy of Europe? What but a 'public debt', my lord, places Upper Canada so far in advance of her elder sister? What but a 'public debt', my lord, will enable Lower Canada to avail herself of all the advantages of even 'the noblest river in the world'? Your lordship's 'triple' revenue will be utterly inadequate to the accomplishment of so magnificent an end. Was it wise, my lord, to represent a *public debt* as being ill an unqualified manner a *public evil*.

Your lordship is pleased to hazard the assertion, that, in Lower Canada, there are 'no poor who require any other aid than the natural impulses of charity'. This language, my lord, is not quite so 'precise' as your 'instructions'.—Whether does your lordship mean, that the 'vast and beautiful country' contains little poverty or much benevolence? You have merely affirmed that the moral virtue is commensurate with the physical misfortune. As your lordship could not have had any personal knowledge of the subject you must have drawn the complimentary inference from the presumed absence of any legal provision for the poor. Your lordship's experience in Ireland must convince your lordship of the untenable nature of such a position. But your lordship has rashly mistaken the very facts of the case. In this country, there are 'poor, who require any other aid than the natural impulses of charity'. In almost every session of the legislature, the means of supplying unskilful or improvident *habitans* with seed-corn are furnished from the provincial revenue.

In my next letter, I shall close the consideration of your lordship's speech.

I have the honor to be,
My Lord,
Your Lordship's most obedt. humble servant,

CAMILLUS.

***

No. LX.

Montreal, 11th January, 1836.

My Lord,

I subjoin your lordship's thirty-fourth paragraph:

"If you extend your views beyond the land in which you dwell, you find that you are joint inheritors of the splendid patrimony of the British Empire, which constitutes you, in the amplest sense of the term, citizens of the world, and gives you a home on every continent and in every ocean of the globe. There are two paths open to you: by the one you may advance to the enjoyment of all the advantages which lie in prospect before you; by the other, I will not say more than that you will stop short of these and will engage yourselves and those who have no other object than your prosperity, in darker and more difficult courses."

The 'precise' bearing of the first sentence, my lord, I cannot discover. To 'the Canadians' of 'French origin,' who are not much less stationary than so many vegetables, 'a home on every Continent and in every Ocean of the globe' must seem to be a somewhat speculative blessing, a 'flattering and kind' sentence of restless banishment. But try the test of experience, my lord, and tell any one of your French friends, whether a shopkeeper or a farmer, how highly he ought to appreciate the liberty of expatriating himself to the Cape of Good Hope or Sincapore or Gibraltar or St. Helena. Does not the minute specification of the general compliment bring down the sublime to the level of the ridiculous? May I not, my lord, justifiably allude to 'the circulating-library style' or even repeat the critical dissyllable of the *Minerve*? But even in 'the Canadians' of 'British origin' your lordship's sketch of 'the splendid patrimony' can only excite a smile. Most of them, my lord, have adopted this country as a permanent residence and have not the slightest intention of migrating to Newfoundland or Jamaica or Demerara or Sierra Leone or the magnetic pole. It is, however, consolatory to them to know, on your lordship's authority, that, if they should, by an anti-national policy, be driven from their adopted country on account of their 'British origin,' thay may still find 'a home on every Continent and in every Ocean of the globe.'

But does your lordship seriously mean, that none but British subjects find 'a home' in the British Empire? Are American citizens, on account of the 'darker and more difficult courses' of their fathers, excluded from the full and free enjoyment of 'the splendid patrimony'? Does your lordship again seriously mean, that British subjects have 'a home' only in the British Empire? Is there a civilized spot, my lord, along the length or the breadth of either continent—with the exception of your lordship's vice-regal dominions—on which the name of Englishman is not a passport to favour, hospitality and respect?

But how could your lordship, while actually placing 'the English inhabitants of this province' under the feet of a French faction as the presumed organ of 'the great body of the people', guarantee to an Englishman 'a home' in every quarter of 'the splendid patrimony'? Has an Englishman, my lord, 'a home' even in the 'vast and beautiful' dominions of your lordship? No, my lord, he is stigmatised as a foreigner; and what is still more remarkable, your lordship's confidence.—But it is not in words merely, that an Englishman is denied 'a home' in a land conquered by his fathers. Offensive words are backed by more offensive deeds. Your lordship, for instance, will soon be required to sanction or reject or reserve a bill, which degrades the Englishmen not only of Lower Canada but every portion of 'the splendid patrimony', which confers an invidious privilege on French law-students and disqualifies the Broughams, the Scarletts and the Copleys of England for exercising their profession in the King's Courts of this province among the Vanfelsons,[246] the Debleurys[247] and the Gugys.[248] Your lordship's pleasing language about 'a home' is 'incompatible or incongruous' with the sanctioning or even the reserving of such a bill. Let not the anti-national imbecility of the Legislative Council be your model on this point. The bill is not the less Anti-English, that Englishmen permitted it to reach your lordship.

The *two paths*, to which your lordship emphatically alludes, may be presumed to be the path of *peace* and the path of *war*. A more acute analysis, my lord, would have discovered at least *four paths*. The 'two parties' may be both quiet or both warlike; or either of them may be warlike, while the other remains quiet. May I presume, my lord, to conjecture, that your opinion, as to the probable choice of 'paths', is not now the same as that which you entertained on 27th October, 1835? Your disappointment, my lord, has been equally bitter and complete. You vainly flattered yourself, that unjust and illegal measures would lead to 'the conciliation of adverse parties' and lay deep and wide the foundations of general harmony. Has your unconstitutional nostrum, my lord, succeeded? You vainly believed, that the danger of physical resistance was to be apprehended only from the French-Canadians. Has your belief, my lord, been justified by the visible and tangible results? No, my lord; for the results have convinced you, that 'the English inhabitants of this province' are alone likely to vindicate their rights by force of arms and that the French demagogues have uttered a wilful falsehood in every threat of physical resistance.—Pardon me, my lord, for requesting you to read a few editorial remarks on the British Rifle Corps in the last number of the *Vindicator*, the English organ of your French allies. So far from attempting to counteract that corps by fulfilling their own threats of physical resistance—even with a special example and a special justification before them—the demagogues exhibit nothing but fear, distrust and confusion.[249] The journal, my lord, to which I have alluded, has been deservedly styled the French *Vindicator*. The article in question justifies the national epithet; and your lordship's philological taste may be delighted to find such un-English expressions as 'citizens of the city' and 'in our midst'.

As to the 'darker and more difficult courses,' my lord, we dread them not, for English soldiers will not plant the tree of French democracy in English blood. The bare supposition, which is implied in your lordship's threat, would certainly have been realised against French republicans and French rebels; but, as matters, my lord, now stand, such a supposition is absolutely monstrous and utterly incredible.

Those who have pledge themselves to resist your lordship's present course of policy, by any and every means—and their number, my lord, is hourly increasing—have been stigmatised as rebels, because your lordship, forsooth, is HIS MAJESTY'S REPRESENTATIVE. That your lordship, like any other executive officer, represents his Majesty as to the discharge of special duties, I willingly admit; but to give your lordship the benefit of an unqualified interpretation of the complementary phrase, savours of servility, for your lordship, under the cloak of the King's name, has been defended, as if you could do no wrong, for having done that, which the King himself could not have done with impunity; it savours of disloyalty, for it loads his Majesty with the crime of having robbed the public chest of Lower Canada.

I have the honor to be,
My Lord,
Your Lordship's most obedt. humble servant,

CAMILLUS.

ABBREVIATIONS

CAM   Constitutional Association of Montreal

HA   Herald Abstract (Abridged weekly edition of the *Montreal Herald*)

KMH   Montreal Herald (Scrapbook prepared by Charles Kadwell)

ENDNOTES

Chapter 1. The Historical and Political Context

1. This brief overview of the historical and political context is based partly on Chapter 6 of *A People's History of Quebec* by Jacques Lacoursière and Robin Philpot (Baraka Books 2009).

Chapter 2. Who Was Adam Thom?

1. Biographical notes based on the *Dictionary of Canadian Biography* and Deschamps, 2015a.

Chapter 3. Introduction

1. *Getting it Wrong. How Canadians Forgot Their Past and Imperilled Confederation* (Romney, 1999). On the issue of forgetting, see the chapter entitled, "Memory and Forgetting" in B. Anderson ([1983], 2006, 187-206), Agamben, 2015, as well as Assmann and Shortt, 2012.
2. *Canadiens* refers to the indigenous French-speaking population of Canada. The term dates back to the late 1600s, when the local population began self-identifying as *Canadiens* to distinguish themselves from the French, who also used the term to describe the "country born." In the 1830s, very few English-speaking people in Canada referred to themselves as "Canadians."
3. Colonel Grey visited Montreal in August 1839 (Ormsby, 1965, 97).
4. Here is what T. B. Macaulay wrote in December 1838: "I fear that the victorious caste will not be satisfied without punishments so rigorous as would dishonor the English Government in the eyes of all Europe and in our own eyes ten years hence. [...] The savage language of some of the papers

both in Canada and London makes no doubt whether we are as far beyond the detestable Carlists and Christinos of Spain as I had hoped" (William, 2008, 112-113).

5. "They are political Tory Societies, composed of persons confessing Orangeism in its worst shade… They are struggling for political ascendency of the few over the many. […] They assumed the sacred garb of charity to conceal their dark and real design…. But we cannot be imposed upon by the hypocrites, whether they herd together in a St. Andrew's Society, St. George's or a German Society. Their sole aim is political power. And they threaten to fight, too." See Senior, 1985, 13, who quotes articles from the *Vindicator,* December 9 et 15, 1835, whereas Thom's reply appears in letter XLIII on December 1.

6. The myth that the English descended from the Romans mainly through the Trojan hero Aeneas has a long history. See Bradley, 2010.

7. Reference to the battle of Marathon in Byron, *Childe Harold Pilgrimage*, 2, XC, 1812-1818. Thom set the tone at the beginning of his mandate: "It was a profound maxim of Solon, that in all civil commotions every individual should attach himself to one or other of the contending factions; for that philosopher well knew that every gentleman, whose cowardice or indolence would incline him to be neutral, would rather espouse the right cause than subject himself to the penalty of outlawry. Solon's law would be very useful in Lower Canada". (*HA*, 25 January, 1835). "Solon's law" is excerpted from *The Athenian Constitution* (VIII, 5) Aristotle; see Koselleck, 1988, 187-189, Agamben, 2015, 23-24 and Deschamps, 2015a, 11-13.

8. See Deschamps, 2015a, 46-47.

9. Use of the pseudonym "Hampden" shows how the Montreal Tories saw themselves. John Hampden was "one of the leading parliamentarians involved in challenging the authority of Charles I of England in the run-up to the English Civil War". See https://en.wikipedia.org/wiki/John_Hampden.

10. "W.O.M." sounded the alarm similarly, likely early in October: "Sir – The blood is boiling in my veins while I endeavour to write these few and hurried lines; no language can express the indignation and abhorrence I now feel at having just witnessed a band of revolutionary ruffians parading through the streets of Montreal, preceded by the tri-coloured flag, and headed by a Band of Music, (such as it was) playing, or trying to play the Marseilles Hymn. 'Oh,' I exclaimed, 'where is the Rifle Corps?' 'where is the vaunted British Legion?' 'where are the Axe Handle Guards?' 'where, oh where! is the Doric Club that used always to be first at the post of danger or of honor?' Though the revolutionary cowards dare not show themselves in the open day nor produce their dirty tri-coloured "while the sun shows its light,' still that is no reason why they should be permitted with impunity to carry the

flag of revolution through our streets, and insult the loyal subjects of our gracious Queen after sun down." (KMH, n.d.)

11. E. K. Senior articulated it brilliantly and concisely when she wrote that the burning down of the Parliament in Montreal in 1849 was to mark the demise of the "old alliance between the garrison and the British party that had begun in 1832 and matured in the rebellion years" (Senior, 1981, 107).

12. See below for an excerpt from his address and Deschamps, 2015a, 237.

13. Far from being peripheral, tangential and late-coming, as Ducharme claims, the ethnic dimension of the conflict can be grasped within the overarching context of the cultural and commercial rivalry between France and England that dates back, according to Thom, to ... William the Conqueror (XXV)!

14. "Every conflict has an emergent occasion" (À tout conflit, il faut une occasion), wrote M. Séguin (1995, 25), for whom the notion of kairos is present in the prison tax, budget quarrels (subsidies), the crisis over the sharing of customs duties, etc. (1995, 87; 97; 103; 119; 155) as well as in the term "separatistes d'occasion" ("occasional separatists") (196)! On this fundamental point of interpretation, see J. Pigeaud (2006) and R. Koselleck [1959], 1988.

15. Jackson, 2009.

16. It is difficult not to see a coded reference to the famous, "Smooth runs the water when the brook is deep/ And in his simple show he harbours treason" (Shakespeare, Henry VI, part 2, III, 1, 55-56). Moreover, here too it is a question again of discovering signs of treason. Regarding the notion of the inevitable advancement of democracy, see Bell, 2009, 41.

17. "Something of the nature of this political love can be deciphered from the ways in which languages describe its object: either in the vocabulary of kinship (motherland, Vaterland, patria) or that of home (heimat or tanah air [earth and water, the phrase for the Indonesians' native archipelago]). Both idioms denote something to which one is naturally tied. As we have seen earlier, in everything 'natural' there is always something unchosen. In this way, nation-ness is assimilated to skin-colour, gender, parentage and birth-era - all those things one can not help. And in these 'natural ties' one senses what one might call 'the beauty of gemeinschaft'. To put it another way, precisely because such ties are not chosen, they have about them a halo of disinterestedness." (Anderson, 2006, 143).

18. The term "nostalgie" in French—return (nóstos) and pain (álgos)— appeared in the Dictionnaire de l'Académie in 1835, the very year of the Anti-Gallic Letters. On the invention of this "mal provincial," see Jean Starobinski, 2012, "La leçon de la nostalgie," 257-337.

19. It would be interesting to study Thom's variations on the theme of regression to 'original violence' in light of Stanley Cavell's writings, 1983. In

letter XXXVI, for example, alluding to the theme of the god Saturn eating his children, which was the theme of a recently finished Goya painting (1819-1823), Thom submits that it is the "English inhabitants of this province" who are cannibalized. The idea implicitly taken from Plautus is that "man is wolf to man." See also XXXIX, note 184.

20. Virgil, *The Aeneid* VII, v. 312.

21. John Molson Jr. and James Quinlan, "To men of British and Irish descent" (20 December 1834). The document is reprinted in *HA*, 8 January 1835. See Deschamps, 2015a, 25-32.

22. The furthest that Papineau would go in this area was joint action with the Reformers of Upper Canada. In an August 1837 letter to Wolfred Nelson, he wrote: "Agitation is active. They (the Reformers) intend to send a deputation of seven members to the Convention, or as they call it, the Congress of the two provinces, at which there will be prepared a constitution purely democratic, and England will be told that on the principles of that Constitution alone will we continue the connection with her, *and that if she does not concede to us, we will have justice INDEPENDENTLY of her*" (*HA*, 1 February, 1840).

23. Should an infraction occur, Thom challenges Gosford to send a magistrate or an officer from among the loyalists "hardy enough to attempt the seizure of a single citizen of English blood" (XLIV).

24. John Ralston Saul, *Louis-Hyppolyte Lafontaine and Robert Baldwin*, Penguin 2010.

25. See Deschamps, 2015a, 48-54. In the nineteenth century, from 1815 to 1875, eight million British people left their country and settled elsewhere than Europe. Two thirds of them chose to settle in the United States. Between 1815 and 1850, 600,000 people from England, Scotland and Wales left, while at that time two million Irish emigrated. That tendency increased in 1850s and 1860s, reaching 1.3 and 1.5 million respectively. See Darwin, 2009, 58 and Vaughan, 2010, 119-153 and the brilliant analysis of James Belich, 2009, 279-305.

26. Montgomery Martin wrote: "I do not use the fiction of saying *nominated by the Crown*, — I wish the colonists in every part of the Empire to know that the king has nothing to say to any appointments, his Majesty's sanction even being a matter of course after the approval of the Ministry, it is therefore a question of patronage to the Colonial Secretary and Primer Minister for his relatives, friends — and political friends (or foes who may be dreaded,) rather than a question of the prerogative of the Crown as artfully put forth.]" (Martin, 1834). On the evolution of the British parliamentary system, see Marcel Gauchet, *La voie anglaise*, 1995, 259-266.

27. In January 1835, Thom already made fun of a cabinet headed by Prime Minister Papineau; see Deschamps, 2011, 98-99. On Dalhousie, see XXXIV, note 157.

28. Vaugeois, 1992, 25-26; 92-94; 120; 141-142.
29. Deschamps, 2015b.
30. Seeley, 1883, 56-57.
31. See Bell, 2007, 66 and 74.
32. On the extension of British citizenship in the rival multicultural approach defended by William Gladstone of the Select Committee on Aborigines in 1835 and 1836, see Kumar, 2012. For her part, Kolsky, 2005, emphasizes the resistance of British settlers in Bengal in the 1830s.
33. Since Tocqueville does not distinguish between the British and the Americans, in one of his striking general observations he writes: "The four hundred thousand Frenchmen of Lower Canada are today like the debris of an ancient people inundated by the flood of a new nation" [1835], 2004, 471.
34. See J. I. Little, 2008.
35. Deschamps, 2015a, 189-233.
36. KMH, n.d.
37. Lefebvre, 1970, 155. Yet Thom has already said all this. See XXXIX, note 184.
38. Écrits français, Paris, Gallimard, 1991, 435 (our translation).

Anti-Gallic Letters

1. Not dated; *Montreal Herald*, 28 September 1835.
2. Curtis, 2015.
3. The notion of "secret" was still very much alive in English political culture at this time and it ends up in the fear of a "conspiracy," either the establishment of a double *Canadien* majority in the House of Assembly and the Legislative Council with good will of the Melbourne cabinet; see the Introduction for the excerpt from the address to the British House of Commons made in 1839 by the former governor of Upper Canada, Francis Bond Head; see also below Letters XVII, XXX, XLVIII and XLIX.
4. The distinction here is vital: the plan for a legislative union developed the following year by the CAM involved the indefinite suspension of the representative body of the "La Grande Nation."
5. Moderate newspaper in Quebec City published by Étienne Parent.
6 *DCB*.
7. *DCB*.
8. In Montreal, *The Morning Courier*. On Christopher Dunkin, the publisher, see Curtis, 2012.
9. An indication of the new democratic legitimacy stemming from the Reform Bill of 1832 was that in 1835 the Peel cabinet in England was dismissed

244 · The Prophetic Anti-Gallic Letters

and the Melbourne cabinet returned to power. Moreover, in the wake of the Canadian Revenue Control Act of 1831, except for the Crown duties, the budget was virtually in the hands of the majority party in the House of Assembly. See "APPENDIX E. GRIEVANCES OF LOWER CANADA, BY THE HON. D. B. VIGER, MEMBER OF THE LEGISLATIVE COUNCIL OF THE PROVINCE" in Montgomery Martin, 1834, 577-586; and *Lord Durham's Report on the Affairs of British North America*, Oxford: Clarendon Press, 1912, vol. II, 141-142 and M. Ducharme, 2010, 211.

10. Thom, under pseudonym "Anti-Bureaucrat," had just lambasted the imperial policy of conciliation towards the Patriote Party that was being implemented since the Canada Committee of 1828; in Thom's eyes the policy stemmed from fear of a rebellion whose ultimate goal was "the establishment of a French Republic"; See Anti-Bureaucrat, *Remarks*, 1835, "On the presumed necessity of conciliation," 4.

11. This rapprochement is dubious since the Patriote movement was divided, with a radical and a moderate branch.

12. The theme of violence is introduced in a negative form. Thom brings to bear his most powerful rhetorical devices.

13. At issue here is the right of the imperial Parliament to intervene, which was rigorously circumscribed since the Declaratory Act of 1783. The Russell resolutions of April 1837 go beyond this right to intervene in the local affairs of the colony and give rise to a vast popular "anti-coercion" movement that grows around the assemblies prohibited by Governor Gosford in the Proclamation of June 15, 1837. See below Letter XXVI.

14. Thom's key argument: deprived of adequate representation, the British merchants contribute massively to the provincial budget.

15. Following the defeat of the Tory candidate in the close election in Montreal's West Ward, the "British Party," as Durham described it, founded the Montreal branch of the Constitutional Association in December 1834. In spring 1835, Thom began developing the notion of "physical resistance" to which will be driven the Montrealers of British stock who consider themselves to be "outlaws."

16. Crécy, 1346; Poitiers, 1356; Agincourt, 1415 (Shakespeare's play *Henry V* deals with these battles); Minden 1759: whereas the first three battles refers to the War of Roses between France and England, the fourth battle took place during the Seven Years War, in which the taking of Quebec by the armies of General Wolfe in 1759 and the surrender of Montreal in 1760 were the high points. See Buckner, 2012, Buckner and Reid, 2012, F. Crouzet, 2008, as well as Fonck and Veyssière, 2013.

17. The medical metaphor appears throughout: see "the homeopathic principle of modern liberals" (XXIII) and the many uses of "remedy," "injury," "evil." "moral medicine," etc.

18. When the British Rifle Corps and the district committees, the Executive Committee of the Montreal Constitutional Association turns to the idea of a congress clearly of a republican nature (See Introduction, 20). An article in the *St. Catherine Journal* alludes also to it: "let Constitutional Associations be immediately formed in every district of the Province, based upon the same principles and having the same objects in view, as those of our Lower Canadian friends – let Delegates be chosen, to meet in a general Congress, of the British Colonies of North America" (*HA*, 23 January, 1836).

19. Thom lumps together the members of the Patriote Party led by Louis-Joseph Papineau for the past 15 years and former supporters of that party who had gone over to the "conciliatory" camp, such as D. Debartzch and S. de Bleury. The imperial authorities, resisting Patriote Party demands to make the Legislative Council an elected body, would nonetheless make appointments in October 1837 that ensured the predominance of *Canadiens*.

20. "Outlaw" was a favourite term used by Thom and encompassed other notions that could include "desperado" or even "mobster" and others.

21. A significant part of the executive still remained in the hands of civil authorities, as can be observed at the municipal level in the judiciary, the police and the militia; see Fyson, 2015.

22. Papineau also spoke of the "*droit de n'obéir à aucune autre loi qu'à celles que nous avons formées et adoptées nous-mêmes par nos représentants*" (the right to obey no other laws that those we have drafted and adopted ourselves through our representatives) (Lamonde, 2013, 63) (our translation). In *England and America* (1833), E. G. Wakefield wrote similarly: "[l]et colonies be societies in new places, and they will have the power to choose between self-government and government from a distance. That they would choose to govern themselves cannot be doubted by any one who is at all acquainted with the evils of being governed from a distance"; quote from Bell, 2007, 76.

23. Creation of the great "Province of Quebec" that neutralized certain provisions of the Royal Proclamation of 1763 with regards to British settlers.

24. Until the burning down of the Canadian Parliament and the annexation manifesto of 1849, the republican tendencies of the Montreal Tories was very strong. Their loudly expressed "loyalism" failed to impress Durham; see Deschamps, 2013a and 2015c. 35-37 and, for a sampling, Letters XLIII and LIII.

25. How long can one tolerate an uncomfortable situation? This was a decisive issue with respect to an aspect of skin-deep British sensitivity; see Montesquieu, 1748, XIV, 13 and Letter XXV below.

26. James Leslie. "The learned member for the East Ward of Montreal would make an excellent President of the Board of Trade" (*HA*, 29 January 1835). Thom spoke this way when he was sketching out the shadow cabinet under the leadership of Prime Minister Papineau.

27. In *An Historical View of the English Government* (1770), John Millar wrote concerning this "voice of mercantile interest": "The prevalence of this great mercantile association in Britain, has, in the course of the present century, become gradually more and more conspicuous. The clamour and tumultuary proceedings of the populace in the great towns are capable of penetrating the inmost recesses of administration, of intimidating the boldest minister, and of displacing the most presumptuous favourite of the backstairs. The voice of the mercantile interest, never fails to command the attention of government, and when firm and unanimous, is even able to controul and direct the deliberations of the national councils. The methods which are sometimes practised by ministry to divide this mercantile interest, and to divert its opposition to the measures of the crown, will fall more properly to be considered hereafter." See, http://oll.libertyfund.org/titles/millar-an-historical-view-of-the-english-government, 727-728.

28. To be attributed to the Tories' "occasional separatism" *"séparatisme d'occasion."*

29. The Montreal Tories in the CAM considered themselves no less than "the temporary guardians of the interests of Lower Canada and even of British America"; see *HA*, 25 June 1836. Already in December 1834, a correspondent wrote: "Our flag, the pride of Britain and the dread of France, must float for ever over the citadel of Quebec, the impregnable guardian of half an empire" (*HA*, 1 January 1835).

30. Thom alludes obliquely here to the essential role of the army in case the conflict radicalized. Maintaining the colonial link and the concomitant fear of the "dismemberment of the empire" are explicitly Orangemen's themes that can be found in the oath ritual; see Harland-Jacobs, 2008, 27 and Deschamps, 2015a, 176.

31. See the quote from la *Minerve* in Letter XIX. Papineau never went as far as proposing a joint colonial emancipation movement with Upper Canada radicals. See *HA* 1 February 1840, which quotes a letter from Papineau to Wolfred Nelson dated 19 August 1837: "Agitation is active. They (the Reformers of Upper Canada) intend to send a deputation of seven members to the Convention, or as they call it, the Congress of the two provinces, at which there will be prepared a constitution purely democratic, and England will be told that on the principles of that Constitution alone will we continue the connection with her, and that if she does not concede to us, we will have justice INDEPENDENTLY of her." The only explicit reference to the political independence of Lower Canada is in Robert Nelson 1838 (see Bernard, 1986, 301-304).

32. Harvey, *Les cahiers des dix*, 2014.

33. On the importance of Wolfe and the Battle of the Plains of Abraham in English culture, see P. Buckner, 2012 et L. Colley, 2003.

34. Reference to Louis-Joseph Papineau and the shooting on 21 May 1832 when on the orders of Tory magistrates the army fired on civilians following an extremely close by-election in the West Ward won by the Patriote Daniel Tracey. Thom returns to those events, XVIII and XLI. It was a founding moment when a critical threshold was reached. See the quote from Senior in the Introduction (27, n. 11) as well as Lamonde and Larin, 1998, 239-247, Jackson, 2009 and Sicotte, 2016, 99-107.

35. This is a central theme towards which the positions of radical Tories and Patriotes converge.

36. See Greenwood and Lambert, "Jonathan Sewell," *DCB*.

37. Papineau.

38. On the danger of "elective attraction" between soldiers and civilians, see Burke, 1790 and Knox, 1795.

39. See J. C. Grant and J. G. Scott, "Report of the Select general committee of the delegates of the constitutionalists of Lower Canada (Deschamps, 2015a, 48-54); G. Moffatt and W. Badgley, "Representation on the Legislative Union of the Provinces, &c." (Deschamps, 2015, 48-54.

40. The searing article "Canada Question" published in the June issue of *Blackwood's Magazine* savaged the tyrannical action of the House of Assembly. See Introduction, 43, n. 29.

41. D. Creighton's (1937) entire thesis on the establishment of the "commercial State" is based on the superior geostrategic interests that this privileged access route to the heart of North American offered financiers in the City in London.

42. Denis Benjamin Viger, member of the Legislative Council.

43. Allusion to the Sack of Rome in 390 before our era by the Gauls led by Brennus. Cf., the editorials of Thom under the mask of Manlius, in December 1835 when the British Rifle Corps was being formed. Christopher Dunkin, publisher of the *Morning Courier*, remembered shortly before the riot of 6 November 1837: "Somebody, (we know not who, but presume it must have been a lineal descendant of the feathered biped that whilom saved the Roman capitol by cackling, who was emulous of the famous ancestor's renown,) had set up handbills calling a meeting on the Place d'Armes at noon, 'to crush rebellion in the bud'" *HA*, 11 November 1837.

44. British Prime Minister agreeing to separation of the great province of Quebec into Upper and Lower Canada. The Montreal Tories' complex of being a minority stems from that decision. See *DCB*, D. Roberts, "Adam Lymburner," on line A. Lymburner, "*Paper read at the bar of the House of Commons, by Mr. Lymburner, agent for the subscribers to the petitions from the province of Quebec, bearing date the 24th of November 1784. . .* (Quebec, 1791)" and Deschamps, 2013a.

45. Vaugeois, 1992.

46. Stuart, 1824 and Deschamps, 2015b. The plan to annex Montreal to Ontario would reappear in the news in 1836 among other scenarios, including the annexation of Lower Canada to Upper Canada; the latter would end up being retained by the Tories on the MCA, purged of is liberal elements, and the clandestine paramilitary organization, the Doric Club. See Deschamps, 2011 and 2015a, 48-54 and 139-141.

47. A contemporary echo of the debate on the influence of Thom in public opinion in "English Montreal" (Young, 2014). The *Morning Courier* had just written: "We have positive evidence that the Constitutional cause has suffered, both here and at Home, from the false impression that has been propagated, that such illiberal and ultra-Tory principles as those which load the columns of the *Herald* are in unison with the sentiments of the British party in this Province. We need scarcely appeal to our fellow-Constitutionalists to prove how false such an impression is, and how little such doctrines are sympathised with. The principles of 'A REFORMER'S' letter, we reassert, are the same as those held by an overwhelming majority of the Constitutionalists of Lower Canada" (*HA*, 26 September 1835). Before leaving the *Herald*, a disenchanted Thom wrote: "[…] we had almost resolved to let the good folks of Montreal make out their own case in their own way, for, with certainly one exception and perhaps two or three others, they have met our public labours of the last three years and upwards with nothing but discouragement and neglect" (*HA*, 7 July 1838).

48. Irishman or someone who provokes riots.

49. Incomplete quote from R. R. Madden, M. D., *A Twelvemonth's Residence in the West Indies, during the Transition from Slavery to Apprenticeship; with incidental notices of the State of Society, Prospects, and Natural Resources of Jamaica and other Islands*, vol. I, London, James Cochrane and Co., Waterloo Place, 1835, 273. The sentence goes on after "galley-wasp": " — a press, that can so exaggerate the idea of its natural dimensions as to diminish its powers by the very effort it makes to enlarge its volume, but that fortunately scatters its venom on all sides with such lavish prodigality, that no individual is injured by its virus." In a note, the author quotes several respected Jamaican newspapers.

50. See Louise-Crête-Bégin, "Charles-Christophe Malhiot," *DCB*.

51. Thom emphasized this passage. Making the *Canadiens* inevitably into a minority through massive immigration from the British Isles was at the heart of the Tory plan for legislative union. See among others the devastating report of the tandem Moffatt-Badgley in March 1837 in Deschamps, 2015a, 52-54, as well as Belich, 2009, "Canada Boom."

52. See in Letter L what Thom says about the threats of a popular uprising by the man who became Gosford's *eminence grise*, P.D. Debartzch. In October 1837, in Montreal, in the parades, the Fils de la Liberté proudly

carried the Tricolour flag to the horror of the "young men" of the Doric Club: "On Monday evening last, a *pro re nata* meeting has held by a few of the young men in this city who are determined to use their best exertions to crush the incipient symptoms of rebellion displayed by the "Sons of Liberty," and to trample in the dust the tricolored flag should they again have the temerity to carry it through the streets" (*HA*, November 4 1837).

53. Lamonde, Larin, 1998, 251-288 and Sicotte, 2016.

54. See Stuart, 1824, Deschamps, 2015a and 2015b and the quote in the *Minerve* in Letter XX where the link between political independence and saving "our nationality" is established.

55. Thom would have the chance to rethink his judgment: "Disguise not the fact, that the whole country is in a state of rebellion; when we say the whole country, we know what we are saying: — it is not necessary to prove our words that each village should be stockaded as was St. Charles, or garrisoned as was St. Denis, — it is sufficient for us to know that one spirit animates the French Canadian peasantry, from Kamouraska to Coteau-du-Lac" (*HA*, 9 December 1837). Until the real recourse to arms, Thom would waver between alarmism and provocative bravado.

56. Thom's remarks are aimed particularly at P. D. Debartzch. See Letter L.

57. A variant of the garrison mentality. The Tories have the impression they live "in the midst of a foreign and hostile population, and that watchfulness and discipline are strongly recommended" (*HA*, 14 December 1837). At the 1839 St. George's Society activities at the Orr Hotel, before a large group of senior officers—including Major General Clitherow, a new and distinguished member of the masonic lodge St.Paul who presided over the Court Martial and of the garrison and Colonel G. A. Wetherall, "the *Savior* of Canada" (*HA*, 11 May 1838)—, the president of the Society, George Moffatt, proposed to modify the toast "the land we live in." The reason for doing so was interpreted by the journalist from the *Herald*: "while martial law was in existence, and the majority of the population was decidedly hostile to the Government and the prosperity of the country, he could not, with consistency, propose "the land we live in," but would give in its stead (…) the loyal Volunteers of the land we live in, three times three. […]."

58. Mill, 1838, notes that a quarter of its 88 members are English-speaking.

59. See Peter Burrows, *DCB*, "John Arthur Roebuck." He was a salaried spokesman of the Patriote Party at Westminster; during his mandate as member for the riding of Bath (1832-1838), he published T. Falconer *Orange Societies* (London: John Longlay, 1835), republished in Pamphlets for the People (2V, London: Charles Ely, 1835) and published again his own work *Remarks on the Proposed Union of the Canadas* [1822], 1836. H. S. Chapman was a close collaborator of Roebuck. See Woollacott, 2015.

60. "I have not taken by violence, but received." All taken together: Governor Gosford is as guilty as the Secretary of State for the Colonies (S. Rice).

61. F. Bond Head, *HA*, 15 August 1839.

62. Debartzch and company who abandoned Papineau to support the policy of conciliation.

63. A local variant of the frontier in fashion at that time in the Midwest; see Patricia Nelson Limerick, *The Legacy of Conquest: The Unbroken Past of the American West*, New York, W.W. Norton & Co., 1987 and M. Crouzet, *Stendhal et l'Amérique*, 1. *L'Amérique et la modernité*, Paris, éditions de Fallois, 2008.

64. Rearguard action. In the wake of the Reform Bill of 1832, the trio of "King, Lords & Commons" is replaced by a structure comprising another trio: electoral body, Communes, Cabinet; see F. M. Greenwood, 1979, M. Gauchet, 1995, Deschamps, 2011, 96-100 and 2015a, 2-3; the disastrous consequences of such a transfer of legitimacy towards the modern parliamentary democracy did not escape the Tories; see Letter XXXIV.

65. "Unity in a phalanx creates a shield."

66. It should be remembered that the policy of conciliation was devised to divide the Patriote camp into moderate and radical branches. Similarly, it aimed to divide those of British in the Constitutional Association of Montreal.

67. In fact no riot occurred following this election. Warned by excited Tory magistrates, the soldiers commanded by Colonel Macintosh shot three innocent *Canadiens* who happened to be walking by on Saint-Jacques (St. James). See Jackson, 2009. Reference to the shooting of 21 May1832 was still very much alive in the minds of the Tory militia in 1837, as the song attributed to Isaac Valentine illustrates: "*On the Twenty first of May, boys/ Now more than twice two years,/They* [Papineau and its Clique] *first became acquainted/With the British Grenadiers;/Then fill a glass of Farintosh/And let us give three cheers,/For the gallant Colonel M'Intosh/And the Fifteenth Grenadiers,*" *HA*, 5 July 1837.

68. Allusion to the possible involvement of the army in civic affairs as would in fact be the case during the carefully orchestrated riot of 6 November 1837 in Montreal.

69. Greenwood, 2002, 279-352.

70. See Deschamps, 2015a and Letter XXXVII.

71. Illustrious soldier whose heroic death propelled him among the great English officer like Cook and Wolfe. A column was erected to honour him in 1809 on Place Jacques-Cartier in Montréal. The one in Trafalgar Square was only erected thirty years later. The Nelson column in Dublin, also erected in 1809, was blown up by Irish Republicans in March 1966. Nelson

is also known to this day as the "Butcher of Naples" for his actions against the short-lived republic of Naples in 1800.

72. England is paradoxically the agent of destruction, transformation, and conservation of communities. See for example the case of Bengal, Chatterjee, 2011. For a general overlook, see Dorsett and McLaren, 2014.

73. "Contradictions in policy were exposed at the battle of Navarino (October 1827) when Vice-Admiral Edward Codrington, leading a combined force of British, French, and Russian vessels, destroyed a Turkish-Egyptian fleet. This satisfactorily advanced the cause of Greek independence, but the damage to Turkey worked to Russia's advantage." See Hilton, 2006, 378, n. 28 and https://en.wikipedia.org/wiki/Battle_of_Navarino.

74. http://www.thebookofdays.com/months/sept/3.htm

75. https://en.wikipedia.org/wiki/Guy_Fawkes_Night

76. Opposing the concept of cultural homogeneity, Defoe, in *The True-Born Englishman*, subscribes to the notion of the mixed ancestry of the English: "Thus from a Mixture of all kinds began,/That Het'rogeneous Thing, *An Englishman*:/In eager Rapes, and furious Lust begot,/Betwixt a Painted *Britton* and a *Scot*:/Whose gend'ring Offspring quickly learnt to bow,/And yoke their Heifers to the *Roman* Plough:/From whence a Mongrel half-bred Race there came,/With neither Name nor Nation, Speech or Fame./In whose hot Veins now Mixtures quickly ran,/Infus'd betwixt a *Saxon* and a *Dane*. While their Rank Daughters, to their Parents just,/Receiv'd all Nations with Promiscuous Lust./This Nauseous Brood directly did contain/The well-extracted Blood of *Englishmen* . . .." Quoted in Anderson, 2006, *x*.

77. *Canadien* newspaper published by Ludger Duvernay.

78. *Canadien* newspaper owned by the Seigneur Debartzch.

79. http://www.westpoint.edu/history/sitepages/napoleonic%20wars.aspx

80. Greenwood, 1992.

81. See Introduction, 38-39.

82. "From one learn to know all."

83. Joseph de Maistre, *Du Pape*, II, 7 (1819).

84. As can be seen, Thom uses the same language against his opponent.

85. Deschamps, 2015a, 116-120.

86. British-American Land Company. See Little, 2008.

87. "Something of the nature of this political love can be deciphered from the ways in which languages describe its object: either in the vocabulary of kinship (motherland, *Vaterland, patria*) or that of home *(heimat* or *tanah air* [earth and water, the phrase for the Indonesians' native archipelago]). Both idioms denote something to which one is naturally tied. As we have seen earlier, in everything 'natural' there is always something unchosen. In this way, nation-ness is assimilated to skin-colour, gender, parentage and

birth-era - all those things one can not help. And in these 'natural ties' one senses what one might call 'the beauty of *gemeinschaft*'. To put it another way, precisely because such ties are not chosen, they have about them a halo of disinterestedness."(Anderson, 1998, 143). Closing in on and encircling of *Canadien* peasants in the seignories and their being blocked from expanding west. See A. Greer, 1998 and Letter L.

88. Lamonde and Larin, 1998, 325-356.

89. Horace, *Satires*, I, 10: "that of the bilingual people of Canusium."

90. Voltaire seems to be the author of this quote : "*Les Français seront toujours moitié tigres et moitié singes. Ils se réjouissent également à la Grève et aux grands danseurs de cordes aux boulevards.*" See, *Œuvres complètes*, 1838, 403.

91. Paraphrase of "Egyptian servitude" inspired by Adam Lymburner: "if the Province is to be divided, and the old System of Laws continued, if it is expected that either Part of the Province, separated as proposed in the Bill, shall in its present exhausted and impoverished State [...] the Supplies for the whole Expenses of the Government – it will be reducing the Province to a Situation as bad as the Children of Israel in Egypt, when they were required to make Bricks without Straw" (1791, 31-32).

92. Notions of heredity and trans-generational solidarity are common to all nationalism.

93. Earlier that year Thom had developed this notion: "A despotic majority is not subject to any one of the ordinary checks of monarchical despotism, such as law, conscience, public opinion, and physical resistance" (*HA*, 21 February 1835); and in June: "as the supremacy of the revolutionary faction would be tantamount to a dismemberment of the empire, it would force on the constitutionalists a virtual separation from the mother country, and leave them, therefore, Hobson's choice of physical resistance on their own account to an unprincipled and oppressive majority" (*HA*, 26 June 1835).

94. Once again it can be seen that "Canadians" = French-Canadians.

95. See Copy of a Dispatch from the Earl of Gosford to Lord Glenelg, dated Castle of Sr. Lewis, Quebec, 12 November 1835 included in Papers Relative to the Affairs of Lower Canada. (Presented to Parliament by His Majesty's Command.) Ordered by the House of Commons, to be Printed, 20 February 1837. Online: http://static.torontopubliclibrary.ca/da/pdfs/37131055459416d. pdf

96. Deschamps, 2015a, "*Antagonisme ethnoculturel et dynamique triangulaire*", 103-130.

97. A Conservative paper published from 1805 to 1903 whose founder and publisher at that time was Thomas Cary. Curiously, Nabokov in *Lolita* gives some amusing developments to this paper.

98. Thom once again uses the epithet "Canadian."

99. Deschamps 2015a, 34. The expression appears often in *The Wealth of Nation*, 1776, by Adam Smith.

100. The first, being E. B. O'Callaghan, 1797-1880, publisher of the *Vindicator*, freemason and member of the Grand Lodge of Montreal in 1828 where he rubbed shoulders with McCord, McGill, J. Molson, Badgley, and many more; the second "renegade" being James Leslie, 1786-1873, businessman. Concerning the masonic connection, see the list of the members of St. Paul's lodge in the 1830's from official sources in Deschamps, 2015, Annexe A, 253-255.

101. "Britons, attend: be worth like this approv'd,/ And show you have the virtue to be mov'd"; See http://www.bartleby.com/203/46.html

102. Prime Minister in 1835 before the Whig-Radical coalition led by Lord Melbourne returned to power thus signifying the end of Royal prerogative and the supremacy of the Imperial parliament.

103. Downing Street was the seat of the Colonial Office at that time and not the Prime Minister's residence as it is today.

104. On this point and on many others, Lord Durham in his report comes across simply as an officer carrying out the Ultra-Tory program.

105. See Montesquieu, *L'esprit des lois*, XIV, 13: "*Effets qui résultent du climat d'Angleterre.*"

106. Reference to William the Conqueror. Flagrant anachronism: the English vernacular had yet to develop in the 11th century. Benedict Anderson (1991) writes: "English history textbooks offer the diverting spectacle of a great Founding Father whom every schoolchild is taught to call William the Conqueror. The same child is not informed that William spoke no English, indeed could not have done so, since the English language did not exist in his epoch; nor is he or she told 'Conqueror of what?'. For the only intelligible modern answer would have to be 'Conqueror of the English,' which would turn the old Norman predator into a more successful precursor of Napoleon and Hitler. Hence 'the Conqueror' operates as the same kind of ellipsis as 'la Saint-Barthelemy,' to remind one of something which it is immediately obligatory to forget. Norman William and Saxon Harold thus meet on the battlefield of Hastings, if not as dancing partners, at least as brothers" (201).

107. On the two "classic" models, see Kumar, 2012.

108. Maréchal Michel Ney, shot 7 December 1815.

109. 21 August, 1765-20 June 1837; See https://en.wikipedia.org/wiki/William_IV_of_the_United_Kingdom

110. Reference is to Canada Revenue Act de 1831; See D.-B. Viger in Martin, 1834, Durham, [1839], 1912, II, 141-142, as well as Ducharme, 2010, 211.

111. 1 May, 1769-14 September 1852. Wellington is one of the heroes of the young gentlemen of the Doric Club who propose a toast to him at the well-heeled public banquet in January 1837: "The Duke of Wellington and the

254 · The Prophetic *Anti-Gallic Letters*

House of Lords, the citadel of British Liberty – Three times three. Song, The old English gentleman" (*HA*, 31 January 1837).

112. Axel Oxenstierna, 1583-1654: "with how little wisdom the world is governed!"

113. 1783, Declaratory Act; see Viger in Martin, 1834.

114. See https://en.wikipedia.org/wiki/Daniel_O%27Connell

115. https://en.wikipedia.org/wiki/Royal_Military_Academy,_Woolwich

116. See Deschamps, 2015a, "*Une orange britannique*" (153-187) based among other documents on the *Select Committee Report into the Origin, Nature, Extent, and Tendency of the Orange Institutions in Great Britain and Colonies* (1835).

117. See Fyson, 2006 and 2015.

118. https://en.wikipedia.org/wiki/John_Russell,_1st_Earl_Russell

119. See Hogg, 1835.

120. On the notion of "neutrality" between the two rival parties on social struggles, see Introduction, 24-25.

121. https://en.wikipedia.org/wiki/Charles_Grant,_1st_Baron_Glenelg

122. "Men of the Twilight of the moon."

123. This is a favourite turn of phrase taken from *Lochiel's Warning* (1802), a ballad by Thomas Campbell (1777-1844). It appears regularly in the *Montreal Herald* throughout the period 1835-1840.

124. Elzéar Bédard (1789-1849), son of Pierre-Stanislas Bédard and Luce Lajus. Said to be the author of the 92 resolutions. See *Dictionnaire des parlementaires du Québec*, 1792-1992, Bibliothèque de l'Assemblée nationale, Sainte-Foy, 1993.

125. See "Chief Justice John Marshall and the Origins of Judicial Review," in Gordon S. Wood, 2011, 433-468.

126. Robert Weir and the young bucks in the Doric Club hit on the same point: "if deserted by the British Government and the British people, rather than submit to the degradation of being subjects of a French Canadian republic we are determined by our own right arms to work out our deliver[a]nce from the galling yoke" (*HA*, 21 March 1836). These strong supporters of the imperial link have a plan B in mind.

127. The retrospective testimony by Francis Bond Head in 1839 quoted in the Introduction is in perfect synchronism with what Thom says here. The democratic conspiracy controlled by the puppet masters of Downing Street as imagined by the "High Flown Tories" is a self-fulfilling prophecy.

128. The long quote from John Adams is taken from a 1787 document; See http://press-pubs.uchicago.edu/founders /print_documents/v1ch2s12.html

129. Publisher of the *Mercurius Politicus* (1650). Also written "Nedham." See N. H. Keeble, 2001 et https://en. wikipedia.org/wiki/Marchamont_Nedham.

130. Richard Price, 1777, *Additional Observations on the Nature and Value*

of Civil Liberty, and the War with America, http://www.constitution.org/price/price_4.htm; on Price see also https://en.wikipedia.org/wiki/RichardPrice

131. Adams's point of view is close to the criticism of the anthropology of interest in Hume; See Raynaud, 2013, 100-107.

132. See Pocock, [1975], 2003, "The Eighteenth-Century Debate. Virtue, Passion and Commerce," 462-505.

133. That how the "renegades" O'Callaghan and Leslie are perceived. See Letter XXIII, n. 100.

134. 14 February 1755-7 April 1831; https://en.wikipedia.org/wiki/Henry_Phipps,_1st_Earl_of_Mulgrave

135. 2 *Samuel*, 12:7.

136. Lord Aylmer's reputation was sullied because of the cover-up of the military shooting of 21 May 1832.

137. Lamonde, Larin, 1998, 382-416.

138. Deschamps, 2015a, 110-116.

139. Sir George Gipps. Curtis, 2015: "Gosford and Gipps shared a position in which the best course was to pursue the substance of the 1828 Canada Committee's recommendations, without making any fundamental constitutional changes."

140. The Radical-Whig coalition in Westminster did not reject the idea of sharing British citizenship with, and virtually extending the modern democratic principle to, the various national communities in the empire. Thom's position is similar to that of 'Loyal Scotchman': "If numbers are to determine the future condition of a British subject leaving his native country for the Colonies encouraged by the Government, why is not the principle carried out in the other British Colonies. — We do not hear of a British subject on his arrival in the East Indies being compelled to adopt the laws and customs of the Parsees or Hindoos, or when he goes to the Cape of Good Hope that he must become a Hottentot. And then in the West Indies, the slave population is by far the most numerous, and the blacks might possibly prefer their condition of slavery to the freedom that has been offered to them — and who shall say that the weight numbers ought not in their case to prevail as much as with the French Canadians — and that they should not be permitted to say to the British emigrant arriving on their shores — if you remain here you must adopt such laws and customs and form of government as we choose to impose upon you" (*HA*, 31 October 1837). On this point, see the quote from Lord Palmerston in 1850 in Kumar, 2012, 94.

141. The *Morning Courier*; on its publisher, Christopher Dunkin, See Curtis, 2012, 352-355.

142. *Morning Courier*, October 30, 1835.

143. *Morning Courier*, November 13, 1835.

144. *Ibid.*

145. *Ibid.*

146. https://en.wikipedia.org/wiki/Andrew_Jackson

147. *Ibid.*

148. Two leading figures in the Constitutional Association of Montreal sitting on the Legislative Council. They preside respectively over the St. George's Society and the St. Andrew's Society.

149. He alludes here to the dissolution of the Constitution, recourse to arms, and to the conditions for implementation of martial law. See in particular, Fecteau, 2002 and, in the American context, Barbisan and Bonafé, 2011.

150. 22 October 1770-21 March 1838. Head of the Natural History Society where members of the St. Paul Lodge met sometimes. The Tories yearned for the old days and Dalhousie's paternal administration: "Were we under the vigorous administration of a man like Lord Dalhousie, we should have had a few of the leading rebels hanged by this time as high as Haman [*Esther*, 7:6-10], and the Province would be in a state of peace and tranquility" (*HA*, 28 October 1837). On the crisis of 1827, See particularly G. Gallichan, 2013 et Dessureault, 2007.

151. He was still in charge of the Royal Mail in August 1837: "We have been informed, that the tenth letter of L. M. N. has been printed in town on a separate sheet of paper in French and English, and has been extensively circulated through the province. We wonder if they were allowed to go through the Post Office free; if so, Mr. Stayner ought to look into the matter. Our readers will recollect that the letter alluded to attempts to instruct the Canadians how to raise barricades, and how to organize the whole machinery of bush fighting" (*HA*, 4 August 1837).

152. On the "democratic conspiracy," see Introduction.

153. Another name of the House of Assembly of Lower Canada.

154. Allusion to Virgil, *Aeneid*, VI, 417: Merriam-Webster "a concession or bribe to conciliate a person otherwise liable to be troublesome."

155. Attribution unknown. The article was reproduced in *The People's Press*, Gettysburg, Pennsylvania, 20 November, 1835; See https://www.newspapers.com/newspage/37112436/

156. Martin Van Buren, Vice President of the United States from 1833 to 1837, then President 1837-1841.

157. Shakespeare, *Hamlet*, I, V, 108.

158. https://en.wikipedia.org/wiki/On_the_Crown

159. Lord Gosford: "In 1835 he was created Baron Worlingham, of Beccles in the County of Suffolk, in the Peerage of the United Kingdom, which gave him and his descendants an automatic seat in the House of Lords." See https://en.wikipedia.org/wiki/Earl_of_Gosford.

160. "And now justice returns, honored rules return (or return of Saturn's reign);" Virgil, *Ecloge*, IV, 6.

161. *Et Thybrim multo spumantem sanguine cerno*; "I see the Tiber foaming with much blood"; Virgil, *Aeneid*, VI, 87.

162. Jacques Viger. see http://www.biographi.ca/en/bio/viger_jacques_8E. html.

163. Allusion to the "cabinet of all the talents" (1806-1807) under Lord Grenville, the man who conceived the Constitutional Law of 1791. See https:// en.wikipedia.org/wiki/William_Grenville,_1st_Baron_Grenville #The Ministry_of_All_the_Talents.2C_February_1806_.E2.80.93_March_1807

164. Reference to the statue of Wolfe of Montcalm burning their flags. "Immediately before leaving the colony, Dalhousie presided at a ceremony for placing the top stone on a monument to James Wolfe and Louis-Joseph Marquis de Montcalm. Erected in a prominent position near the Château Saint-Louis, overlooking the river, this memorial, which Dalhousie considered "Wolfe's monument," had been an enthusiasm of the earl's, completed with his own subscription to compensate for Canadian indifference." See Peter Burrows, "George Ramsey, 9th Lord of Dalhousie," *DCB*.

165. 14 June, 1807.

166. Robert Weir, owner of the *Montreal Herald*, would repeat this prophetic statement: "His Lordship of Gosford did certainly open a brilliant career for Sir John Colborne, and both he and the Earl of Durham must quail before the eagle eye of Baron Seaton, when meeting him on an equality in the House of Peers, of which he is a worthy member, at the expense of the imbecility of the one and the moral cowardice of the other, as was well expressed in a verse we quote from memory, 'And when again against the Queen/ Dark hearted rebels rush,/ Who'd change the glow on Colborne's brow / For Durham's shame dyed blush!' From all appearances we fear that, in the latter part of the above extract, Camillus will be mistaken, and that both the second and third conquests of the Canadas, achieved under the superintendence of Sir John Colborne, will yet be characterised, "like the shock of nations at Friedland," as battles won but victories lost, for the dearly bought lessons of conciliatory experience seem [not] to have been thrown away, and traitors are honored and rewarded for their treason while loyalists are punished for" (*HA*, 21 March, 1840).

167. In running public affairs, the governor is assisted by an executive council (comparable to the Privy Council in English and not to the cabinet or the "ministry" as such), whose number of members was set a nine in Lower Canada according to the instructions the Colonial office gave Lord Dorchester in September 1791. The dilemma of ministerial responsibility began with the imbroglio over the appointment of the member Dominique

258 · The Prophetic *Anti-Gallic Letters*

Mondelet to the Executive Council in 1833. See Elizabeth Gibbs, "Dominique Mondelet," *DCB*.

168. The reference is to Judge Joseph Story, whose *Commentaries on the Constitution of the United States* (Boston, Cambridge, 1833) are quoted in G. Bowyer, Philadelphia T. & J. W. Johnson, Law Booksellers, 1854, 273-275. The author submits that recourse to "congresses" should be exceptional in a constitutional monarchy. Thom rehashes an earlier Anti-Bureaucrat editorial that included a long quote from Judge story; See *Remarks*, 1835, 27-34.

169. Wolfred Nelson? Henry Samuel Chapman, "What is the result of the elections? &c. Lower Canada, 1834, *The Montreal daily transcript and commercial advertiser*, McGill University, AP5 M 57, 410;"Progress of event in Canada," The Westminster Review, 26 (1837), 468-482; An Impartial and Authentic Account of the Civil War in the Canadas, London: J. Saunders, Jr., 1838. On Chapman, see Woollacott, 2015.

170. In passing, Thom evokes the chronic problem of the weakness of the government's executive branch in a colonial perspective.

171. Here Thom focuses on the imperial administration's Achilles' heel. M. Martin writes that the promoters of ministerial responsibility in Canada "in order, as it is supposed, to assimilate the colonial government to that of England," neglect to consider the essential difference between the executive in the imperial government and the executive in the colonial government: "that the former must of necessity have a control over the latter so long as they maintain towards each other their relative positions of protecting and protected states" (1837, 67). As with Arlequin, the members of the executive under the Union (1841-1867) must serve two masters, the Secretary for the Colonies and the electoral body in their ridings.

172. Virgil, *Georgics*, II, 490: "*Blessed* is *he* who *has succeeded* in *learning* the *laws* of *nature's* working."

173. Paul, *Epistle to the Corinthians*, XV, 33.

174. See Jacques L'Heureux, "Hugues Heney," *DCB*.

175. Étienne Parent.

176. An equivalent to "appeal to the sword" in Letters XXXIV; XXXV; XXXVI.

177. The theme of "cannibalism" reappears in the columns of the *Herald*: "The English inhabitants of this province" will no longer submit to an "experiment," of which every step has been begun, continued and matured at their expense. They will no longer endure to be the victims, from whom pounds of flesh are to be periodically extracted for the speculative purpose of making out "a strong case" of cannibalism against the revolutionary ruffians. They must command the imperial cabinet at its peril to abandon the maxim *Fiat experimentum in corpore vili*. To dissolve the existing legislature,

merely that the ignorant electors of French origin might have the opportunity of returning the same disturbers of the public peace, the same slanderer of every public officer, the same insulters of the imperial authorities, the same oppressors of their English fellow-subjects, would be the sure method of alienating the affections of every Englishman of spirit, probity or intelligence. The legislature must be dissolved; but, before another be called together, the constitution must be amended" (*HA*, 8 April, 1836). And at least two more times in 1838: "[...] even at this juncture, there [is] contemporaries to be found who ring, word of conciliation as hard as ever. What do those people mean, what is their object? do they think the British inhabitants of Lower Canada are Cannibals, and that, unless the government interpose its protecting shield, the French will be massacred that they may ban[quet] on their flesh and blood!" (*HA*, 2 April, 1838); "[...] though members of the British Government and of the British Parliament have stigmatised the Volunteers as bloodthirsty, the truth will triumph at last, and they will yet receive that need of credit which is their due, for the loyalty and humanity they have exhibited, and the suffering and sacrifices they have patiently endured. Because they were urgent in their demands to be enrolled to protect their lives and properties, and to preserve the connection of the colony with their fatherland, a Whig Lording accused them of ferocity against the rebels, almost amounting to cannibalism, and because they were a little awkward in some military manœuvres [...]" (*HA*, 1 May, 1838). On this theme, see the meticulous analysis of Shakespeare's *Coriolanus* by Cavell, 1983.

178. Papineau had fully understood the nature of this "elective attraction". Here we get to the heart of the "garrison mentality" analysed until 1815 by F.M. Greenwood. In a letter to Roebuck, Papineau wrote on March 13, 1836: "Sir Charles [Grey] [...] is but the passive instrument, as you all are [Elliott, Gosford, Gipps], if the old oligarchy [the Sewell brothers], J. Richardson, W. Robertson, G. Moffatt and P. McGill]," who uses the military to get around you and make you adopt the old routine;" see Papineau, 2006, 329, Knox, 1795 and Letters V and XLVIII.

179. Francis Bacon, 1561-1626; see http://www.iep.utm.edu/bacon/.

180. See Richard Chabot, "Édouard-Étienne Rodier," *DCB*. On news of his death, the following note, likely penned by the owner of the *Herald*, appeared: "As Dr. Johnson loved a good hater, so do we admire an honest rebel, however much we may be opposed to him. We formerly expressed our opinion on this subject in noticing the decease of Mr. Rodier [...]" (*HA*, 2 April, 1840).

181. The reference is to P. D. Debartzch and E. Bédard respectively, which is a clear indication of the erroneous lumping together by Thom of Papineau's

Patriote Party and those he called "Anti-British lip-loyalists" (*HA*, 9 December, 1837).

182. See Claude Vachon, "George Vanfelson," *DCB*.

183. Boston, New England, 1767.

184. Not to be confused with the youngest son of his brother, Jonathan Sewell Sr., "a prominent loyalist who was the last British attorney general of Massachusetts"; See F. Murray Greenwood, *DCB*.

185. Lieutenant Colonel, Assistant Adjutant General.

186. See above, Letters III and XVIII.

187. The conflict centred on the attributes of the House of Assembly. In reaction to an article in the *Vindicator*, Thom concluded: "the quotation from the constitutional history of England, that forms part of the article in the *Vindicator*, is fatal to the conclusions of the writer. The powers of the house are limited to "any purposes of their constitutional duties." Let the Assembly have the full benefit of a similar privilege. Did the bill, on which Mr. Jessop's evidence was to bear, fall within the limits of the "constitutional duties" of the Assembly? If not, the analogy is clearly fatal. It falls to the ground, and, muddy as are our streets, carries the Assembly's partisans along with it" (*KMH*, n.d.).

188. "Nip it in the bud," as Sewell put it to the grand jury in 1812. The Doric Club rally around the same motto during the riot of 6 November 1837 with the appeal to "crush the rebellion in the bud."

189. The inquiries conducted by the majority party, as with the inquest into the military shooting of May 21 1832, were clearly constitutional inasmuch as they concerned exclusively the internal affairs of the colony.

190. See Evelyn Kolish, "James Stuart," *DCB*.

191. See J. C. Bonenfant, "Samuel Gale," *DCB*.

192. See Bolingbroke, 1738, *The Idea of a Patriot King*, https://www.google.ca/?gws_rd=ssl#q=patriot+king+ bolingbroke and Armitage, 1997.

193. Another allusion to the military shooting of 21 May 1832.

194. Prototype of the ritual around deployment of the army in civilian affairs such as the planned riot of 6 November 1837 in the streets of Montreal, which is a perfect illustration: under the pretext of protecting Papineau from the unbridled hoard of demonstrators, the officers a few streets away ignored the orders of the French-speaking magistrates and allowed the rioters of the Doric Club to ransack the presses of the *Vindicator*. On the double dealing of the military following proclamation of Martial Law in the District of Montreal during the ambush in Longueuil on 18 November 1837, see Deschamps, 2015, 209-215.

195. In the Tories' eyes, Papineau is a coward. "Hampden's" attack on 14 October 1837 provides a good example of this. "Hampden" also refers to the

tumultuous election of November 1834 in the West Ward: "The coward Papineau, whose nose and seat of honour were so unceremoniously visited by the hand and foot of the late Honorable Mr. Muir, this miserable wretch who submitted when a young man to such an insult, had the hardihood, (the blustering poltroon,) to charge the English merchants and lawyers of Montreal, with being unable, through cowardice, to face the rough-handed artisans of the clique. He made that charge in his celebrated West Ward Address! He make that charge! the leprous coward! not a drop of chivalric blood can there be in his veins, or he never could have survived the infamy of the hour when his nose spouted forth blood under the sinewy strength of Mr. Muir." (See Kadwell n.d.).

196. The prophetic vision of Thom comes clear as he foretells the thesis defended by Creighton [1937], 1970. Montreal is at the geopolitical heart of the struggle for domination between the two founding national communities. In the century that would follow, the entire British North America would develop around it. Recourse to violence and savage military repression would bring about the annexation of Lower Canada and the indefinite strangling of the House of Assembly of Quebec, whose "days are counted" prophesied the author of the article in the *Blackwood Magazine* of June 1835. See Letter VI and note 41.

197. John Molson Jr. had basically written the same thing a year earlier: "Numbering in our ranks many who, both in Britain and Ireland, were foremost in the cause of reform; independent in our principles; unconnected with office; of all classes and creeds; bound together by the endearing recollection of a common origin, and the powerful sentiment of a common danger, we are prepared to resist to the uttermost the efforts of a party, which, under the specious guise of a popular institutions, would sever wisdom from power, and respect for His Majesty's Government" (*HA*, 1 January, 1835).

198. The "myrmidons" appears to refer to the municipal policemen under the orders of Mayor Jacques Viger, as suggested by the letter of a leading Ultra-Tory, William Badgley, alias "Civis": "Is your Lordship aware, that subsequently to the election the citizens of Montreal would not tolerate a watchman in the streets for two months, when your friend the mayor had to withdraw his myrmidons, and that, during that period, not one robbery was committed in the city" (*HA*, 21 April, 1836).

199. In the wake of the Gosford on the criminality of the Orange Order in England, O'Callaghan had just published articles in which he revealed the alarming degree of infiltration by the Orange Lodges in the army, civil society and, especially, the Constitutional Association of Montreal. See the quote from O'Callaghan in the Introduction, Deschamps, 2015, Chap. V, "*Une orange britannique*" and Harland-Jacobs, 2013. For the radical Montreal merchants

262 · The Prophetic *Anti-Gallic Letters*

and magistrates, the creation of a *Canadien* Republic on the shores of the St. Lawrence River would automatically result in the "dismemberment of the Empire." This overpowering fear could be described as a "self-fulfilling prophecy." It represents without a doubt the point were the editorial line of the *Montreal Herald* is in lockstep with the Doric Club, the Orange Lodges and the Executive Committee of the CAM. See, for example, the annual report of 1837 signed P. McGill and W. Badgley pleading for "the immediate adoption of the means necessary for crushing the blighting influence of French provincial ascendancy, and for rendering the colony a British province in fact as well as in name, and upon a re-union of this province with Upper-Canada, as the only means for promoting the prosperity of both provinces, of securing their dependence upon the British Government, and of preventing a dismemberment of the Empire" (*HA*, 30 December 1837).

200. A verse attributed to Jonathan Swift.

201. To Viceroy Gosford.

202. About the liberal radical supporters of the Patriote Party in Westminster, the anonymous author of *Blackwood's Magazine* had already referred to it: "Here they publish not, but prefer to work with the mole in the underground burrows of 'secret committees' of the Reformed House."

203. To which De Quincey applied his seal in his famous essay, *The English Mail-Coach*.

204. The example of the monarch.

205. Reference to the sacred individual right of habeas corpus against arbitrary arrest that only can be transgressed under martial law in cases of emergency.

206. William Hoggarth, 1697-1764; see https://en.wikipedia.org/wiki/William_Hogarth.

207. See https://en.wikipedia.org/wiki/George_Hamilton-Gordon,_4th_Earl_of_Aberdeen

208. In the last public statement of the Doric Club, Glenelg, like Melbourne and Brougham, is held to be "one of the sleeping beauties, who were hanged, drawn and burned in Doric Square in the City of Montreal, on the evening of Wednesday, the third day of October, 1838, for *having been* found guilty of High treason to their countrymen in Canada by persecuting the Earl of Durham and acquiring for themselves the enviable title of 'Traitor's friends.'" (*KMH*, n.d.).

209. *Epistles*, VI.

210. Cobbett, *Parliamentary History*, vol. XXXII, 930-944.

211. 1828. See https://en.wikipedia.org/wiki/George_Canning

212. On the wavering of the Montreal Tories on these options up to the annexationist manifesto of 1849, see Deschamps, 2013a.

213. Thom juggled with the idea since at least the Saint-Jean-Baptiste festivities of June 1835: "On this point the past and the present constitute an infallible index of the future. Against such robbery and oppression, what remedy would there be but physical resistance? But, if physical resistance be the only remedy, the constitutionalists ought not to wait, till the triumph of an elective principle shall have invested their revolutionary oppressors with the majesty of legal authority, and hurled down themselves from the proud height of conquerors to the grovelling debasement of slaves" (*HA*, 28 July, 1835).

214. Gosford's Speech from the Throne was a turning point in the division of the generic term "*Canadiens*/Canadians" (which designated until then the descendants of French settlers) and the later invention of the term "French Canadian," which would be used for more than century thereafter. See Deschamps, 2015b.

215. Biblical expression referring to Israel.

216. "In 1835, during the Murrell Excitement, a mob from Vicksburg attempted to expel the gamblers from the city, because the citizens were tired of the rougher element treating the city residents with nothing but contempt. They captured and hanged five gamblers who had shot and killed a local doctor. The historian Joshua D. Rothman calls this event 'the deadliest outbreak of extralegal violence in the slave states between the Southampton Insurrection and the Civil War.'" (https://en.wikipedia.org/wiki/Vicksburg). In a striking about turn, Thom himself proposed in November and December 1837 to "feed the greedy gallows" (*KMH*, n.d.).

217. https://en.wikipedia.org/wiki/Whiteboys.

218. "All that is unknown fascinates."

219. The *Herald* often referred sarcastically to the case of "his Honor the Mayor, Jacques Viger, Esquire, the Hero of Sackett's Harbour, and now Colonel of Militia" (*HA*, 1 February 1838) basing their writings on J. Richardson et Stephen Sewell, *The Letters of Veritas*, 1815. Viger was a captain in the Voltigeurs regiment during the War of 1812.

220. Under the pseudonyme Anti-Bureaucrat, Thom quoted long excerpts from l'*Écho du pays*, a newspaper funded by Debartzch: "*LES CANADIENS COMPRENNENT QUE S'IL Y A DES INCONVENIENS A TIRER L'ÉPÉE, IL Y EN A DE BIEN PLUS GRAVES A LE REDOUTER, ET DE NUISIBLES A LEUR NATIONALITÉ, EN LA LAIS[S]ANT DANS LE FOURREAU*"; and further: "*Des flots de sang couleraient; mais au prix de ce sang les Canadiens gagneraient ils la liberté et la force? Pourquoi non? Seraient-ils aveugles pour ne pas See la lumière qui brille aux Etats-Unis*" (*Remarks*, 1835, 110-111).

221. The Tories were watching the movement of "Captain Charles Clement Sabrevois de Bleury and his Rifle Corps abroad" (*HA*, 27 August 1835).

222. A change of tone occurred with the parades of the Fils de la Liberté in October 1837 as they marched to the sound of *La Marseillaise*. McCord did not forget it. Four months before Colborne took power ("assumption") at the head of the Special Council in February 1838, he evoked "[...] with what deep anxiety did we watch the proceedings of a wilfully blind Executive, ever crying out peace, peace, when there was no peace, — whilst treason openly marched through our streets, and men, self-styled patriots, were permitted, in open day, to drill and organize themselves for the avowed purpose of overthrowing everything we held sacred, whilst the services of our loyal fellow-citizens, eagerly tendered in the hour of need, were not only coldly refused, but their energies attempted to be crushed by *proclamation*, as if there were treason in the offer to defend our country (Cheers.)" (K*MH*, n.d.).

223. The same "strange dilemma" would come to the mind of the author of a short dispatch in June 1839 during the procession of *Fête Dieu*: "During the imposing procession of the *Fete Dieu* on Sunday week, it struck us as an extraordinary circumstance, that so many thousand Canadians should follow the representation of the Host, with heads uncovered and with looks of such apparent devotion, while these same men, several of whom we know to be as rank rebels as breathe, totally and universally disobeyed the strict injunctions of their priests to act as loyal subjects, and have nothing to do with those who are given to change" (*HA*, 11 June, 1839).

224. *Review of the Report made in 1828, by the Canada Committee of the House of Commons.*

225. Among the leaders of the delegation to meet Lord Durham were Peter McGill and George Moffatt, and Judges Gale and Reid. On 13 June 1838, Durham had some comforting words for the "commercial classes": "After having delivered the written answer to the address, his Lordship proceeded to offer, 'most directly,' as he feelingly expressed it, 'from the heart,' his most positive assurances of ample justice to the commercial classes in the province" (K*MH*, 13 June 1838).

226. https://www.google.ca/?gws_rd=ssl#q=Sir+Henry+Parnell.

227. Anti-colonial criticism in England goes back to the 1770s. In addition to Bentham, Adam Smith and Richard Price were associated with it, as was the School of Manchester later in the 1830s. On this point see Bell, 2009, 63-74.

228. The opening with great fanfare of the first railway linking Laprairie and Saint-Jean sur le Richelieu was to take place 21 July 1836. It is credited to the St. Lawrence and Champlain Railroad Company founded in 1832 par the Molson family.

229. The problem concerns the absence for Upper Canada of direct access to the ocean. The demographic and economic interaction between Upper Canada and the State of New York can be perceived in Stuart (1824), but it had grown

by June 1835 in the "Canada Question" article in *Blackwood Magazine*, and in the *Rapport of the Select General Committee of the Constitutionalists of Lower Canada* of November 1836 (See Deschamps, 2015a 41-45 et 2015b).

230. https://en.wikipedia.org/wiki/Nation_of_shopkeepers.

231. Two dates are to be retained here: 1807, which marked the abolition of the slave trade followed by the abolition of slavery throughout the empire in 1833.

232. On India, see, E. Kolsky, 2005 and 2015; for an overview, see Darwin, [2009], 2011.

233. Chateaubriand, *Les martyrs* (1826).

234. Walter Scott, 1771-1832, *The Lay of the Last Minstrel*, Canto VI.

235. A Scotchman quotes the passage from an article in *La Minerve* of 5 October 1835: "Mais, en comparant le sort éprouvé dans les anciennes colonies avec celui réservé en Canada, on ne peut échapper à une réflexion pénible. A New York, c'est un Ecossais qui le premier se dévoue pour le succès des idées liberals, qui appele [ses] concitoyens à la résistance contre l'oppression: en Canada, ce sont les Ecossais qui se montrent les ennemis les plus acharnés des libertés publiques, ce sont eux qui s'érigent en petits potentats et qui prétendent tenir toute une population sous [leur] domination odieuse; leur conduite parmi nous [est] sans doute le résultat d'une opposition de principe[s] religieux, d'une rivalité nationale vis-à-vis d'hommes qu'ils regardent comme n'etant pas du sang [des] Douglas, des Bruce et de tous ces Clans montagnards dont Walter Scott nous a si minutieusement décrit la misère, la brutalité, l'esprit vindicatif, les rapines, la fierté, la bassesse et la nullité, s'il en est ainsi, il est urgent d'en revenir a l'idée qui preside à l'octroi de notre constitution: une séparation entre tout ce qui est Breton et tout ce qui veut [être] Canadien. Jamais les deux origines ne s'amalgameront. Que ceux qui préfèrent les lois anglaises se transportent dans la province voisine […] bienfait leur est assuré ou que ceux dont les […] et les affections sont liés au sol du Bas-Canada s'identifient avec nos bons Jean-Baptistes, [se] considèrent comme leurs égaux, leurs frères. […] donnent franchement la main et travaillent d'un commun accord à la prospérité du pays. […]" (*HA* 12 October 1835).

236. See the twelfth resolution of the paramilitary and clandestine Doric Club (Letter XXX, n. 134).

237. See the eighth resolution of the same assembly of the Doric Club: "That as our sole aim and object is to secure equal rights and privileges to all classes of our fellow-subjects in this province […]." (*HA*, 21 March 1836).

238. *Daniel*, 3:23.

239. http://www.biographi.ca/en/bio/neilson_john_7E.html.

240. Echoes of this can be found in the Annual Report of the CAM of P. McGill and W. Badgley in December 1837: "Since the last Annual General

Meeting of this Association, the Reports of the Royal Commissioners specially appointed for the investigation of grievances affected Her Majesty's
subjects in Lower Canada, in what relates to the administration of the
Government thereof, have been published ; and whilst your Committee, in
common with the generality of the British inhabitants of this province,
deplore the lost of time and waste of money lavished upon their unprofitable
labours, they have like wise to express their deep regret, not only at the
confused and partial views taken by the Commissioners of the real cause of
discontent in the province, "of the extent to which it has a reasonable foundation", and of the inadequate and inefficient remedies proposed by them
for its removal, but also at their disregard of the substantial grounds of
repugnance existing among the different races of the provincial inhabitants,
their neglect of the acknowledged grievances of those inhabitants of British
origin, and the cautious avoidance of their claims for a just participation in
the enjoyment of rights deservedly dear to Englishmen, and their utter
indifference to the important measure of the legislative union of the
Canadas." (*HA*, 31 December 1837).

241. One of the fashionable slogans of the CAM was, "a long pull, a strong
pull, and a pull altogether" (K*MH*, n.d.).

242. Thom keeps driving his point home: "Even up to that [time], nothing
was heard from Governor or government officer but "Conciliation, conciliation, conciliation." – The very word [stin]ks in our nostrils. –" (*HA*, 2 April,
1838). It is hard to understand, in these conditions, how he accepted a sine-
cure from Durham without being himself in some ways venal and
opportunist.

243. *Macbeth*, V, iii, 40.

244. Byron, *Childe Harold's Pilgrimage*, 1, LXXXIV, To "Ines."

245. See William Robertson charge against neutrality in the Introduction,
24.

246. Claude Vachon, "George Vanfelson," *DCB*, http://www.biographi.ca/
en/bio/vanfelson_george_8E.html

247. In collaboration, *DCB*, "Clément-Charles Sabrevois de Bleury" http://
www.biographi.ca/en/bio/sabrevois_de _bleury_ clement_charles_9E.html

248. Renald Lessard, "Louis Gugy," *DCB*, http://www.biographi.ca/en/bio/
gugy_louis_7E.html; Jacques Monet, *DCB*, "Bartolomew Conrad Augustus
Gugy," http://www.biographi.ca/en/bio/gugy_bartholomew_conrad_augus-
tus_ 10E.html

249. Creation of Les Fils de la Liberté in September 1837 resulted in a considerable change of tone concerning the use of physical resistance among
their opponents; see Introduction, 26, n. 10, Letter XI, n. 52 and Letter L,
n. 223.

BIBLIOGRAPHY

Printed Documentary Sources

Agamben, Giorgio. *La guerre civile. Pour une théorie politique de la stasis.* Paris, Éditions Points, 2015.

Assmann, Aleida and Linda Shortt (eds.). *Memory and Political Change.* Basingstoke, Macmillan, 2012.

Blackwood's Edinburgh Magazine, "The Canada question," June 1835 (reproduction, Mackay).

Bernard Jean-Paul (dir.). *Assemblées publiques, résolutions et déclarations de 1837-1838.* VLB Éditeur et Union des écrivains québécois. Montréal, 1986.

Burke, Edmund. *Reflections on the Revolution in France and on the Proceedings in Certain Societies in London Relative to that Event in a Letter Intended to have been sent to a Gentleman in Paris.* London: Dodsley, in Pall-Mall, 1790.

Chapman, H. S. "What is the result of the elections? &c. Lower Canada, 1834, *The Montreal daily transcript and commercial advertiser,* McGill University, AP5 M 57, microfiches 410.

Chapman, H. S. "Progress of event in Canada," *The Westminster Review,* 26 (1837), 468-482.

DCB, http://www.biographi.ca/en/bio.php?id_nbr=5167

Dilke, Charles Wentworth. *Greater Britain: A Record of Travel in the English-Speaking Countries during 1866 and 1867.* London, Macmillan and Co., 1868.

Disraeli, Benjamin. *The Maintenance of Empire.* 1872, http://www.ccis.edu/faculty/dskarr/discussions%20and%20readings/primary%20sources/disraeli,%20speech%201872.htm

Herald Abstract, MIC BAnQ, 1 January 1835 - 22 December 1840.

Hogg, Thomas Jefferson. *Copy of the Protest by Mr. Hogg, one of His Majesty's Commissioners for Inquiring into Municipal Corporations, House of the Commons,* 1835.

Kadwell, Charles. *Canadiana: Or Medley of Sundry Matters in Print and in Manuscript Relating Principally to the Canadas (during the period of the rebellions); the Other British North American Colonies; and the Neighbouring United States, with Views, Plans, Portraits, &c. and Private Sources.* Rare Books and Special Collection Division, McGill University, Ms 255.

Kennedy, W. P. M. (William Paul McClure). *Statutes, treaties and documents of the Canadian constitution, 1713-1929,* 1930.

Knox, Vicesimus. *The Spirit of Despotism.* 1795.

Lucas, Charles Prestwood. *Lord Durham's Report on the Affairs of British North America.* Oxford: Clarendon Press, 1912, 3 vol.

Lymburner, Adam. *Paper read at the Bar of the House of Commons by Mr. Lymburner, 23 March 1791).* Printed by William Moore (Herald Printing Office), Quebec, 1791.

Mackintosh, James, *Vindiciae Gallicae and other Writings on the French Revolution* [1791], http://oll.libertyfund.org/titles/1665.

Martin, Robert Montgomery, "From Montgomery Martin's work on the British Colonies", in Charles Kadwell, Rare Books and Special Collection Division, McGill University.

— *Colonial policy of the British Empire* (London: [s. n.] 1837).

— *History of the British Colonies,* vol. III, London, James Cochrane and Co., 1834.

Mill, John Stuart. "Lord Durham and the Canadians," *London and Westminster Review,* VI & XXVIII (Jan. 1838), 507-12.

Millar, John [1770] 1818. *The Advancement of Manufacture, Commerce and the Arts; and the Tendency of this Advancement to diffuse a Spirit of Liberty and Independence.*

Papers Relative to the Affairs of Lower Canada. (Presented to Parliament by His Majesty's Command.) Ordered by the House of Commons, *to be Printed,* 20 February 1837.

Papineau, Louis-Joseph. *Histoire de l'insurrection au Canada* (1839). Leméac, 1968.

— *Lettres à divers correspondants. Tome I: 1810-1845.* Montréal, Varia, 2006.

Rapport de l'Archiviste du Canada pour 1923; "Correspondance entre Lord Durham et l'ambassadeur anglais à Washington, les lieutenants-gouverneurs des provinces et le gouvernement des Bermudes";

— "Missive secrète et confidentielle de Lord Durham à Lord Glenelg (Château Saint-Louis, Québec, 9 août 1838)."

Report from the Select Committee of the House of Assembly of Upper Canada appointed to report on the State of the Province, 1839. Lande Collection, S 22S0, Rare Books and Special Collections Division, McGill University.

Roebuck, J. A. "Affairs of Canada" (account of the *Report of a Select Committee of the House of Commons on the Affairs of Canada, 1828* and *Statistical Sketches of Upper Canada, 1833*). *The Westminster Review*, 23, (October 1835), 269-291.

Seeley, John Robert. *The Expansion of England*. London: Macmillan & Co., Limited, St. Martin's Street, [1883], 1914.

Sewell, Jonathan. "Plan for A General Legislative Union of the British Provinces in North America." London: Printed by W. Clowes, Northumberland-Court, 1824.

Stuart, James. *Observations on the proposed Union of the Provinces of Upper and Lower Canada under one Legislature*. London: Printed by W. Clowes, Northumberland-Court 1824.

Thom, Adam. *Remarks on the Petition of the Convention, and on the Petition of the Constitutionalists, by Anti-Bureaucrat*. Montreal: Printed at the Herald Office, May 1835.

Viger, Denis-Benjamin. "GRIEVANCES OF LOWER CANADA, BY THE HON. D. B. VIGER, MEMBER OF THE LEGISLATIVE COUNCIL OF THE PROVINCE." in Martin, Montgomery, *History of the British Colonies*, vol. III, *Possessions in North America*. London: James Cochrane and M'Crone, 1834, 577-586.

W[illiam] M[olesworth]. "Orange Conspiracy," *The London and Westminster Review*, 3 (1836), 181-234.

W[illiam] M[olesworth]. "Orange societies in Great Britain – their illegality and criminality," *The London and Westminster Review*, 3/25 (1836) 480-513.

W[illiam] M[olesworth]. "Parliamentary conduct of the Radicals," *The Westminster Review*, 27 (1837), 270-283.

Articles and Books

Anderson, Benedict. *Imagined Communities. Reflections on the Origin and Spread of Nationalism*, London. New York: Verso, [1983], 2006.

Armitage, David. "A Patriot for Whom. The Afterlives of Bolingbroke's Patriot King," *The Journal of British Studies*, 36, 4, 1997, 397-418.

— "Greater Britain: A Useful Category of Historical Analysis?" *The American Historical Review*, 104, 1999, 427-445.

— *The Ideological Origins of the British Empire*. Cambridge; New York, Cambridge University Press, 2000.

— "Empire and Liberty: A Republican Dilemma," in Golderen, Martin van and Quentin Skinner (eds.). *The Values of Republicanism in Early Modern Europe: A Shared European Heritage*, vol. 2, Cambridge, Cambridge University Press, 2003.

Armitage, David and Sanjay Subrahmanyam. *The Age of Revolutions in Global Context, c. 1760-1840*. New York, Palgrave Macmillan, 2010.

Bannister, Jerry and Liam Riordam (eds.). *The Loyal Atlantic. Remaking the British Atlantic in The Idea of the Revolutionary Era*. Toronto, Buffalo, London, University of Toronto Press, 2012.

Barbisan, Benedetta and Beatrice I. Bonafé. "Preventing an Appeal to the Sword:" The Role of the Judiciary in American Federalism and European Integration, *International Journal of Public Administration*, 34, 2011, 123-128.

Bayly, C. A. "The First Age of Global Imperialism," *Journal of Imperial and Commonwealth History*, 26, 2, 1998, 28-47.

— "Rammohan Roy and the Advent of Constitutional Liberalism in India, 1800-30," *Modern Intellectual History*, vol. 4, no. 1, 2007, 25-41.

Belich, James. *Replenishing the Earth. The Settler Revolution and the Rise of the Anglo-World, 1783-1939*. Oxford, Oxford University Press, 2009.

Bell, Duncan. *The Idea of Greater Britain: Empire and the Future of World Order, 1860-1900*. Princeton, NJ, Princeton University Press, 2007.

Bradley, Mark (ed.). *Classics and Imperialism in the British Empire*. Oxford, New York, Oxford University Press, 2010.

Brown, Stewart J. (ed.). *William Robertson and the Expansion of Empire*. New York: Cambridge University Press. 1997.

Buckner, Phillip A. *The Transition to Responsible Government. British Policy in America, 1815-1850*. Westport: Connecticut: Greenwood Press, 1985.

— "Presidential Address: Whatever happened to the British Empire?" *Journal of the Canadian Historical Association/ Revue de la Société historique du Canada*, 4, 1, 1993, 3-32.

Buckner, Philip and Douglas R. Francis (eds.). *Rediscovering the British World*. Calgary, Calgary University Press, 2005.

Buckner, Philip (ed.). *Canada and the British Empire*. Oxford, New York: Oxford University Press, 2008.

— *Remembering 1759. The Conquest of Canada in Historical Memory*. Toronto, Buffalo, London: University of Toronto Press, 2012.

Buckner, Phillip and Bridge, Carl. "Reinventing the British World," *Round table* 368, *Journal of Imperial and Commonwealth History*, 92, 2003.

Buckner, Phillip and Francis, R. Douglas (dir.). *Canada and the British World. Culture, Migration, and Identity.* Vancouver: The University of British Columbia, 2006.

Burroughs, Peter. *British Attitudes Towards Canada, 1822-1849.* Scarborough: Prentice-Hall, 1971.

Canny, Nicholas. "The Ideology of English Colonization: From Ireland to America," *The William and Mary Quarterly*, vol. 30, 4 (Oct., 1973), 575-598.

— "Writing Atlantic History: or, Reconfiguring the History of Colonial British America," *The Journal of American History*, vol. 86, 3, The Nation Beyond: Transnational Perspectives on United States History: A Special Issue (Dec., 1999), 1093-1114.

Cavell, Stanley. "'Who Does the Wolf Love?' Reading Coriolanus," *Representations*, 3, 1983, 1-20.

Chatterjee. "The Curious Career of Liberalism in India," *Modern Historical History*, 8, 3, 2011, 687-696.

Christie, Robert. *A history of the Late Province of Lower Canada parliamentary and political from the commencement to the close of its existence as a separate Province*, vol. 3 and 4. Montreal: Richard Worthington, 1866.

Christie, Nancy (ed.). *Transatlantic Subjects. Ideas, Institutions, and Social Experience in Post-Revolutionary British North America.* Montreal & Kingston: McGill-Queen's University Press, 2008.

Class, Monika and Terry F. Robinson (dir.). *Transnational England: Home and Abroad, 1780-1860*, Cambridge Scholars. Newcastle upon Tyne, 2009.

Colley, Linda. "Whose Nation? Class and National Consciousness in Britain, 1750-1830," *Past and Present*, N° 1113, 1996, 97-117.

— *Britons. Forging the Nation 1707-1837: with a new preface by the author*, London: Pimlico, 2003.

Condon, Ann Gorman. *"The Circuitous Career of Loyalist Plans for Colonial Union in America and Canada, 1754-1914," in* The Treaty of Paris and the International States System: Papers from a conference, January 26-27, Gifford Prosser (ed.), Washington, D.C. and Lanham, MD: University Press of America, 1985.

Cooper, Frederick. "Imperialism and the Victorians: The Dynamics of Territorial Expansion", *English Historical Review*, 112, 1997, 614-642.

Constant, Jean-François and Michel Ducharme (eds.). *Liberalism and Hegemony. Debating the Canadian Liberal Revolution.* Toronto: University of Toronto Press, 2009.

Crouzet, Michel. *Stendhal et l'Amérique, 1. L'Amérique et la modernité.* Paris, éditions de Fallois, 2008.

Creighton, Donald. *The Empire of the St. Lawrence.* Toronto, Macmillan [1956],
1970.

Curtis, Bruce. *Ruling by Schooling Quebec. Conquest to Liberal Governmentality
– A Historical Sociology.* Toronto, Buffalo, London: University of Toronto
Press, 2012.

— "La Commission d'enquête comme réflexivité gouvernementale," *Bulletin
d'histoire politique,* 23, 3, 2015, 21-37.

Darwin, John. *The Empire Project. The Rise and Fall of the British World-System,
1830-1970.* New York, Cambridge University Press, 2009.

Deschamps, François, "Le combat du *Montreal Herald*, organe du Doric Club,"
*1811: de Québec à Montréal, essor de la presse et affirmation d'une parole
publique francophone,* Nova Doyon (ed.). Montréal, Petit musée de l'impression, 2009, 85-119.

— "Le radicalisme *tory* à travers le prisme du *Montreal Herald* et la mobilisation
des milices dans le district de Montréal (1834-1837)," M.A. UQAM, 2011.

— "L'incendie du parlement et le manifeste annexionniste: la face cachée du
torysme montréalais (1832-1849)," *Bulletin d'histoire politique,* 22, 1, automne
2013a, 28-57.

— "La réforme des institutions politiques au Québec (1834-1848): un héritage
contesté," *Bulletin d'histoire politique,* 22, 1, automne 2013b, 93-129.

— *La "rébellion de 1837" à travers le prisme du* Montreal Herald. *La refondation
par les armes des institutions politiques canadiennes.* Québec, PUL, 2015a.

— "La coexistence des communautés canadienne et britannique vue par le
Montreal Herald (1837-1839), *Cap-aux-Diamants,* 21, printemps 2015b, 9-12.

— "1840 et la jonction du discours radical *tory* montréalais avec le libéralisme
impérial anglais," *L'action nationale,* vol. 105, 7-8, septembre-octobre 2015c,
92-109.

Dorsett, Shaunnagh and John McLaren (eds.). *Legal Histories of the British Empire.
Laws, Engagements and Legacies.* Abington and New York, Routledge, 2014.

Dorsett, Shaunnagh and Ian Hunter. *Law and Politics in British Colonial Thought.
Transpositions of Empire.* New York, Palgrave Macmillan, 2010.

Ducharme, Michel. *Le concept de liberté au Canada à l'époque des révolutions
atlantiques, 1776-1838.* Montréal, McGill-Queen's University Press, 2010.

— "Macdonald Roundtable," *The Canadian Historical Review,* 94, 1, 2013, 80-112.

Fecteau, Jean-Marie. "Les dangers du secret: Note sur l'État canadien et les sociétés secrètes au milieu du 19e siècle," *Revue canadienne Droit et Société,* 6 (1991): 91-112.

Fecteau, Jean-Marie, F. Murray Greenwood and Jean-Pierre Wallot. "Sir James Craig's 'Reign of Terror' and Its Impact on Emergency Powers in Lower Canada, 1810-1813", *Canadian State Trials I. Law, Politics, and Security Measures, 1608-1837.* Toronto, Buffalo, London: University of Toronto Press, 1996, 323-378.

Fecteau, Jean-Marie. "'This Ultimate Resource': Martial Law and State Repression in Lower Canada, 1837-1838," *in* Greenwood, F., Murray and Wright, Barry (ed.). *Rebellion and Invasion in the Canadas, 1837-1839. Canadian States Trials, II,* 2002, 207-247.

Fonck, Bertrand and Veyssière, Laurent (dir.). *La guerre de sept ans en Nouvelle-France.* Québec: Septentrion, 2013.

Fyson, Donald, *Magistrates, police and people: everyday criminal justice in Quebec and Lower Canada* (Toronto: Published for the Osgoode Society for Canadian Legal History, University of Toronto Press, 2006).

— "The Canadiens and the Conquest of Quebec: Interpretations, Realities, Ambiguities," in Rudy, Jarrett et al. (ed.). *Quebec Question: Quebec Studies for the Twenty-First Century.* Toronto: Oxford University Press, 2010.

— "La gouvernance municipale avant la municipalité: Montréal, 1760-1840," Léon Robichaud, Harold Bérubé and Donald Fyson (ed.), *La gouvernance montréalaise: de la ville à la frontier.* Montréal, Éditions MultiMondes, 2015, 25-41.

Gallichan, Gilles. "La crise parlementaire de 1827 au Bas-Canada", *Les cahiers des dix,* 66, 2012, 95-166.

Gauchet, Marcel. *La Révolution des pouvoirs. La souveraineté, le peuple et la représentation, 1789-1799.* Paris: Gallimard, 1995.

Gould, Eliga H. "To Strengthen the King's Hands: Dynastic Legitimacy, Militia Reform and Ideas of National Unity in England, 1745-1760," *The Historical Journal,* vol. 34, n° 2, 1991, 329-348.

— "A Virtual Nation: Greater Britain and the Imperial Legacy of the American Revolution," *The American Historical Review,* vol. 104, n° 2 (Apr. 1999), 476-489.

— "Persistence of Empire. British Political Culture in the Age of the American Revolution.* Chapel Hill, N.C: The University of North Carolina Press, 2011.

— "Review of Armitage, David. *The Ideological Origins of the British Empire: Ideas in Context 59.* H-Albion, H-Net Reviews. July 2001.

Greenblatt, Stephen. "Murdering Peasants: Status, Genre, and the Representation of Rebellion," *Representations*, 1, 1989, 1-29.

Greene, Jack P. (ed.). *Exclusionary Empire: English Liberties oversees, 1600-1900*. Cambridge, New York, Cambridge University Press, 2010.

Greenwood, F. Murray. "Les patriotes et le gouvernement responsable dans les années 1830", *Revue d'histoire de l'Amérique française*, 33, 1, 1979, 25-37.

— *Legacies of Fear: Laws and Politics in Quebec in the Era of the French Revolution*. Toronto: The Osgoode Society, 1993.

Greenwood, F. Murray and Wright, Barry. Parliamentary Privilege and the Repression of Dissent in the Canadas, *Canadian State Trials I. Law, Politics, and Security Measures, 1608-1837*. Toronto, Buffalo, London: University of Toronto Press, 1996, 409-449.

— "The General Court Martial at Montreal 1838-9: Operation and the Irish Comparison" in *Canadian State Trials*, vol. II. Osgoode Society and Canadian Legal History, 2002, 279-324.

— "The Montreal Court Martial, 1838-9: Legal and Constitutional Reflections" in *Canadian State Trials*, vol. II. Osgoode Society and Canadian Legal History, 2002, 325-352.

Greer, Allan and Radforth Ian Walter (eds.). *Colonial leviathan: state formation in mid-nineteenth-century Canada*. Toronto, Buffalo: University of Toronto Press, 1992.

Harvey, Louis-Georges. "Une Constitution pour l'Empire: sur les origines de l'idée fédérale au Québec, 1765-1815," *Les cahiers des dix*, n° 66 (2012), 25-54.

Harland-Jacobs, Jessica. ""Maintaining the connexion": Orangeism in the British North Atlantic World, 1795-1844," *Atlantic Studies*, vol. 5, n° 1, (2008), 27-49;

— *"Builders of Empire. Freemasonry and British Imperialism, 1717-1927*, Chapel Hill, N.C, The University of North Carolina Press, 2007.

Hilton, Boyd. *A Mad, Bad, Dangerous People, England, 1783-1846*. Oxford, Oxford University Press, 2006.

Hirschman, Albert O. *The passions and the Interests, Political Arguments for Capitalism before its Triumph.* Princeton, Princeton University Press, [1977], 1997.

Jackson, James. *The Riot That Never Was. The military shooting of three Montrealers in 1832 and the official cover-up.* Montréal: Baraka Books, 2009.

Keeble, N. H. *The Cambridge Companion to Writing of the English Revolution.* Cambridge, Cambridge University Press, 2001.

Knorr, K. E. *British Colonial Theories (1570-1850)*. Toronto: University of Toronto Press, 1944.

Koebner, Richard and Helmut Dan Schmidt. *Imperialism. The Story and Significance of a Political Word, 1840-1960*. Cambridge, Cambridge University Press, 1964.

Koselleck, Reinhart. *Critique and Crisis. Enlightenment and the Pathogenesis of Modern Society*. Cambridge, Massachusetts, [1959], 1988.

Kolsky, Elizabeth. "Codification and the Rule of Colonial Difference: Criminal Procedure in Colonial India," *Law and History Review*, 2005, 23, 3, 631-683.

— "The Colonial Rule of Law and the Legal Regime of Exception: Frontier "Fanaticism" and State Violence in British India," *American Historical Review*, 2015, 120, 4, 1218-1246.

Kumar, Krishan. "Greece and Rome in the British Empire: Contrasting Role Models", *Journal of British Studies*, 2012, 51, 1, 76-101.

Lamonde, Yvan. *Histoire sociale des idées au Québec, 1760-1896*, vol. I. Montréal, Fides, 2000.

— "Britannisme et américanité de Louis-Joseph Papineau à l'époque du deuxième projet d'Union (1822-1823)," *Les Cahiers des dix*, 66, 2013, 55-94.

Leask, Nigel. "Irish Republicans and Gothic Eleutherarchs: Pacific Utopias in the Writings of Theobald Wolfe Tone and Charles Brockden Brown," *Huntington Library Quarterly*, 63, 3, British Radical Culture of the 1790s (2000), 347-367.

Lefebvre, André. Les "Montrealers" et la crise politique du Bas-Canada (juillet 1835-mars 1836), mémoire prédoctoral, s.é., Université de Montréal, 1960.

— *La Montreal Gazette et le nationalisme canadien (1835-1842)*. Montréal, Guérin, 1970.

Limerick, Patricia Nelson. *The Legacy of Conquest: The Unbroken Past of the American West*. New York, W.W. Norton & Co., 1987.

Little, J. I. *Loyalties in Conflict: a Canadian Borderline in War and Rebellion, 1812-1840*. Toronto, Toronto University Press, 2008.

Martin, Ged, *The Durham Report and British Policy. A Critical Essay*, Cambridge, Cambridge University Press, 1972.

— "Empire Federalism and Imperial Parliamentary Union, 1820-1870", *The Historical Journal*, XVI, 1, 1973, 65-92.

— *Britain and the Origins of Canadian Confederation*, UBC Press, 1995. Vancouver, 1995.

Mason, Keith. "The American Loyalist Diaspora and the Reconfiguration of the British Atlantic World" in *Empire and nation: the American Revolution in the Atlantic World*, Eliga H. Gould and Peter S. Onuf (eds.). Baltimore: Johns Hopkins University Press, 2005, 239-259.

McLaren. "The Uses of the Rule of Law in British Colonial Societies in the Nineteenth Century", in Shaunnagh Dorsett and Ian Hunter (ed.), *Law and Politics in British Colonial Thought. Transpositions of Empire*. New York, Palgrave Macmillan, 2010, 71-90.

Montesquieu. *L'esprit des Lois*. Paris, La Pléiade, t. 1, [1748], 1951.

Ormsby, William (ed.). *Crisis in the Canadas: 1838-1839. The Grey Journals and Letters*. London, Macmillan & Co LTD, 1965.

Pigeaud, Jackie. *La crise*. Nantes: éditions Cécile Defaut, 2006.

Pocock, J. G. A. "The Limits and Divisions of British History: In Search of the Unknown Subject," *AHR*, LXXXVII (1982), 311-336.

Pitts, Jennifer *A Turn to Empire: The Rise of Imperial Liberalism in Britain and France*. Princeton: Princeton University Press, 2005.

—   "Empire and Legal Universalisms in the Eighteenth Century," *The American Historical Review*, 117, 1, 2012, 92-121.

Raynaud, Philippe. *Trois révolutions de la liberté. Angleterre, Amérique, France*. Paris, Presses Universitaires de France, 2009.

—   *La politesse des lumières. Les lois, les mœurs, les manières*. Paris, Gallimard, 2013.

Romney Paul. "From the Types Riot to the Rebellion: Elite Ideology, Anti-legal Sentiment, Political Violence, and the Rule of Law in Upper Canada, *Ontario History*, 79, LXXIX, 1987, 115-144.

—   *Getting it Wrong. How Canadians Forgot Their Past and Imperiled Confederation*. Toronto; Buffalo, London, University of Toronto Press, 1999.

Séguin, Maurice. *Histoire de deux nationalismes au Canada*. Montréal, Guérin, 1997.

Senior, Elinor K. *British Regulars in Montreal: An Imperial Garrison, 1832-1854*. Montreal, McGill-Queens University Press, 1981.

—   *Redcoats and Patriotes. The Rebellions in Lower Canada 1837-1838* (Ontario: Canada's Wings, Inc. in collaboration with the Canadian War Museum, National Museum of Man, National Museums of Canada, 1985.

Sicotte, Anne-Marie. *Histoire inédite des Patriotes. Un peuple libre en images*. Fides, 2016.

Skinner, Stephen. "Blackstone's Support for the Militia," *The American Journal of Legal History*, 44, 1 (Jan., 2000), 118.

Smith, Allan. "Seven Narratives in North American History: Thinking the Nation in Canada, Quebec and the United States", in *Writing the Nation. A Global Perspective*, Stefan Berger (ed.). Basingstoke, Palgrave Macmillan, 2007.

Starobinski, Jean. *L'encre de la mélancolie*. Paris, Seuil, 2012.

Taylor, Alan. *The Civil War of 1812. Americans Citizens, British Subjects, Irish Rebels, & Indian Allies*. New York: Vintage Books, 2010.

Tocqueville, Alexis. *De la démocratie en Amérique*. Paris, Gallimard, [1835], 1986.

Tousignant, Pierre. *Documents relatifs au projet d'Union législative du Bas et du Haut-Canada, 1922-1828*. Montréal: La librairie des presses de l'Université de Montréal, 1968.

Vaugeois, Denis, *Québec 1792. Les acteurs, les institutions et les frontiers*. Montréal, Fides, 1992.

Vaughn, Géraldine. Clarisse Berthezene, Pierre Purseigle and Julien Vincent, *Le monde britannique 1815-1931. Historiographie, Bibliographie, Enjeux*. Paris, CAPES Agrégation, 2010.

Watt, Stephen. "State Trials by Legislature: The Special Council of Lower Canada, 1838-1841" in Greenwood, F., Murray and Barry Wright (ed.). *Rebellion and Invasion in the Canadas, 1837-1839. Canadian States Trials*, II, 2002, 248-278.

William, Thomas (dir.). *The Journals of Thomas Babington Macaulay*, vol. 1, 2008.

Wilson Kathleen (ed.). *A New Imperial History. Culture, Identity, and Modernity in Britain and the Empire, 1660-1840*. Cambridge, Cambridge University Press, 2004.

Wood, Gordon S. *Empire of Liberty. A History of the Early Republic, 1789-1815*. Oxford: Oxford University Press, 2011.

Woollacott, Angela. "A Radical Career: Responsible government, settler colonialism and Indigenous dispossession", *Journal of Colonialism and Colonial History*, 16, 2, 2015,

Young, Brian. "The Volunteer militia in Lower Canada, 1837-50", in *Power, Place and Identity. Historical studies of social and legal regulation in Quebec*: proceedings of a Montreal History Group conference, May 1996, Tamara Myers, editor, 37-53.

— *Patrician Families and the Making of Quebec. The Taschereaus and McCords*. Montreal; Kingston, McGill-Queens University Press, 2014.

ACKNOWLEDGEMENTS

"Readiness is all." I jumped at the idea of doing this book first proposed to me by Robin Philpot, publisher of Baraka Books. I was able to count on his encouragement and enthusiasm at every stage, particularly with the translation that François Robichaud carefully revised. My warmest thanks are extended to both of them, and to book designer Josée Lalancette. With this book, we have turned the wish of Maurice Séguin (1918-1984) into reality, albeit posthumously. Leader of the École de Montréal (Montreal School), Maurice Séguin hoped to see Adam Thom's *Anti-Gallic Letters* be made known to all. They were a crucial part of his teachings.